Law School Basics

Basics

A Preview of Law School and Legal Reasoning

By David Hricik

NOVA PRESS

Other law-related products from Nova Press:

Master the LSAT (560 pages, includes an actual LSAT!)

LSAT PrepCourse Software (includes three actual LSATs!)

Copyright © 2000, 1998, 1996 by David Hricik
Published by Nova Press
All rights reserved.

Duplication, distribution, or data base storage of any part of this work is prohibited without prior written approval from the publisher.

ISBN 1–889057–06–1

11659 Mayfield Ave., Suite 1
Los Angeles, CA 90049
Phone: 1-800-949-6175
Email: info@novapress.net
Website: www.novapress.net

TABLE OF CONTENTS

Pages

ACKNOWLEDGMENT

This book is dedicated to my mother.

I would like to thank Jennifer Smith, George Goolsby, Parker Binion, Carolyn Southerland, Buddy Perkel, Janet Guillory, Tim Headley, and Karen Maston. Jennifer, George, Parker, Carolyn, Buddy, and Tim provided me with many of the humorous cases I used. Janet typed most of this. Without their help, I could not have done it.

I would also like to thank Baker & Botts, L.L.P., which allowed me to take the time to teach at the University of Houston Law Center, and encouraged me to write articles and be involved in educational and bar activities.

Paul Klenk taught Law School Basics with me on America Online. Angelini F. Delaney Wallace was a first-year law student at the University of Houston when I "met" her through America Online, and she gave me three single-spaced pages of excellent comments on an earlier draft. Kay Wilson and Cindy Schiesel gave me significant suggestions for improvement. In addition, Jeff Schlegel and Louise Shearer assisted with the "problem words" examples. Patrick Stellitano, a former student, gave me permission to publish his memorandum.

Finally, I would like to thank my students at the University of Houston Law Center. I learned as much from them as they did from me.

— David Hricik

The author gratefully acknowledges permission to reprint from the following source:

WNS, INC. v. James Larry FARROW and Mary Dee. Reprinted from West's Federal Reporter, with permission of the West Publishing Company, St. Paul, Minnesota.

I. Introduction

When starting law school, I knew everything about "the law" that your average liberal arts major did: there was an executive branch, a legislative branch, and a judicial branch. The judicial branch interpreted the laws that the legislative branch enacted upon recommendation by the executive branch. The courts also decided civil and criminal law suits of some kind or another.

Before law school, I did not understand the difference between criminal and civil matters. Neither did many of my law school classmates. On the first day of class, however, we all learned. One student responded to the contract professor's question by stating that the defendant in the case we were discussing had been "found guilty of breaching a contract." This seemed to cause the hair on the back of the professor's neck to go straight back as he turned his attention to the issue, vigorously questioning my classmate in front of us all, making him seem foolish for not knowing something so basic as the distinction between civil and criminal wrongs.

As the professor used the "Socratic method" to show that the student had no idea of the difference between criminal and civil suits, between civil wrongs and criminal wrongs, I remember thinking: "There, but for the grace of God, go I." If there is a silver lining to that experience, I'm sure that my classmate has always gotten the two straight ever since, as have I. (For the record: a criminal proceeding may only be brought by the government; a civil proceeding is usually between private individuals.)

The point is that when I started law school, I had a general notion of the functions of government, a vague idea of what courts did, and an understanding that there was something out there called "law" which you shouldn't break or else you'll go to jail, or be sued.

I entered law school believing that the classes would teach me all the things I had not learned about the law. I thought law school would *explain* the law and the legal system to me. For example, I expected that someone would explicitly and directly teach me the difference between civil and criminal matters.

I was wrong.

Law school is concerned with forcing you to learn legal reasoning through the arduous (and at the time, seemingly never-ending) task of reading cases. Law school teaches you how lawyers think. It does not teach you "about" the subject in any direct way. Very few professors ever *explain* what you are reading and—more importantly—*why* you are reading it. Instead, you learn rules of law about torts, property, contract, and only by reading the cases and extracting the rules from them.

No one explains much of anything.[1] No one tells you the facts about the structure of the judicial system. No one tells you the nuts and bolts of how a lawsuit is structured. No one gives you any context to help you see the forest from the trees. Law school is little concerned with giving you the means to understand what you are going through, or about explaining the basics of the American legal system, or about the "big picture" of what you're reading.

Although the structure of the judicial system and the basics of the trial process *slowly* became clear while in law school, I never did understand the structure of lawsuits—what a motion was; how it differed from a brief; things like that. I also only slowly began to realize *why* we were reading cases—the earlier cases *were* "the law" that governed any later similar disputes. Once I realized that I was supposed to pull the "rules" out of the cases, I thought that I was learning the entire law of contracts in my contracts class, all of torts in my torts class, and the entire body of criminal law in "crim"

"That must be why I am reading all these cases," I thought to myself.

But I slowly came to realize that that is not what law school is about, either. You can't learn all of contract law in nine months. You just can't. It was not until late in my third year that I fully understood what law school was really about.

Not until four years later, after two years of teaching legal writing, did I understand how to make the whole process a lot easier and more meaningful for my students. My own frustrations during law school and my own revelations obtained while teaching in law school for the past three years led me to write this book.

Don't misunderstand me: I did well in law school. The frustration I experienced came from the belief that the learning process does not have to be so difficult.

This book arose from that frustration. It has three overriding goals. First, it gives you an overview of daily life in law school. Second, it seeks to explain how the legal system works, so you will have the details of the "big picture" illuminated for you *before* you begin your studies—instead of three years afterward. Third, it explains the common law process of legal reasoning—how

---

1   The silver lining: all first-year law students go through pretty much what you will, no matter which school they attend, and every lawyer before you had to go through it, too. If you find solace through the suffering of others, you'll be a fine lawyer.

courts develop and apply legal rules on a case-by-case basis—so that you can more quickly become a better legal writer, which will improve your law school grades.

The book is organized to achieve those three primary goals. The first part of the book gives an overview of law school and the federal and state judicial systems in the United States. Then, it briefly discusses the common law system and how legal "rules" develop. That way, you will know what is coming because you will have a basic understanding of how and why we have cases.

The second part of the book is organized the way most first-year legal writing or "legal methods" courses are taught. Those classes cause tremendous anxiety to first-year students. This section will give you a larger view of case law and how lawyers write about the law, so that you will better understand what cases and "the law" really are. More importantly, it will show you why the fundamental characteristics of the common law system forces law school to use the "case method" for learning purposes, which will better prepare you for law school. This book also gives a short overview of legal research, giving some shortcuts, some tips, and a few ideas to help pull together what you will learn during the first half of your first semester.

The book was written with a purpose always firmly in mind: to give you a look at case law—so you can see how lawyers write about "the law"—and to give you a preview of some of the fact patterns you will face during your first year. Real outlines are also included from my law school days and real examples from my teaching experience. By the time you finish, you will have seen two actual opinions, a legal memoranda, an appellate court brief, and three actual law school outlines. You will also have read a book which discusses legal issues and cases as a lawyer does.

By design, some of the more useful concepts are repeated. The entire book is written to make understanding all of this a little easier by emphasizing the lighter side of the law.

I hope you find it useful.

Finally, the views expressed in this book are only my views, not necessarily those of Baker & Botts, L.L.P. or the University of Houston Law Center.

David Hricik
E-Mail: PrfHricik@aol.com

II. An Overview
of Law School

A word about the organization of law school is probably the best place to start. The students in your law school class will be organized about the same no matter which school you attend. Typically, each entering first-year class is divided into two or more "sections," which take their classes as a group. During your first year, you will take every class with the same group of people, and quite possibly have no classes or at most only one class with the other half or third of your class. Often there is little interaction in the classroom between the sections during the first year, which leads to little social interaction as well. After the first year, when the required courses are over, students are free to take whatever courses they like, with a few mandatory exceptions, and then mixing more readily occurs.

Some schools also offer night classes for part-timers or students with jobs. Usually these students are older than their day-time counterparts, and their course load is different because they usually don't take 15 hours per semester, like most students. Apart from that fact, the rest of what follows generally applies to anyone in law school anywhere.

A.   First Year.

Although each law school varies slightly from the norm, your curriculum during first year will be substantially the same no matter where you go. Your course load will include contracts, torts, property, legal writing, criminal law, and constitutional law or possibly one elective.

You will have a big, thick casebook for each class which will contain edited versions of cases, arranged by topic. For example, your contracts case book will be organized by issues such as "formation of contract," "excuse for breach," and "remedies for breach." Each section of the book will have lengthy excerpts from cases in which the courts addressed those issues. For example, the "remedies for breach" section of your contracts book will have several excerpts (lengthy, naturally) from cases which discuss certain aspects of damages, such as the measure of damages when the subject matter of the contract is unique (a piece of art, for instance).

Each day of class, your professors will assign several cases to read. Reading assignments of 50 pages per class are not uncommon. Remember, too, that you will sometimes have three or four classes a day. (Recall, too, that you're willingly about to pay substantial sums of money to go through this process.)

Thus, a good portion of every one of your law school days will be spent preparing for the next day's class by reading cases and "briefing" them. A "case brief" has very little in common with a "legal brief," which you will write in your legal writing class. A case brief is a short synopsis of the case which you write for your own use (many people then use case briefs as the basis for their class "outlines"—discussed below). Example case briefs are contained in the *outline* from my employment discrimination class (see Appendix A).

Take a quick look at the "case briefs" in the "outline" in Appendix A now; we'll take a longer look at them later.

Law school classes are not taught like undergraduate courses. Instead of simply listening to a lecture and taking notes, law school classes—particularly most first-year classes—are taught using the so-called "Socratic method." In the Socratic method, the professor teaches not by lecturing, but by engaging in a dialogue with one or more students in the class. The teacher may often stay with one student for the entire class period. It can be stressful, and some professors enjoy showing off their intellect at the expense of their students.

Professors who use the Socratic method teach by asking questions based upon hypothetical fact patterns slightly different from the cases that were assigned as reading. The professor will see how far the rule from the case can be stretched: when should a different result be reached, or a different rule applied? For instance, suppose in the assigned case the court had reasoned that a person's trespass[2] across somebody else's property was unlawful, even though the person did not know he was trespassing. The professor may ask: "Suppose he was trespassing across someone's land in order to rush another person to the hospital?" The professor wants to test the *limits* of the "rule" from the case *and* the student's ability to think on his or her feet. Does the case *really* mean that *all* trespasses are *always* illegal; that *is* what the court said that it "held"; but can't some trespasses be "justified" or "excused?" If so, what rules or tests should be used to determine whether such an exception should apply—whether someone should not be held liable for trespass even though he went onto another's land without permission. The Socratic method is used to explore the factual, logical, and policy boundaries of legal rules as stated by the cases.

---

2   A trespass occurs when a person goes onto someone else's land without permission.

The Socratic teaching method is less widely used in law schools than it was in the past, particularly after the first-year classes. Whether that is good or bad as a pedagogical matter is an open question. From personal experience, however, I can say that knowing you will not be grilled about the assigned reading makes it easier to go to classes during your third year, when often you are too detached to care about being prepared for class.

Another common feature of most law schools is that you will have only one test in each class, a final, given at the end of the semester. In some year-long classes, you will have only one test at the end of the school year. Unlike undergraduate courses, your grade for each law course will depend entirely upon how well you do on one test. (Legal writing classes are different because an evaluation of writing ability is not best based on one sample, and so grades in legal writing are based upon several assignments turned in over the semester.)

Thus, except for legal writing, during your first year your daily routine will consist of reading cases and other materials, such as law review articles, and showing up for class to discuss them by the Socratic method. Unlike your typical undergraduate experience, during your entire law school career you will rarely turn in any paper or other assignments. There will only be one final in each class. That one test will determine your grade for the entire, semester-long course, or in some cases, for the entire year-long course. During your first year, this routine will be punctuated every four to six weeks by the need to turn in an assignment in your legal writing class.

"Briefing cases" is something you will hear a lot about even before your first day of class. Everyone will be talking about how it is important to "brief" the cases you are assigned to read before the class begins. What is a case brief? It is *not* what lawyers call "briefs," which are documents written to file in a court to persuade a judge on a particular issue. Instead, a "case brief" is a way for you to break down each case you read for class into useful, categorized information.

Some of this discussion is premature (so I suggest you read this discussion of case briefs again just before you turn to the section on legal research since case briefs will be mentioned so often and so early in law school), discussing them now seems appropriate.

There is no One True Way to write a case brief. Their purposes, in my view, are two: to make it so that (a) I never had to re-read the case again, and (b) so that if I were called on in class, I could answer likely questions without having to pour over the case. (Cases can be very long, and the ones chosen for inclusion in law school casebooks seemed to be deliberately longer and more opaquely written than they are in "real life.") To meet these two purposes, my case briefs typically followed this format:

Name of case (court/year)
Facts:
Issue:
Holding:
Rationale:
Dissent:
Class Notes:

We will discuss each part in detail.

In the name of the case, I included information which let me know who was the plaintiff. So, for example, in the "name" section, I might have written: "Smith (Δ) v. Jones (π) (Tex. S.Ct. 1987)." "π" means plaintiff; "Δ" means defendant. You can't tell from the name of an appellate case who sued whom. On appeal, the *loser* in the trial court will be listed first in the caption of the case, even if that party was the defendant (the party who was sued) in the trial court, because it is the party which is appealing—the party listed first is the party who lost in the court below and is the one appealing to a higher court. Professors often asked basic questions such as who won below. In addition, understanding the basic facts of cases made them a lot easier to understand. (You will be amazed, though, at how difficult it can be to figure out who sued whom about what.)

The "Facts" section was usually a chronological, short explanation (three or four sentences, or less) of what seemed to be the relevant facts. (You can know which facts are relevant only *after* you have read the whole case.) I might have written, for example, "π went to Δ-doctor to get nose job. Δ allegedly made the nose worse. π then sued Δ, and jury found for π, awarding damages equal to the difference between the value of the nose as promised and the value of the nose actually delivered."

The "Issue" section would lay out the primary legal issue in the case. For example, "Was the proper measure of damages the difference between the nose as delivered and the nose as promised, or should it have been the difference between the nose as delivered and the nose as it had been before surgery?"

The "Holding" would be what the court held the answer to the primary legal question was. For example, "The correct measure of damages was *expectancy* damages—the difference in value between as delivered and as promised." This was, in essence, the "rule" from the case.

The "Rationale" section could be quite long. Again, my goals were not to re-read the case and to have something I could rely on were I called on in class. I learned a lot by "outlining" the rationale of the court in some detail, usually following the court's own structure. Look at the outlines in the appendices to see how I did this. Some are quite elaborate and detailed. It varied a lot, depending primarily upon my mood.

Next, if a judge dissented from the case, I would summarize what he said.

Finally, after class, I would type into my computer my notes from class. I figured that whatever the professor emphasized would probably be on the final. Sometimes it was.

That fairly describes case briefs. Again, understanding much of what we just discussed depends on information contained below, primarily in the first half of the book. Re-read about case briefs before you start law school.

For me, the process of preparing case briefs for each day of class was part of the process for preparing *outlines*. Like briefing cases, you will hear a lot about outlines before you take your first law school class.

Much of your preparation time for finals will be spent on a computer preparing "outlines" for each class final. There are even commercial outlines, usually referred to by the original publisher's name. So you will buy, out of fear, *Gilbert's* for torts, *Legallines* for contracts, and so on. I wasted a lot of money on commercial outlines. Buy them used, and see if they help you—they probably won't.

Everyone has a different notion of what level of detail they feel comfortable with in their outlines. Some people use outlines which are a hundred pages long for *each* class. Others use a bare bones approach. Length and level of detail should serve a purpose, and the purpose of an outline, however long, is to provide an organized, topical outline of the legal "rules" you learned from reading the cases. It will be "the law" for that class in a format you can use during the (typically) three-hour-long final exam.

Each outline in the appendices is slightly different. One thing they have in common is lots of abbreviations.[3] The outline in Appendix A is from my employment law class. I never could understand a word the professor said in class, so I made a very detailed "outline" in which I briefed every case, so that I would learn the law.

The outline in Appendix B is from my professional responsibility class. It is not finished. It was a code-based course, with far more emphasis on the codes of professional responsibility than cases, so there is little reference to case law.

The outline in Appendix C is from my Administrative Law class. It is an "issue-spotting" outline. I tried to break the class into issues to watch out for on the final exam. It is sort of a "checklist" to use on the final.

Why do law students make these outlines? I did it because everyone else did. (That explains the motive for much of what goes on in law school: fear.)

---

[3]   Some common abbreviations used in class and in outlines: "π" means plaintiff, the party who sued. "Δ" means defendant, the party who got sued. "K" is often used to mean "contract." "B/c" means "because."

They do serve a key purpose. To understand that purpose you need to understand law school. Each of your finals will probably consist of hypothetical fact patterns which you must write an essay about. For instance, a final exam in a typical torts class will have a few short paragraphs stating the facts of a car accident, an explosion, an injury caused by a defective product, or something along those lines. During the final exam, and under severe time restraints (though each test is typically three hours long), you will have to "issue spot" while analyzing the facts. To do so, you will apply the "rules" which you learned from reading the cases for class to the facts in the hypothetical to analyze whether the fact pattern on the test presents a tort of one sort or another. That is what your outline is for—to help you learn and then write about the issues on the final exam.

For instance, in a contracts final, the professor might give you a hypothetical in which the parties thought they were agreeing to buy/sell a particular item, but in reality the seller thought that he was selling a different item. The buyer thought he was buying the original Mona Lisa; the seller thought he was selling just a print. You would have to analyze whether a contract was actually formed (after all, they never truly agreed on what they were trying to do), and if so, whether there was a breach of it, and if so, what were the damages. You do that by writing down the legal rules relevant to the issues, applying them to the fact pattern, and then writing down a conclusion. So, for example, you might write:

> Whether there was a contract depends on whether there was a meeting of the minds between the buyer and the seller. The seller will argue there was not because a mistake occurred. The seller did not intend to sell his original Mona Lisa, just the print. The buyer will argue . . . .

Again, outlines help you study for finals, and during the finals (many exams are "open book"), they help you locate and write down the relevant legal rule and spot issues as you read the fact patterns. They are very important. For that reason, there will be lots of anxiety throughout law school about outlines. Your classmates will hear of great outlines done for the class the year before, and everyone will want one. People stress out over not sharing outlines. You will be amazed, appalled, and amused.

Outlines are useful in every class except legal writing. Grades in legal writing class are determined differently, and outlines play no part. There are usually no finals in legal writing class. Instead, grades are determined much like they are in undergraduate composition classes. You will be graded on the three to five memoranda, pleadings, and briefs, which you turn in during the semester. (Because legal writing class will be the source of your' first feedback and grades, anxiety about legal writing usually runs quite high—even at those schools where it is taught pass/fail.)

Legal writing classes typically focus on three general topics during the year. The first topic, sometimes taught by third-year students, consists of self-contained ("canned") assignments which are intended to force you to become acquainted with legal research materials: cases, statutes, secondary authorities (like law review articles), and other sources of the law. During this first part, a typical assignment would be to look up certain cases, find statutes from various jurisdictions which relate to certain subjects, and find law review articles discussing specified issues.

The second and third parts of the typical writing program are most often taught by adjunct professors. The second part of the typical writing class consists of writing legal memoranda, which are *objective* discussions of the law. After graduation, during your first year or so of practice, much of your time will be spent writing legal memoranda to lawyers to explain the law in *neutral* terms—describing both the good and the bad possibilities, the strengths and the weaknesses of your client's legal and factual positions. Memoranda are to inform, not to persuade. Memoranda are written only for use by your client and your law firm: the other side hopefully never sees them. During your legal writing class, you will write at least two memoranda.

The third and final part of the usual legal writing program consists of *persuasive* writing—primarily pleadings, motions, and briefs. Unlike memoranda, pleadings, motions, and briefs are not neutral, but are persuasive pieces of advocacy intended to convince the reader (usually a judge) that one view—your client's—is right. Briefs are not intended to explain both sides of the argument in balanced terms. Also, unlike memoranda, pleadings, motions, and briefs get filed with a court and served on the other side. In your legal writing class, you will probably write a motion, a response to the other side's motion, and then a lengthy appellate brief. Chances are, you will also be required to do an appellate oral argument as part of your writing course. The process of going through an appellate oral argument will make you a better writer.

The most important, but commonly overlooked, value of legal writing class is this: it teaches you how to write your finals. Most professors are as impressed or more impressed by a well-organized, well-written final exam as they are by one which is thoroughly-analyzed, but not well written. The impact of a well-organized and clearly written final exam cannot be overstated. In addition, if you use your legal writing class to learn the legal reasoning process, your understanding of your other classes will also improve, and so will your grades.

Thus, even though your legal writing class may be taught only by an adjunct and may be graded on a pass/fail basis, it has tremendous potential to increase the grades you receive in every other class. Moreover, it is the class which gives you the broadest view of the legal reasoning process and may help you better understand the cases you will read for your other classes. For those reasons, and because my teaching experience has shown me that legal writing causes the greatest anxiety (and often the greatest disappointment, especially by those who did well in writing as undergrads), I emphasize legal writing in this book.

In addition to studying, preparing outlines, and writing your memoranda and briefs, you will also want to get a law-related job. (After all, that may have something to do with why you are going to law school.) During the late winter or early spring of your first year, you will send out resumes to law firms, corporations, and other organizations in order to find yourself a job for the summer. Although law firms still hire first-year law students, first-year hiring has fallen off in recent years because of the over-all tightening of the employment market for lawyers. However, many job opportunities exist with judges, government agencies, public interest groups, businesses, and other organizations. They are hard to find, and many may involve little or no pay, but having at least some real-world legal experience can help you get a "real" summer job in a law firm during the next summer. In addition, an unpaid internship with smaller firms, public interest groups, or the state or federal government may help you decide whether certain areas of the law or types of careers are right for you.

Or, you could also enjoy your last summer of freedom for most of the rest of your life by just relaxing, running your Visa or Mastercard (or, more likely, both) up to the limits, and just letting your mind rest. Once you've been working for a few years, you might look fondly back on such a "wasted" summer....

At the end of the first year at many law schools, the attention of the students turns to the competition for, or selection to, the law reviews. Many law schools have at least one law journal, usually the Law Review and one or more "lesser" specialty journals, such as an international law journal, or a journal devoted to intellectual property issues or other substantive legal areas. There are pecking orders at each school: usually the Law Review is the most prestigious and the others follow from there.

Generally, those students near the top of each section will qualify to join a journal. If you are not one of those chosen few, often you can still qualify by participating in a "write-on" competition, which typically involves staying on campus for a week or more after finals in order to write a short (five to ten page) article. The journal's staff will then judge whether you should be allowed on to that particular journal in light of your article and your grades.

With completion of the writing competition, first year ends. Summer clerkships begin for those who obtained them.

B.   Second Year.

Which classes you take during your second year will generally be left up to you, though each school will have certain courses required after the first year—typically, constitutional law, professional responsibility, and perhaps one or two others. Professors tend to use the Socratic method (teaching by question and answer, as opposed to lectures) less often in second and third year classes, primarily because many students, if they show up at all, show up for class unprepared. Consequently, using the Socratic method tends to waste time. Some professors continue to use it, however. If so, you will have to prepare for such classes more rigorously, which is a definite factor to consider in choosing your second year classes. In addition, because you will be having on-campus job interviews the fall semester of your second year can be your most hectic.

During your second and third years, you will also have the opportunity to take clinical classes, during which you will be able to practice taking and defending depositions, arguing motions or appeals, negotiating settlements, and examining witnesses at mock trials. Most schools also have "mock trial" and appellate advocacy competitions, in which many students compete for the experience and the resume enhancement. In addition, but probably only during your third year, you may have the opportunity to work for your school's "legal clinic," where you will be able to get real-world experience by handling family law, minor criminal law, and landlord-tenant disputes under the supervision of a faculty attorney.

If you qualified for a journal at the end of your first year (either by grades or write-on), you will spend far too many hours of the fall semester of your second year researching the topic for your "note" or "comment." (A "note" is an article about *one* recent case, and how it modified the law; a "comment" is a broader, though not necessarily lengthier, article about a single legal issue, not just one case.) As part of your journal responsibilities (and, probably, graduation requirements), you have to write a publishable-quality note or comment. To select a topic, you must first spend a lot of time making sure no one has already written about that precise topic (if someone has, then that topic has been "pre-empted"). Once you find a good, non-preempted topic, you have to research and write your note or comment. That can take *a lot* of time.

In addition, most second-year journal members must "cite check" the notes, comments, and articles written by the third-year students and other authors which their journal has decided to publish. This means spending countless hours in the library making sure the author has cited judicial opinions or other legal authority which actually support the point for which they are cited, and even more mind-numbing hours pouring over the Bluebook to make sure that the citations are done in proper format. (More—unfortunately, much more—about the Bluebook later.) Second-year journal members work hard.

During the fall of the second year, potential employers come to campus to conduct interviews for jobs during the summer between second and third years and, ultimately, after graduation. Law firms, corporations, government agencies, and legal organizations come to interview at many law schools. You can also send your resume and cover letter to any firm, agency, or organization in which you are interested that is not interviewing at your school. At some schools, there only a few on-campus interviews. Even at the best schools, those who do not excel may find it difficult to obtain jobs at the premiere firms because the competition for jobs in the legal market is fierce.

The interview process is time-consuming. In general, the law school's placement office will post the names of the firms, organizations, and agencies that are coming on campus and you will sign up to interview with those in which you are interested. On-campus interviews typically last only 15 or 20 minutes, and never more than 30 minutes. Because of that brevity, there often is a strong emphasis on good law school grades, undergraduate achievements, and a demonstrated writing ability. Many interviewers will request writing samples (which is still another reason this book emphasizes legal writing class).

If the on-campus interview goes well, you will receive a letter from the firm inviting you for a "fly back interview"—if it is an out-of-town firm—or for an "office interview," if it is a local one. You will then fly to the city where the firm is located for an overnight stay followed by an all-day interview consisting of several half-hour long interviews with six or eight partners and associates at the firm. Chances are, you will also be taken out for lunch, dinner, or both. Costs are generally borne entirely by the firm. Spouses are usually not invited.

By the end of your third semester, or by early February at the latest, you will have accepted jobs for the summer between your second and third years. Depending upon which part of the country you will be "clerking" in that summer, you may be able to clerk at only one firm or you may be allowed to "split" your summer by working six to eight weeks at two or more firms or organizations. The practice of "splitting" one summer among two or more law firms varies by region (it is more common in the south and west), but splitting gives you the chance to compare different cities, law firm sizes, cultures, and approaches to the practice of law. Some students work at a company or in the government for one-half of the summer and at a law firm during the other half to see what benefits an "in house" or government position may have over private practice.

If you are on a journal, then at the end of your second year you will have to decide whether to run for election as an editor during the third year. There are several different kinds of editors, ranging from the editor-in-chief (often called "EIC"—"ee-eye-see"), to articles editors, to note and comment editors. Each position has different responsibilities. The third-year editorial board members usually conduct interviews to decide the make-up of the upcoming year's editorial board by voting on the candidates for each office. Editorial board elections can be divisive and mean-spirited, particularly where two or more well-qualified students both want to be editor-in-chief.

Once second year ends, you will probably get your first significant look at the real world when your second-year clerkship begins. The summer associate programs at the larger firms continue to have many social activities, including lunches, dinners, and two or more firm-wide parties during the summer. However, things have toned down significantly since the mid-1980's, when the social activities were arguably ridiculous.

Expect to work hard at your summer clerkship. Although law firms vary so much that generalizing is at best wildly inaccurate, at most firms you will be asked to research and write legal memoranda about several issues, explaining the law to the partner or associate who assigned the work to you. You may write a brief or motion, but most likely it will be a memo. (Remember the difference? Memos are neutral analyses; briefs are persuasive.) Whether you receive a job offer will depend in large measure on how well they think you write compared to the other summer associates. (Which is one more reason why legal writing is so important.)

C. Third Year.

After returning to school from the summer, it's decision time. If you got an offer from one of your summer employers, you will have a choice to make: you either can go through the interview process again and interview for a permanent position at a firm, agency, or organization for which you never worked, or you can accept the offer from one of the firms you worked for during the summer. There are obvious disadvantages in accepting a job offer from a firm where you have never worked. But if you were not happy with what you experienced during the summer, or if they were not happy with you, it may be the only choice. Likewise, if you were not able to get a summer position, you will need to spend a lot of energy seeking permanent employment.

A word about classes is probably in order, though classes and grades are far less important during your day-to-day life as a third-year. Instead, the focus is on getting a job and getting law school behind you.

The third-year curriculum is much like the second year. You will be able to choose nearly all of your classes. Many third-years, recognizing that they will have to take a bar exam, take courses that will be on the bar in order to prepare for it. Others use law school to study the subjects they intend to focus on during their careers. Still others, viewing law school as a place more for academics than pragmatism, take classes which are intellectually interesting, but of no practical value. No one way is right, and few people accurately predict what kind of law they will eventually practice.

If you are an editor of a journal, you will spend a significant amount of your third year editing some very poorly-written manuscripts by well-renowned authors, and turning them into publishable pieces. (I was amazed and appalled that well-known and respected lawyers and professors would submit for publication very poorly written and reasoned material, knowing that their names alone would force the students to make that material worth publishing.) It can take many hours to write the article essentially from scratch.

If you got onto a journal at the end of your first year, but decided not to be an editor, then you probably will have very little journal work to do during your third year. Although you may get called in a pinch to help cite check an article, you will probably spend very little time on journal work. Whether or not you are an editor, though, if your note or comment was chosen for publication, you will have to spend some time updating it and getting it into shape for publication.

If you are an editor during your third year, at the end of the year you will meet with the other editorial board members to interview the second-year students to decide who will serve on the up-coming year's editorial board. This will be your final task for the journal.

Although being on a journal can be a significant achievement, it requires a significant commitment of time and energy and means having less time and energy to spend on your graded courses. It can be and most often is well worth the effort, but think about it before you undertake the responsibilities.

During your final semester, you will probably need to take the "MPRE," or Multi-State Professional Responsibility Exam. It is an ethics test which is required in many states to get licensed. If you are lucky, your firm will pay for a preparatory course. Most people find the MPRE to be pretty easy, at least if you have a good gut-level sense for such complex issues as whether stealing is ethical or not. (It's not—despite conventional wisdom—even for lawyers.)

It is common for students to work at part-time legal jobs during their third year to make some spending money. Some law firms will pay their in-coming lawyers $20 or $30 per hour to do basic legal research and writing, and so part-time work is a common way for third-year students to make it through the last year.

Believe me: during your third year, your central thought will be on getting law school behind you. (Of course, owing to predictable human nature, once you are out, you will reminisce about your leisure-filled, fun-packed law school days.)

D. Post-Graduation.

During the summer immediately following graduation, you will study for your state's bar exam, which is typically a two- or three-day test given at the end of July. Although bar examinations vary by state, typically they include a day-long, nationwide multiple-choice test called the "multi-state exam" and a day or two of short answer, fill-in-the-blank, or essay questions on your specific state's law. These examinations now include a national essay section (called "MEE" for "Multi-state Essay Examination. Again, there are preparatory courses for the bar exam, and taking one of those courses makes passing the bar that much easier. Bar results are typically received by early November.

In my opinion, the pass rates merely limit the number of new lawyers; they do not ensure a minimum level of competence. In some states, 90% pass. In others, 60% fail. It's doubtful that the quality of legal services is significantly better in states where the pass rates are low.

If you pass the bar—and many people do not, particularly in states like Arizona and California (the easy bars include Illinois, for example)—then you get to be sworn in as a lawyer . . . once you pay your state's licensing fees.

After that—finally—you are an attorney!

You now get to bill more than 2,000 hours a year under tremendous stress with the constant threat of malpractice and the incessant complaints of co-workers, bosses, secretaries, opposing counsel, the public, judges, and even your own clients. You also hardly know the first thing about practicing law.

Congratulations! You've made it to square one.

III. The United States Legal System

Here are some basic questions: What is the "law?" Where does "law" come from? What is the purpose of law?

The last question first: What is the purpose of law?

A. What Is the Purpose of Law?

For our purposes, it is easier to begin by saying what the purpose of law is not, rather than what it is. Laws are not the same as personal or individual morality. This is easy to prove: some things are legal, yet are considered immoral by some people. *See, e.g., Roe v. Wade*, 410 U.S. 113, 119 (1973) (holding that abortion is protected by the United States Constitution).

> Note: you have just seen a case cited in Bluebook format, as a lawyer would do in a brief or memorandum. (The Bluebook is discussed below. It is a *long* rule book on how to cite cases properly.) A few words about case *citations* is in order here because one goal of this book is to get you used to how lawyers write about the law. Look at the cite for *Roe*. The words "*See, e.g.,*," mean "See, for example." "*Roe v. Wade*" means that someone named Roe is involved in a suit with someone named Wade. (You can't tell who sued whom, though, not just from the *style* of the case.) "410 U.S. 113, 119" means that the Roe versus Wade case is "reported" (*i.e.*, printed) at volume 410 of the United States Reporters (we will discuss "reporters" below), beginning at page 113, and that the specific words from the case to which I'm referring are on page 119 of that Reporter. The fact that it is in the United States Reporters means it was decided by the United States Supreme Court, as that particular reporter publishes only its decisions. The date in the parenthesis is when the case was decided. The parenthetical explanation of "abortion is protected by the United States Constitution" is what *I* say that the court said. It is one way to let the reader know what a case says.

Moving onward.

Some things which are moral to some people are nonetheless always illegal. *See, e.g., Reynolds v. United States*, 98 U.S. 145, 167 (1878) (holding that polygamy is illegal). Some laws even require people to do things which they find utterly immoral. For example, Christian Scientists may be forced to accept blood transfusions, even though they believe it damns them to eternal hell. *See generally, Holmes v. Silver Cross Hosp. of Joliet*, 340 F. Supp. 125, 129-30 (N.D. Ill. 1972). Laws are not morals—at least not an individual's or a particular group's morals. That much is clear.

There are many theories about why we have laws, about what purpose is served by our explicit, institutionalized and complex legal system. Some view law as merely a tool to oppress people; others argue that laws express reason and order. Many view law as a system of rules which, when applied to facts by judges and juries, should result in rational and reasonable results to particular cases—to particular facts. We will not decide who is right. As with most things, the truth no doubt lies somewhere in between.

For our purpose, we do not care too much about what the purpose of law is, at least not on this fundamental level. For lawyers and law students, the law is a set of "rules" which create "duties," the breaking of which may result in "liability," usually in the form of money damages. Put at its simplest, "the law" is an expression of the social policy that people have a duty to follow the rules, and those who don't will incur liability for any harm they cause.

The "rule" is very often something so vague as having a duty to "act reasonably under the circumstances." Or, the rule can be very specific: having to stop at a stop sign, having to drive no more than 30 miles per hour, having to do what you have agreed in a contract to do.

"Liability" for breaking a rule often comes in the form of a "judgment" for money damages, which is a court's order for one person to pay money to another person. It can also take the form of an "injunction," which is a court order prohibiting someone from doing something. For example, a court could enjoin a party from selling dangerous products. (In criminal cases, "liability" can take the form of a jail or prison sentence or a fine—which is a court's order that a person pay money to the government.)

So the "purpose" of law is to have rules that create duties which, when breached, result in some sort of liability to the injured party. Obviously that is an oversimplification: for example, some of the law comprises those rules that define *how much* someone who breaks a "rule" must pay the injured party. But as a general concept, law is meant to define the duties which people owe one another.

B.   Where Does "Law" Come From?

As to where this "law" comes from, it is again probably easiest to first say what the law is *not*. The western world's legal systems are of two primary kinds: common law and civil law. For our purposes, the "common law" system which we have in the United States can be described by contrasting it to civil law systems. By illuminating the differences, we can better see the common law method. Understanding how the common law system works will help you understand why you spend so much of law school reading cases.

Civil law jurisdictions place their primary emphasis on legislation—statutes or codes enacted by a parliament or similar legislative body. The governing legislatures of civil law countries try to enact comprehensive codes on every subject. These statutes or codes provide the main source of the legal rules. In theory, everything necessary for the legal operation of society is covered in a code or statute. Consequently, in civil law countries, decisions by courts are not as important as those codes. The courts play a role, to be sure, but it is comparatively less than in common law countries.

In contrast, under the common law system, like we have in the United States, the society places less overall emphasis on statutes and codes. The "common" law plays a much greater role because there are *no* statutes or codes governing *most* legal issues. Instead, most of the "rules" are in the form of previously decided judicial opinions, not statutes or codes. Unlike civil law systems, in common law countries, *judicially* developed "rules"—that have never been approved by any voters or elected legislative body, such as a Congress, a state legislature, or even a city council—provide much of the governing legal framework.

The common law method means building up the law by court opinions, case-by-case, as opposed to creating the law by legislative enactment. The facts surrounding origins of the English system are illuminating:

> England had laws just as Continental countries did, even though these laws were not 'written' in the Romanist sense of being declared in authoritative texts. The rules established by general custom were declared not by a single judge alone but by the whole court of the king, which represented the magnates of the kingdom; *but there was no authorized version of these rules*.

2 *Dictionary of the History of Ideas* 694 (emphasis added).

Under our common law system, most law comes in the form of these judicial opinions: there is no big encyclopedia of "rules" setting out what can, must, or should be done under any set of facts or circumstances. You will seldom go to a "rule book" to find an "outline" of legal rules on the issue you are researching. As will become more clear later, the common law is really a series of *cases*—not rules—which can be applied to later fact patterns.

The point is so important that it bears repeating: most "law" in common law systems is case law, decided by judges and memorialized only in written "opinions"—not statutes, codes, or other "rule books." For instance, the "elements" which must be alleged to effectively claim that a party was negligent in injuring another person were essentially created by the courts of England in the sixteenth century and were adopted by America's state courts throughout the nineteenth century. Likewise, most contract law is primarily found only in cases decided over hundreds of years by judges. Similarly, the rules governing real property come from cases which were written by judges in England long, long ago involving fee tails, fee simples, and other legal concepts whose importance has left us, but whose labels have not.

Of course, there are specialized statutes in common law jurisdictions such as the United States. Statutes provide a very comprehensive set of legal rules for some issues. For instance, significant federal legislation, called ERISA, governs employee benefit plans. ERISA is a complex statute, and the government has promulgated hundreds of pages of rules and regulations which further clarify and add to the statute. The patent statutes are comprehensive, as are some of the federal environmental statutes. Similarly, many state legislatures have enacted very detailed state statutes on various subjects. For example, the Texas Deceptive Trade Practices Act (often called the "DTPA"), provides a fairly complex codification of law designed to protect consumers. There are also *a lot* of federal and state regulations which are relatively comprehensive.

Nonetheless, with certain exceptions, statutes play a comparatively insignificant role in the common law system. For example, even though the DTPA is probably one of the longer Texas statutes, the legislature left many issues for the courts to decide by applying the statute to various facts. Those judicial interpretations are as important—if not more so—than the words of the DTPA statute itself.

The main supposed benefit of the common law system is its flexibility: a judge can decide that the facts before him are different enough under the rules so that a different *result* from an earlier case should be reached. Courts can also create a different, new rule when needed to apply to new problems or social changes. The common law has an additional benefit: judges decide cases based on actual, concrete disputes, not hypotheticals. A statute cannot be written which will govern every possible fact pattern, but a court can decide what rule should apply to specific facts, and a jury can decide what result is just under all kinds of different and unforeseeable fact patterns. The common law system allows for a lot of discretion in order to achieve justice in each dispute.

Most people are surprised to learn that many, if not most, of the laws that lawyers rely on in their day-to-day practice were never passed by a legislature or by Congress, but instead evolved over hundreds of years as courts developed and applied judge-made rules to the facts presented in each new dispute brought before them. That arguably makes judges very powerful. That power, in turn, means that *your* ability to effectively argue the law can shape the outcome of your client's cases. Knowing how to find the law and how to write about it, will make you a more effective, and therefore a more powerful, lawyer.

To sum up, the "purpose" of law is to create duties which, if breached, mean that the wrong-doer must compensate the injured party. This "set of rules," however, exists only in the form of case law; there is no "rule book" as there is in civil law countries.

C.   Why Do We Have "Cases" Anyway?

Lawyers use the word "case" to refer to many very different things. "Case" means a dispute: your client has been sued by IBM. That is a case. "Case" also refers to the published opinions which judges have written when they decided earlier disputes. Thus, if IBM's case against your client went to trial and the judge wrote an opinion explaining the case, that opinion is also a "case." I will refer to the latter kinds of "cases" as "opinions" whenever I think the context is confusing.

How are opinions created? As next shown, a court may, when it decides a case, write an opinion that will be published in a reporter (reporters are discussed below). Those published opinions then become *precedent*—the law—for other courts to use when deciding later cases. To understand why opinions get written, you need to understand how lawsuits are resolved. To illustrate, I will give you something you will not get in law school: a brief and over-simplified synopsis of a lawsuit.

The *plaintiff* is the party which sues. The plaintiff files a "complaint." The complaint lays out the allegations in which plaintiff claims to show why the defendant (the party being sued) owes the plaintiff money. Put in terms of the "purpose" of law: the plaintiff alleges facts which show that the defendant owed a duty to the plaintiff, breached that duty, and injured the plaintiff. For example, in a case you will read as a 1-L, the plaintiff claims that the defendant had agreed to deliver a load of coal to the plaintiff's lumber mill; because the defendant failed to deliver the coal on time and as promised, the mill had to shut down, causing the plaintiff to lose business; because he had no coal, he could not run the mill, and so could not cut wood to sell to his customers.

After being served with the plaintiff's complaint, a defendant must file an "answer." The defendant will "deny" those allegations in the plaintiff's complaint which, the defendant contends, are not true and will assert any "affirmative defenses" he might have. Again, for example, the defendant will deny that there was a contract to deliver coal; if there was a contract, it is legally unenforceable because it was not in writing; even if there were an enforceable contract, the damages were caused or at least exacerbated by plaintiff's failure to order coal from some other supplier.

The judge will then issue a "scheduling order." Scheduling orders typically set the case for trial in a year or so, and establish certain deadlines along the way, the most important of which is a "discovery cut-off" deadline. The parties will have up to that date to take "discovery" of each other. Discovery consists of asking each other written questions (called "interrogatories"); asking each other to produce documents which are relevant to the suit (called "requests for production"); and taking each other's sworn answers to oral questions (called "depositions"). We are not going to talk about discovery much. You will study many exciting discovery issues in your civil procedure class. *See, e.g., King v. Loveable Co.*, 506 So.2d 1127 (Fla. Ct. App. 1987) (analyzing whether defendant was entitled to inspect plaintiff's breasts in a case where she alleged that bra had permanently stained her).

Typically, at some point near the end of the discovery period, one side or the other will file a "motion for summary judgment." This motion says that the moving party is entitled to "win as a matter of law": the *movant* will argue that given the undisputed facts and under the controlling case law, it is entitled to have the court enter judgment in its favor. For example, the defendant coal supplier could file a motion for summary judgment contending that there had been no enforceable written contract, and so a judgment should be entered in the defendant's favor ordering that the plaintiff "take nothing" for the lawsuit. The other side will oppose this motion by filing a response in which it argues either that a jury must be allowed to decide the case because there are disputed facts, or, for various legal reasons, that the controlling opinions do not mean that the movant should win as a matter of law. So the plaintiff in our coal case might contend that there really was a written contract and that a jury needs to decide whether to believe the plaintiff's story that his dog had eaten it.

When the trial court judge grants or denies the motion for summary judgment, he may write an opinion which explains the facts of the case and the controlling legal principles, and then *applies* those legal principles to the facts of that particular lawsuit to explain why the court reached the result it did. Judges write opinions so that the parties understand why he ruled as he did; so that the appellate court can review whether his decision was correct (if there is a later appeal); and, in a larger sense, so that in the future other parties can conduct themselves in accordance with the law. This is one way the published opinions are created: district court judges sometimes write and publish opinions when deciding cases.

If the trial judge determines that the movant is entitled to win the case as a matter of law, the losing side can appeal after he writes the opinion. If the judge denies the motion, then there must be a jury trial, after which the losing side can still appeal. Judges sometimes write an opinion even after a jury trial, when denying the losing party's motion for new trial or motion for judgment as a matter of law (formerly, and in some states still, called judgment *non obstante verdicto*, or "JNOV").[4] This is another way published opinions are created: by district judges when explaining why the result reached after a trial by jury was correct and fair.

Any appeal will be decided by an intermediate appellate court (the exact name of which depends on whether the suit is in state or federal court). The party that *lost* in the lower court will appeal, and will be called the "appellant." The party that won will be called the "appellee." The parties will file their *briefs* in the appellate court. After reading the briefs and perhaps allowing a short oral argument, the appellate court will write an opinion that either *affirms* the trial court's judgment as correct, or *reverses* the trial court because it committed some reversible error. Any appellate court opinion which is published becomes part of the common law that can be applied by later courts. This is another way the published opinions are created.

The loser in the court of appeals can then try to appeal to the highest appellate court. (Usually called a supreme court.) As with appellate court decisions, the published opinions of the supreme court join the common law decisions.

Thus, we have opinions because of the way by which we resolve lawsuits in the common law system. The parties need to know *why* one side won. The reviewing appellate court needs to be able to check whether the lower court got it right. Society needs to know what the legal rules are so that in the future, people can avoid breaking the rules. That's why we have all these opinions.

D. The State and Federal Court Systems.

The next piece of the puzzle which no one will ever *explain* to you in law school is how the courts are structured. You are just supposed to already know it, or you are supposed to figure it out from reading opinions for class.

There are at least two reasons why you need to understand the court systems. (System*s*, not system.) First, it will help you understand cases better when you are preparing for class. When you read the case, and it says that the plaintiff lost in the trial court, but won a reversal in the appellate court, you will know that the plaintiff will be the appellee in the decision in the supreme court.

---

[4]   A motion for summary judgment is thus brought *before* trial; a motion JNOV is brought *after* trial.

Second, the fundamental principle of legal reasoning is the doctrine of precedent. You have to know which earlier cases are *controlling* precedent over the particular court your case is in. In order to know which cases are *binding* on your court, you have to understand how the state and federal judicial systems in the United States are structured. (You'll see why in a moment.) The doctrine of precedent is crucial in the practice of law and in the United States legal systems.

The fact that the United States has the federal judiciary, along with fifty independent state court systems, as well as countless administrative and quasi-judicial bodies, makes it probably the most complex judicial system in the world. Welcome to it!

1. The Structure of the Federal Court System.

The federal court system has a pyramid structure. The federal district courts, of which there are about ninety, are at the base. Twelve federal appellate (or "circuit") courts make up the middle. At the top of the judicial pyramid sits the United States Supreme Court.

We'll study the federal judicial pyramid from the bottom up.

a. United States District Courts.

As mentioned, there are about ninety federal district courts. Each state has at least one, and most states are divided into several districts.

Lawsuits must originally be filed in district courts. All federal trials take place in the district courts. Witnesses testify, evidence is received, and juries reach their decisions *only* in these district courts. District courts are the only courts which *find facts*; appellate courts cannot do so, but instead merely apply the law to the facts as found by the district court, or determine whether there is evidence to support the district court's fact-findings. Appellate courts merely review the written "record" of testimony and exhibits taken in by the trial court and apply the law to double-check whether the trial court was correct.

Federal district court opinions are published in the "F. Supps." (Federal Supplement) Reporters. (More about reporters later.)

b. United States Courts of Appeal—the Circuit Courts.

Appeals from district courts, with few exceptions, are heard by federal appellate courts, called "circuit courts." The United States is divided into twelve regional circuits—the first through eleventh, plus the Court of Appeals for the District of Columbia. (There is also the "Federal Circuit," which takes appeals from all over the country, but only on certain issues, like patent cases.)

An appeal from a district court must go to the circuit court for that particular region. For example, Texas is within the Fifth Circuit. California is within the Ninth. New York is in the Second. Illinois is in the Seventh. The District of Columbia has its own circuit. If you look in the front of any volume of the "F.2d's" (the Federal Second Reporters), you'll see a map of which states are in each circuit. (Again, reporters are discussed below.) So, if you lose a case in a federal district court in Texas, you file your appeal with the Fifth Circuit. If you lose one in a California federal district court, you appeal to the Ninth Circuit.

Whoever lost in the district court may appeal. The loser—called in the appellate court the "appellant"—will file an opening brief in the circuit court which explains why the district court's decision was wrong. Typically, the circuit courts limit appellants' briefs to fifty pages. Whoever won below will file an appellee's brief, which is also typically fifty pages. The appellant then usually gets a 25-page reply brief.

The appeal will be assigned to a "panel" from among the judges in that particular circuit. A panel usually has three judges. These three judges then read the briefs and sometimes permit a 30-minute (15 minute per side) oral argument. (Oral argument is becoming rare, which—you guessed it—is another reason why legal writing is so important.) Some time after oral argument, the court will issue a written opinion explaining why the district court was right or wrong, and so whether it is affirming or reversing the decision of the district court.

Lawsuits may not originally be filed in the appellate courts—each appellate court only *reviews* the decisions of the district courts in its circuit. As Justice Thurgood Marshall was quoted by The Wall Street Journal, "such appeals should await the outcome of the trial." It is hard to argue with that.

The opinions from the federal circuit courts are printed in the F.2d Reporters, and now the "F.3d's." Only circuit court opinions appear in the F.2d's. (Again, more about Reporters later.)

c. The United States Supreme Court.

If the loser in the court of appeals wants to try, it can ask the United States Supreme Court to review the case.[5] Again, the United States Supreme Court sits alone at the top of the federal judicial pyramid.

---

5   There are some circumstances where a party in a *state* supreme court can appeal to the United States Supreme Court, such as where the party claims a federal constitutional issue is involved. This is one of the few times when a state court case can be appealed to a federal court. Other than that, and the use by people convicted in state court of state crimes of federal petitions for writs of habeas corpus to review their convictions, the systems generally operate separately.

The principal way by which cases reach the Supreme Court is through the writ of *certiorari*. Whoever lost in the appellate court will write a "petition for a writ of *certiorari*," which argues why the Court should issue an order (a "writ of *certiorari*") directing the lower court to send up records of the case so that the Supreme Court can consider the issues which it is interested in, to see if the result reached in the case was correct. The loser is called a "petitioner" in the Supreme Court because that's what it's doing: it is petitioning the Court for a writ of *certiorari*. The winner in the circuit court will write a brief opposing *cert* (pronounced like the candy), arguing that either the circuit court decided the issues correctly, or that essentially the issues are just not important enough to warrant the Supreme Court's time, or both. The winner below is called a "respondent" in the Supreme Court because that is what it is doing: it is responding to a petition for a writ.

Nine justices (not, mind you, "judges") sit on the United States Supreme Court. Like all federal judges, they are appointed by the President, subject to approval by the Senate, and serve for life unless impeached. One of the nine is appointed Chief Justice, also subject to Senate approval. He (there has never been a female Chief Justice) presides over the Court's sessions and determines which justice will write each opinion.

If the Court grants *cert*, then the parties write briefs, much like they did in the circuit court. The Supreme Court then holds an oral argument and will later issue an opinion deciding the case. The Supreme Court's opinions are published in three different reporters: the United States Reports, the Supreme Court Reporters, and the Lawyer's Edition Reporters. (Again, more on the Reporters later—you try organizing all this stuff in a way that does it better!) The Supreme Court is the ultimate judicial tribunal: if you lose there, it's "game over."

As a final note, this structure—of written decision followed by appeal—has certain practical consequences, which we'll discuss in detail later. Primarily, if you are reading an opinion, you need to make sure that a court further up the pyramid has not already issued a later, different opinion because it heard an appeal. For example, you're reading the circuit court opinion in *Roe v. Wade*; if you are not careful, you will rely on "bad law" because later a reviewing court (the United States Supreme Court) took an appeal and issued a different opinion. (We will discuss these issues more in connection with how to "Shepardize" cases.)

2. The Structures of the State Court Systems.

The vast majority of cases are handled by state courts. Why? There are far more state courts than federal district courts, there are far more disputes which can be heard only in state court, there are more state laws than federal laws, and there is virtually no federal common law—only federal statutory law. *Erie Railroad Co. v. Tompkins*, 304 U.S. 64 (1938). (*Erie* is a famous case you will read as a 1-L.) Federal courts are courts of *limited jurisdiction*. Only suits which are expressly recognized by federal law may be filed in federal court. Everything else must go to state court.[6] There is very, very little federal law governing divorce, car wrecks, breach of contract, products liability, and most common disputes. Thus, most cases must go where most of the governing law subsists: in state court.

The structure of each state court system varies by state. Each state has between two and four levels of courts. Generally, most states have lower courts of limited jurisdiction. Examples of this kind of court include county courts, family courts, municipal courts, JP (justice of the peace) courts, or small claims courts. The next higher level consists of the district or superior courts, which also act as appellate courts for cases decided by the courts of limited jurisdiction. Next up are the "true" appellate courts often thought of as intermediate appellate courts. Finally, at the top, sits a court of last resort, usually, but not always, called the state's "supreme court."

a. Courts of Limited Jurisdiction.

At the bottom of each state court "pyramid" are its courts of limited jurisdiction. These can include municipal courts, JP courts, small claim courts, family courts, and the like. These courts have limited jurisdiction. This means

---

6   There is something called "diversity jurisdiction," which allows people to file a lawsuit in federal court only because the defendant resides in a different state than the state in which suit is brought. Even in such suits, however, state law is applied to the merits of the dispute.

that they have jurisdiction[7] to handle cases involving only smaller amounts of money, or only certain kinds of cases (for example, landlord-tenant disputes).

Generally, these courts are informal. Parties often file suits without a lawyer; the rules of evidence may not apply; and the judges probably never write opinions that will be published in the reporters. These courts are critically important to solving the problems that confront people every day, but they

---

[7] The word "jurisdiction" has many different meanings in the law. Here, it essentially means that the court does not have the legal authority, or power, to even address the parties' claims. For a case illustrating another meaning of "jurisdiction," see *Searight v. New Jersey*, 412 F. Supp. 413 (D. N.J. 1976). There, the defendant alleged that he had been taken to a speech clinic while in the custody of the state of New Jersey and had been "unlawfully injected . . . in the left eye with a radium electric beam. As a result, he claims that someone now talks to him on the inside of his brain. He asks money damages of $12 million." 412 F. Supp. at 414. The district court dismissed for lack of jurisdiction—of a different sense than we are using here—reasoning as follows:

> The allegations, of course, are of facts which, if they exist, are not yet known to man. Just as Mr. Houdini has so far failed to establish communication from the spirit world, so the decades of scientific experiments and statistical analysis have failed to establish the existence of "extra sensory perception" (ESP). But, taking the facts as pleaded, and assuming them to be true, they show a case of presumably unlicensed radio communication, a matter which comes within the sole jurisdiction of the Federal Communications Commission. And even aside from that, Searight could have blocked the broadcast to the antenna in his brain simply by grounding it. See, for example, *Ghirardi*, "Modern Radio Servicing", First Edition, p. 572, ff. (Radio & Technical Publishing Co., New York, 1935). Just as delivery trucks for oil and gasoline are "grounded" against the accumulation of charges of static electricity, so on the same principle Searight might have pinned to the back of a trouser leg a short chain of paperclips so that the end would touch the ground and prevent anyone from talking to him inside his brain.

> But these interesting aspects need not be decided here. It is enough that . . . the court lacks jurisdiction. The complaint will be dismissed with prejudice.

412 F. Supp. at 414-15 (citations omitted).

generally do not add much to the common law, because they do not write opinions that are published in the reporters.

b. District or Superior Courts.

Just above the courts of limited jurisdiction are the district courts. In some states, they are called superior courts. District courts handle the bulk of the state court caseload. They also handle appeals from the courts of limited jurisdiction: the loser in a lawsuit filed in a court of limited jurisdiction can "appeal" up to the district or superior court, although usually the "appeal" takes the form of a completely new trial—"*de novo* review"—rather than the review only by written briefs which takes place in the typical appeal.

Practice before a state district court is, in broad view, much the same as in a federal district court (discussed above). The procedural rules can be quite different, however, and so the actual daily practice may be very different. For our purposes, however, they are quite similar: the written practice consists of pleadings and motions supported by briefs.

The state district courts generally do not issue written opinions for publication in the reporters. For that reason, they do not directly add much to the law. However, they *apply* the law to the facts of the bulk of the disputes.

c. Intermediate Appellate Courts.

Intermediate appellate courts exist in many states and are much like the federal circuit courts. In most states, as a matter of right the loser in a district court can appeal and have a state court of appeals review the district court's decision for error.

The briefing practice in state appellate courts is much like it is in the federal circuit courts: main brief, response; reply, followed (perhaps) by oral argument.

State appellate courts often publish their decisions in the reporters. The bulk of state law is written by state intermediate appellate courts. The state appellate court opinions are published in the Regional Reporters (called by their regional name—Northwest, Southeast, Southern, *etc.*).

d. Courts of Last Resort: State Supreme Courts.

At the top of state court systems is a court of ultimate review. In a deliberate scheme to confuse you, New York calls its supreme court the "court of appeals," and Texas has *two* supreme courts—one for criminal matters and the other for civil suits. Most states, thankfully, have only one highest court, and they call it the supreme court.

Most state supreme courts act like the United States Supreme Court, taking only those cases in which they are interested and ignoring the others. They will decide whether to take your case based only on the written briefs. This means that only your *writing* can persuade the court to review your case (which, you guessed it, is yet another reason writing is so important).

Like the state appellate courts, state supreme courts usually publish their opinions, and they are printed in the Regional Reporters. As in the federal system, if you are reading a case written by a state appellate court, you need to make sure that the state supreme court has not, after an appellate court published its opinion, taken review of the case and reversed or otherwise disagreed with it in a later opinion.

3. The Structure of the Courts and the Concept of *Controlling* Precedent.

The concept of *controlling* precedent has two different but interrelated aspects. First, is the *spatial* aspect. For precedent to be controlling, the opinion must have been written by a court directly up the pyramid from the court in issue. The second aspect relates to the source of the law at issue (state or federal) and whether the earlier opinion was written by a court *based in the same system as the law at issue*.

The first aspect is easy to describe. An earlier decision by a court directly above the court in issue is binding on the lower court. As explained above, both the federal and state court systems are shaped like pyramids. On top of the federal system sits the United States Supreme Court, and on top of each state system sits a supreme court. Below each are several intermediate appellate courts. At the bottom are many trial courts.

Within each system, whether a prior case is binding precedent depends on whether the case was decided by a court *directly* up the pyramid. So a state supreme court's decision is *binding* on every court in that state. A state appellate court's decision is *binding* only upon the trial courts which are in that appellate court's geographic region. (State appellate courts, like the federal circuit courts, usually take appeals from the state district courts in their particular and statutorily defined area of the state.) State district court opinions are *binding* only on the same state district court.

These same principles apply with equal force in federal court: the United States Supreme Court's interpretation of federal law controls all the circuit courts and all the federal district courts. Each circuit court's opinion controls only the federal district courts which are located in that circuit. A federal district court's opinion is *binding* only on itself.

For example, if the Supreme Court of Oregon had held in a published opinion that under *Oregon state law* failing to warn that cigarettes are dangerous always constitutes a breach of duty, then every Oregon state court is bound by that decision, and must apply that same rule to all future cases which come before them that involve that issue. If an Oregon appellate court had made that same holding, then the Oregon Supreme Court would not be bound (it's *up* the pyramid), but every trial court within the geographic region controlled by that particular appellate court would be bound.

The same principles operate in federal court. If the Ninth Circuit held that the use of inside information to buy stock constituted a violation of *federal law*, that decision would be binding on all federal district courts in the Ninth Circuit (the West Coast area), but it would not be binding on any federal district court in any other circuit (they are not directly below the Ninth Circuit in the pyramid); nor would it be binding on any other circuit (they are at the same level on the pyramid, not directly below). Plainly, it would not bind the United States Supreme Court, which is *up* the pyramid.

The concept (and law) of binding precedent gets murky when you move to the second aspect: whether the prior opinion was written by a court based in the same system as the law at issue. Put in concrete terms the issue is: was the earlier court a federal court applying federal law; a federal court applying state law; a state court applying state law; or a state court applying federal law? (As mentioned above, usually state courts apply state law to their cases because that's what governs since there is so little federal law. However, state courts can decide issues of federal law and federal courts can write about state law.)

In the United States' federal form of government, two primary sets of laws generally co-exist: those of the federal government, and those of each of the fifty states. There are multiple layers of federal law, from the United States Constitution at the top, down to federal statutes enacted by Congress, down to federal regulations promulgated by federal agencies under the authority delegated to them by Congress. Likewise, each state has a constitution, statutes, regulations; and there are county and municipal ordinances, too. Each state also has its own common law; but there is very little federal common law. In addition, the federal system has its own distinct rules of procedure and evidence, as do each of the fifty states.

The federal and state courts are autonomous when applying the law that they have created. That is, a federal court's interpretation of federal law controls a state court's interpretation of federal law; a state court's interpretation of state law controls a federal court's interpretation of that state's law. On the other hand, a federal district judge should follow any state court decisions on state law; a state judge should follow a federal court's opinion interpreting federal law.

However, where one court interprets the other's law, no controlling effect need be recognized. Thus, for example, a New York municipal court judge does not have to follow what the United States Supreme Court unanimously held about New York state law because the Supreme Court's decision is not *controlling.*[8] Similarly, a federal district court does not have to give any weight whatsoever to an opinion by the state supreme court on the meaning of federal law.

To wrap up the concept of controlling precedent: there are two aspects to determining which law controls. First, was the prior case written by a court further up the pyramid from the court your case is in? Second, was that court interpreting its own law or some other jurisdiction's? If it was a court further up the pyramid applying the particular law at issue, then that opinion is a binding interpretation of the law.

These concepts are fundamental to the federal system we have, in which the state and federal courts co-exist. (Although federal law, as the supreme law of the land, controls to the extent state law conflicts with federal law.) They also will help you identify which jurisdictions to research for relevant case law. For example, if you are addressing a problem concerning a lawsuit filed in a Pennsylvania federal district court, and the lawsuit is about a car wreck in Pennsylvania, the decisions of Pennsylvania state courts—from the Pennsylvania Supreme Court on down—would *control.* If you are in Montana state court and the issue is one of federal securities law, then federal law—as interpreted by the United States Supreme Court on down—will control. If you are in Arizona state court and the lawsuit is about an Arizona divorce, the opinions written by the Arizona Supreme and appellate courts control. In each instance, if some *other* court has previously written an opinion about that issue, that opinion may be persuasive authority—especially if the opinion is right "on point" (a concept we will talk about below)—but it is not *controlling* precedent.

4. Precedent and Why the Court Systems Are Structured Like They Are.

Only one district judge works on a case; three circuit judges typically decide an appeal in a federal district court; nine justices hear each case before the United States Supreme Court. The higher you go up the pyramid, the more judges you get. The same holds true in state court.

---

8   As a *practical* matter, of course, if you are in federal court it may be more likely to follow the circuit court's interpretation rather than the state's courts because the federal district judge knows that it is the judges on the federal circuit court, not the state court, who will reverse him.

A related issue arises when courts in one state interpret a sister state's law. As a purely legal matter, those cases should be treated no differently than a federal court within the state interpreting the state's law. However, as a practical matter, cases decided by state or federal courts outside the relevant state are given less weight.

Given that most cases are not appealed, and most cases which are appealed to a circuit court are not taken to the Supreme Court, one would think the allocation would make more sense were it the other way around: you get nine judges at the start, and only one at the end. However, more judges decide each case the higher up it goes because the *controlling* effect of the opinion grows broader. The opinion of a district court is binding precedent on that court. However, an opinion from a circuit court is binding on that court *and* all of the district courts within its circuit. The decisions of the Supreme Court are binding on all the circuits and every district court.

Thus, having an increased number of judges at higher levels on the pyramid is well thought out from the point of view of the controlling effect that the doctrine of precedent will give to the particular court's opinions. The wider the controlling effect of the court's opinions, the more judges are involved in deciding the case.

IV. The Common Law Reasoning Process

A. Introduction.

As just shown, courts decide cases and write opinions about them. Those opinions (also called decisions or cases) are often published in the reporters. Then, judges decide later cases by looking back at what has already been written on a specific legal issue, and those judges *apply* the existing law to new cases.

Because the common law develops on a case-by-case basis, the basic pattern of legal reasoning and argument under the common law is *to reason by example*. A judge will compare the facts of the later case to the facts of earlier written opinions to find out which rules apply to the issue and what result must be reached. This means that the common law method is to reason and write by analogy: No two cases are identical, so lawyers must be able to spot similarities and differences between the facts of the written opinions and the facts of the later case and predict whether a court would find the cases so similar that it would reach the *same result* as was reached in the earlier opinion, or whether it would find the differences between the facts sufficient enough so that the court would reach a *different result* when deciding the later case.

If the facts of the new dispute are not sufficiently different from the published opinion, then the court must reach the same *result* that was reached in the opinion (assuming it was controlling precedent). For example, suppose the earlier controlling opinion stated that the rule was that killing someone is "murder" unless the killing is justified. In that earlier opinion, the court held that killing was not justified where the defendant's only excuse for murdering his neighbor had been that the neighbor's dog was ugly. In a later case, the court must apply the *same rule* (killing is murder unless justified) and it must reach the *same result* (conviction for murder) *unless* the facts of the later dispute are distinguishable from the earlier opinion. Suppose, for instance, that in the later dispute the defendant had killed someone because she had shot at him for no reason. That might be "justified" as self-defense.

This fundamental idea—that two cases which have *similar* facts should be treated as if they were the *same*—is the linchpin of the common law system. It is called the doctrine of precedent.

There are two terms related to these issues which you will hear early in law school, and which you need to understand now. The first is "*stare decisis.*" It means "strict precedent," and stands for the idea that a later court should be strictly bound by an earlier, controlling court's opinion. This basic principle of the common law doctrine of precedent is this: the law (that is, the *result* in light of the facts in the prior controlling opinion) must be followed. If an earlier opinion held that someone who trespasses on another's land is liable for the damage she causes, then that "rule" must be *consistently* applied to later cases, and the same *result* must be reached in all cases which have *facts* which are not legally distinguishable from the earlier opinion. So, a later court cannot simply say that someone who trespasses is liable for all damages she causes, unless the trespass occurred on a Thursday.

Here is an example of one court following the doctrine of precedent by applying the rule from an earlier case to a later dispute. In the first case, *Peek v. Ciccone*, 288 F. Supp. 329, 334 (W.D. Mo. 1968), a prisoner brought a *habeas corpus* proceeding[9] because he had claimed "that he had had a religious experience in which it was revealed to him that he was the reincarnation of Jesus Christ." 288 F. Supp. at 333. The prisoner claimed that because he was the reincarnation of Jesus Christ "he is entitled to communicate his revelation and claims to the Pope for recognition of the fact that he has fulfilled the secret prophecy and is the spirit of Christ reincarnated." 288 F. Supp. at 329. The court held that the state had violated his constitutional rights by prohibiting him from communicating with the Pope because to "forbid this is an invidiously discriminatory and arbitrary denial of religious freedom." 288 F. Supp. at 334.

A later court, following the doctrine of precedent, applied the rule from *Peek* to a *habeas corpus* claim by a prisoner who claimed that he was "not Raymond Collins but the 'prophet Mohammed,' and he was convicted under the wrong name." *Collins v. Henman*, 676 F. Supp. 175, 175 (S.D. Ill. 1987).[10] Pay attention to how the court applied the doctrine of precedent when you read the justification for its decision:

---

9   A *habeas corpus* proceeding is a proceeding in which a prisoner incarcerated in a state prison may bring a federal lawsuit and show that his constitutional rights were violated by the conviction or the conditions of incarceration. *Habeas corpus* proceedings are one of the few times when federal courts review state court decisions.

10   Why was *Peek* not *controlling* authority? Hint: look next to the date of the two opinions.

Central to petitioner's claims is his statement that he is the prophet Mohammed, the authority of Islam in the East and West and presumably the same prophet Mohammed who died in the year 632. It might appear that this action is frivolous and subject to *sua sponte* dismissal for that reason alone; but it is not the place of a federal court to decide which is the true faith or who is a true prophet. We will, therefore, accept plaintiff's claims in good faith in making our threshold determination. *Peek v. Ciccone*, 288 F. Supp. 329, 334 (W.D. Mo. 1968) (Federal prisoner claiming to be the reincarnation of Jesus had a constitutional right to write to the Pope to share his good news; court accepted plaintiff's beliefs as held in earnest).

676 F. Supp. at 176 (citations omitted). Nonetheless, the court dismissed Mr. Collins' petition as frivolous because he had not properly exhausted his state court remedies before seeking federal *habeas corpus* relief. *Id.*

The *Collins* court followed the doctrine of precedent because it applied the rule from *Peek*—that a prisoner's claim that he is a reincarnated deity must be accepted as being made in good faith—and then applied that rule to the slightly different fact pattern of whether Mr. Collins was the prophet Mohammed. It would be an arbitrary world indeed if someone's claim that he was a Christian religious figure must be accepted in good faith, but someone's claim that they were an Islamic religious figure would not be accepted in good faith. The doctrine of precedent helps society by creating certainty—even in areas where certainty might not be so important, such as with claims by people that they are reincarnated religious figures.

The second term that you will hear early and often in law school is "*dicta*." This is what a later court (or a lawyer arguing a later case) can call language from an earlier opinion that was not necessary to that court's decision. For example, suppose an earlier court had said "running a stop sign is always negligence *per se*." ("*Per se*" is a Latin lawyer-word which means "as such" or "by itself;" so "negligence *per se*" means "negligence by itself.") If, in that earlier opinion, the jury had found the defendant had been negligent because he had run a stop sign, there was no reason for that court to "decide" whether, even if the jury had *not* found him liable for negligence, that running a stop sign was *always* negligence. Thus, the language is "*dicta*" because it was not *necessary* for the court to say it in order to uphold or explain the result reached by the jury.

Here is a real example of *dicta*. In *State v. Tweedie*, 444 A.2d 855 (R.I. 1982), the defendant had been charged under a specific statute with "cruelly killing" a cat by placing it in a microwave oven. A state statute, Section 4-1-2, outlawed "cruelly killing" animals. The court, though noting that it "would be absurd for us to conclude that the killing of the cat in this manner was not a cruel killing prohibited by the language of § 4-1-2" nonetheless engaged in the following unnecessary reasoning in *dicta*:

> It is well settled that it is the duty of the factfinder to draw inferences. The evidence before the trial justice was that the cat was found alive in the microwave oven even after it had been burned extensively. It survived briefly after removal from the oven. *Admittedly animals are not capable of communicating verbally.* However, reasonable inferences of severe suffering are easily drawn from the evidence.... After Tweedie admitted placing the cat in the oven, turning it on, and leaving the cafeteria, his only concern was that he might have jeopardized his job.

444 A.2d at 858 (emphasis added).

Dicta can also be characterized as loose language; it's something the court did not have to write in order to reach the result it did. To illustrate the problems created by the *Tweedie* court's *dictum* that animals cannot talk, suppose you have a client who claims that his cat talks to him. Being a zealous advocate, you want to rely on those opinions which have held that cats can talk. *See, e.g., Miles v. City Council of Augusta,* 551 F. Supp. 349, 350 n.1 (S.D. Ga. 1982) (judge heard cat say "I love you" and "I want my mama"), *aff'd,* 710 F.2d 1542 (11th Cir. 1983) ("Blackie even purred 'I love you' to [the district judge] when he encountered Blackie one day on the street."). Thus, you have the explicit findings in *Miles* that cats can talk versus the *dictum* in *Tweedie* that they cannot.[11]

These two concepts—*stare decisis* and *dicta*—provide much of the basis for the common law system: Under *stare decisis*, a court must follow binding precedent which cannot be factually distinguished to the extent the prior court's decision is not *dicta*. If the facts of an earlier controlling case are not legally distinguishable, then the later court *must* reach the same result as the earlier case unless the language was *dicta*.

When are facts "different enough" to warrant a different result? If the judge believes the facts of a prior case are *analogous* to a later dispute, he or she is required by the doctrine of precedent to reach the same result in the later dispute that the earlier court reached unless there is a *distinction* between the facts of the earlier case and the later dispute *sufficient enough* so that justice, efficiency, or logic requires a *different result* in the later dispute. If the facts are

---

[11] It is uncertain whether any court will ever address this split among the courts as to whether cats can talk. Personally, because most cats cannot recognize their own names, I doubt any can talk.

not sufficiently different, the court will (implicitly, at least) *extend* the existing case law to reach the same result even though the facts in the later dispute are *slightly* different from the earlier opinions. *See, e.g., Zanzibar Shipping, S.A. v. Railroad Locomotive Engine Number 2199,* 533 F. Supp. 392, 394 (S.D. Tex. 1982) (defendant railroad "may have forged new ground in railroad history when one of its crews ran their train into the side of the 'Arctic Star'. Neither Lexis [a computer-aided legal research system] nor the Court's manual research has uncovered any other case of a train striking a ship."); *Nicholson v. Memorial Hosp. Sys.,* 722 S.W.2d 746, 748 (Tex. Ct. App. 1987) ("This is a case of man bites dog."). For example, if the earlier opinion held that a seller is responsible to a buyer for money damages when a house burns down before the sale is consummated, then that later court will reach that same result if faced with *similar* facts—unless there is a factual distinction which warrants reaching a different result.

There is an obvious purpose served by the doctrine of precedent. By following precedent—by following the law—courts not only efficiently resolve the disputes before them, they also provide consistent rules to which people can later conform their conduct. If drivers know they will be liable for any accident that happens when they run a stop sign, they'll know not to run stop signs. If sellers know they are responsible for damages to the house they are selling until the time of sale, sellers will have insurance in force until then. If people know they will be liable for trespassing, they will respect property rights. If sellers of coal know they will be liable for *all* losses they cause when they fail to deliver, they will use contracts with their buyers that limit potential damages.

This doctrine of precedent serves "that curious, almost universal sense of justice which urges that all men are properly to be treated alike in like circumstances." Karl Llewellyn, Case Law, 3 *Encyclopedia of the Social Sciences* 249 (1930). The issue for lawyers and judges facing a new case is this: when are two admittedly *different* cases similar *enough* in their *facts* to be treated alike?

This idea is critical. One of the best expressions of it comes from *An Introduction to Legal Reasoning*, where Edward Levi makes the following keen observations about the role of precedent in legal analysis:

> The problem for the law is: When will it be just to treat different cases as though they were the same? A working legal system must therefore be willing to pick out case similarities and to reason from them to the justice of applying a common classification. The existence of some facts in common brings into play the general rule . . . .
>
> Therefore, it appears that the kind of reasoning involved in the legal process is one in which the classification changes as the classification is

made. The rules change as the rules are applied. More important, the rules arise out of a process which, while comparing fact situations, creates the rules and then applies them. But this kind of reasoning is open to the charge that it is classifying things as equal when they are somewhat different, justifying the classification by rules made up as the reasoning or classification proceeds. . . . Not only do new situations arise, but in addition peoples' wants change. The categories used in the legal process must be left ambiguous in order to permit the infusion of new ideas.

Mr. Levi captured the central issue of the common law system: when is it just, when is it fair, when is it right to treat different cases as though they are the same. That should be kept clearly in your mind throughout law school. It explains much of what you will be expected to do and learn.

Because of the doctrine of precedent, courts always look to earlier opinions to see if the facts in the present case differ enough for justice to require a different result. For that reason, it is not much of an exaggeration to say that the only thing that has changed since the Middle Ages is that, instead of analyzing whether the owner of a runaway horse-drawn carriage can be held liable for the injuries his horse caused to bystanders, the courts are analyzing whether cigarette manufacturers can be liable to "passive smokers." *See, e.g.,* *Hinman v. Yakima School Dist.*, 850 P.2d 536 (Wash. Ct. App. 1993). The rule, developed long ago, is that where someone does an "affirmative act," and injures someone while doing it, he is liable to that person if the harm was foreseeable. Courts in England analyzed whether bystanders' injuries were foreseeable to the carriage owner; courts today analyze whether injuries caused by passive smoke were foreseeable. Courts today thus *apply* the rules developed long ago, and reason by *comparing* the facts from the old opinions to the facts of the new dispute to see how the old "rules" should be applied to today's disputes. Occasionally, a court may decide that the facts are so different that the rule from the earlier rule *should not be applied*: that is, that the legal rule should be different. Or a court may decide that the original rule should never have been created in the first place (this can be seen in the debate over abortion since that right was first recognized in *Roe v. Wade*). That is less common than you might think, however. The common law process is pretty much old rules being applied to new facts.

B.   How Do Common Law Rules Develop?

Lawyers make it happen. Law school is about teaching people how lawyers make it happen. If you become a lawyer, you will make it happen.[12]

As shown above, under the common law system, most "rules" are written by courts. When a plaintiff files suit against a defendant, there are essentially three possible outcomes: (a) the case settles privately, and there is no reported opinion from the court; (b) one side or the other wins the entire lawsuit by filing some sort of dispositive motion (*e.g.*, a motion for summary judgment) or part of the lawsuit (*e.g.*, the court decides some discovery issue, dismisses some of plaintiff's claims, or grants partial summary judgment) and the court grants or denies the motion, and writes an opinion explaining its decision; or (c) the case proceeds to verdict, and a written opinion results, either as a consequence of trial or post-trial motions (*e.g.*, motions for directed verdict, motions notwithstanding the verdict, motions for new trial) or as a consequence of an opinion rendered on a later appeal.

Where the case does not settle privately, the trial court, and if there is an appeal, the appellate court, can issue a written opinion, setting forth the facts, the applicable rules, and how the rules operate when applied to the facts of the case. Whenever a court applies the rules to certain facts, those rules *change*, as shown above: no two cases are identical,[13] and so every opinion changes the law in some, perhaps slight and insignificant, way when the court compares the facts of the case at hand with those decided and written about in the published opinions. When explaining a dispute, the court in its opinion will either expressly or implicitly *limit* the earlier cases to facts which are different, or it will *extend* the reasoning of the earlier cases to cover the new, different facts.

In motion practice (either pre- or post-trial), one side will argue to the judge that, based upon the applicable rules and the facts as shown by the

---

[12]   *But cf.* Frank Easterbrook, *The Most Insignificant Justice: Further Evidence,* 50 U.Chi. L. Rev. 481, 485 & n.12 (1983) ("Some men achieve insignificance; others have insignificance thrust upon them.").

[13]   Well . . . maybe some cases are identical. The court's entire opinion in *Denny v. Radar Indus. Inc.,* 184 N.W.2d 289, 290 (Mich. App. 1971), reads:

> The appellant has attempted to distinguish the factual situation in this case from that in *Renfroe v. Higgins Rack Coating and Manufacturing Co., Inc.,* 17 Mich.App. 259, 169 N.W.2d 326. He didn't. We couldn't.

> Affirmed. Costs to appellee.

evidence, it is entitled to win.[14] If the motion is on the merits, the moving party will have to show that it is entitled to win as a matter of law (in other words, there is no reason to have a jury find any facts, because the court can decide the issue by itself). If the motion is directed toward a procedural issue (such as a discovery dispute), then the judge rules on the motion.

In motion practice, each side files briefs which argue that, under the rules as decided in the cases, it is entitled to win. Each side will argue that the case is like, or unlike, the precedential opinions: the lawyer who wants to avoid having the court reach the same result as in the earlier opinion will try to distinguish the case from that opinion, arguing that some difference in the *facts* calls for a different outcome, and so the earlier opinion should be *distinguished* on the basis of certain facts and so a different result should be reached. The other side will say, in essence, "no, the facts of this case and those of the earlier opinion cannot be distinguished, and so the same result reached in that earlier opinion should be reached here." Or it will say "yes, the cases are different, but it makes sense to treat the cases as if they were the same by *extending* the rule from the earlier case to this case because the difference in facts is not legally significant." This is the basic process of common law reasoning.

C. Examples of the Common Law Case Method.

1. Hypotheticals.

The basic issue for lawyers in the common law system is this: In two prior opinions, the courts will reach different results despite confronting similar facts. A lawyer must analyze whether his client's case is more like one or the other of the earlier cases: is it like the case with the good result, or is it like the case with the bad result? The lawyer must argue to the court that the facts are different from the bad opinion, but like the opinion with the good result.

The judge then compares the facts of the new dispute to the prior opinions and reaches a result. If he reaches the same result on slightly different facts, he is *extending* the law slightly. If he reaches a different result on similar facts, he is *limiting* or *distinguishing* the prior opinions.

---

14   In cases which have gone to trial, the jury will listen to all of the evidence and decide its verdict in the case. If the losing party seeks judgment notwithstanding the jury's verdict or a new trial and the trial judge explains in a written opinion why he chooses to grant or deny the motion, or if there is an appeal on the merits or on some procedural ground, then a written opinion will result. Later, if that opinion has been reported and thus becomes precedent, it can be used just like any other opinion.

When a later dispute arises, the judge must look back through all of the opinions and compare their results and facts to the facts of the new dispute to decide what result is just. For example, suppose the court in the earliest opinion, called *"Smith v. Jones,"* wrote that speeding is *per se* (automatically) a breach of duty. A year later, another opinion is written about a car wreck involving speeding, but the later opinion—called *Bob v. Fred*—limits *Smith v. Jones* by stating that in *Smith v. Jones* the court had held that it was negligence *per se* because in *Smith v. Jones* the driver had been going 20 miles per hour over the speed limit. However, in *Bob v. Fred*, the court reaches a different result (no *per se* negligence by the speeding driver) because the speeding driver had been going only 5 miles per hour over the limit. Thus, the judge in *Bob v. Fred* limits *Smith v. Jones* to cases involving speeding of something more than five miles per hour over the limit. The *Bob v. Fred* opinion thus *distinguishes* the facts of *Smith v. Jones* because in *Bob v. Fred* the defendant had not been going 20 miles per hour too fast.

Note: the concepts of *distinguishing* and *limiting* are two sides of the same coin. If a court *limits* an earlier opinion to certain aspects of its facts, it will, no doubt, *distinguish* the facts it is addressing from the earlier opinion.

In law school, your professor will question you in class about *Smith v. Jones* and *Bob v. Fred*, and then he will ask you about a case where the speeding defendant had been going 12 miles per hour over the limit. You need to ask yourself: which is it more "like" or analogous to—5 or 20 miles per hour? Maybe there is another level of analogy: maybe in *Bob v. Fred* the speeding defendant had been going 5 miles per hour over a 55 mile per hour limit; but in *Smith v. Jones*, it had been 20 miles per hour over a 25 miles per hour limit. Maybe that level of comparison and more general level of analogy will make the results of the opinions make more sense and make for a more predictable rule.

Here is another hypothetical (but very likely) example of the common law development of a "rule." It seems likely that when cars first came along courts were faced with the question of whether speeding was automatically (*i.e.*, "as a matter of law") a "breach of duty."[15] Some jurisdictions (*i.e.*, states) probably held that any time someone caused an accident by speeding, that person breached a duty. Other jurisdictions may have recognized that speeding was evidence of a breach, but speeding did not automatically mean a breach of a duty; speeding was just evidence that the defendant had breached a duty. Over time, other states may have developed "bright line" rules which made sense to their judges: they might have held that where a person is speeding, it is evidence of a breach, but where they were speeding more than 20 miles per hour

---

15   Remember: the law is a set of rules defining duties which, if breached, mean that the breaching party must pay money to the injured party.

over the limit, that meant they automatically ("as a matter of law") breached a duty. Put another way: speeding more than 20 miles per hour over the speed limit would be negligence *per se*.

Obviously, these examples are simple. You should be recognizing that the common law is an ever-evolving series of cases. Judges in later disputes look back to the facts of the earlier opinions—to the rules which those courts applied and to the results those courts reached—in an effort to determine what result is just, predictable, and fair in the new dispute with its new facts.

2.   The Common Law Process: Real Opinions as Examples.

This section has three cases which analyze the same general legal principle—when may a person recover damages for "emotional distress." Although the cases were decided by courts in three different jurisdictions, ask yourself whether the results can be harmonized with each other. Is there some level of factual analogy at which the results reached in these cases can be explained and looked at as being consistent with each other?

a.   Emotional Distress for the Loss of a Dog's Corpse.

In *Corso v. Crawford Dog and Cat Hospital, Inc.*, 415 N.Y.S. 2d 182 (N.Y. City Ct. 1979), the plaintiff brought her poodle to the defendant's dog and cat hospital for treatment. The hospital "recommended euthanasia and shortly thereafter the dog was put to death." 415 N.Y.S. 2d at 182-83. The plaintiff and the defendant agreed that the dog's body would be turned over to an organization which would arrange a funeral for the dog. Instead, the plaintiff alleged that the defendant disposed of the dog's body, and failed to turn over the remains of the dog to her for the funeral. "A casket was delivered to the funeral which, upon opening the casket, instead of the dog's body, the plaintiff found the body of a dead cat." *Id.* at 183.[16] The plaintiff brought suit for mental distress and anguish, but had suffered no actual damages. The court held that Ms. Corso "did suffer shock, mental anguish and despondency due to the wrongful destruction and loss of the dog's body." *Id.* The court emphasized that she "had an elaborate funeral scheduled and planned to visit the grave in the years to come. She was deprived of this right." *Id.* Accordingly, the court awarded her $700 for her mental anguish damages. *Id.*

Ask yourself this: If *Corso* was the only opinion in New York, what result would a New York court reach if faced with a suit by the parents of a boy who had lost a spelling bee for mental anguish damages based on the following facts:

---

16   "*Id.*" is Bluebook for "the point I just made is supported by the prior cited case." (The Bluebook is discussed below.)

The spelling bee judges had incorrectly ruled that the boy had misspelled a word, and that after they discovered their error they let him compete in a run-off with the girl who had previously been ruled the winner; but he misspelled the first word, and so the girl won. Can the boy get mental anguish damages? How would you analogize the facts to the *Corso* case if you wanted to argue recovery should be allowed? (Hint: how is losing a pet's body "like" losing a spelling bee?) Think about this before you move on.

b. Emotional Distress for Losing a Spelling Bee.

In *McDonald v. John P. Scripps Newspaper*, 257 Cal. Rptr. 473 (Ct. App. Cal. 1989), parents filed a lawsuit on behalf of their son, who had lost a spelling bee. You guessed it: the boy had been incorrectly disqualified for misspelling a word. When the sponsors recognized their error, they held a run-off. In the run-off, the boy misspelled a word, and a girl won instead. The plaintiff contended that the girl who won the spelling bee should not have been allowed to compete in the run-off, and so he should have won. The parents alleged that the boy had "suffered humiliation, indignity, mortification, worry, grief, anxiety, fright, mental anguish, and emotional distress, not to mention loss of respect and standing in the community." 257 Cal. Rptr. at 476. The court held that mental anguish damages were not recoverable, reasoning:

> A judge whose prescience is exceeded only by his eloquence said that ". . . Courts of Justice do not pretend to furnish cures for all the miseries of human life. They redress or punish gross violations of duty, but they go no farther; they cannot make men virtuous: and, as the happiness of the world depends upon its virtue, there may be much unhappiness in it which human laws cannot undertake to remove." Unfortunately, as evidenced by this lawsuit, this cogent insight, although as relevant today as it was nearly 2000 years ago, does not always make an impression on today's practitioner.

> In *Shapiro v. Queens County Jockey Club*, (1945) 184 Misc. 295, 53 N.Y.S.2d 135, plaintiff's horse was the only horse to run the full six furlongs in the sixth race at Aqueduct Race Track after racing officials declared a false start. A half hour later, the sixth race was run again, and plaintiff's horse came in fifth out of a total of six.

> The *Shapiro* court held that plaintiff had no cause of action against the racetrack. Plaintiff could not support the theory that his horse would have won the second time around if all the other horses had also run the sixth furlongs after the false start. Plaintiff was not content to merely

chalk up his losses to a bad break caused by the vicissitudes of life. The lesson to be learned is that all of us, like high-strung horses at the starting gate, are subject to life's false starts. The courts cannot erase the world's imperfections.

The Georgia Supreme Court in *Georgia High School Ass'n v. Waddel*, (1981) 248 Ga. 542, 285 S.E.2d 7, decided it was without authority to review the decision of a football referee regarding the outcome of the game. The court stated that the referee's decision did not present a justiciable controversy. Nor does the decision of the spelling bee officials present a justiciable controversy here.

Our decision at least keeps plaintiff's bucket of water from being added to the tidal wave of litigation that has engulfed our courts.

257 Cal. Rptr. at 476 (some citations omitted). The court denied the recovery of mental anguish damages, emphasizing that "courts try to give redress for real harm; they cannot offer palliatives for imagined injuries." 257 Cal. Rptr. at 477.

Question: How would a California court rule on a claim by someone who sought mental anguish damages against a pet cemetery which had lost her dog's body? How would you *distinguish* losing a spelling bee from losing a pet's body if you were trying to argue that mental anguish damages should be allowed? (Hint: how is losing a spelling bee different from losing a pet's body?)

c. Mental Anguish Damages for Misidentifying the Number of Wheels on a Tractor Trailer.

The court in *Franklin v. State of Oregon*, 563 F. Supp. 1310 (D. Ore. 1983), held a claim for mental anguish damages was frivolous where the plaintiff sought $2 million in general damages and $1 million in punitive damages "for the mental frustration he says a Portland television station caused him when one of its programs allegedly misidentified a '14-wheeler tractor and trailer rig' as an '18-wheeler.'" 563 F. Supp. at 1326.

Question: Oh, never mind . . . .

d. Mental Anguish Damages and Agreements Concerning Divorces.

What follows is almost the entire opinion from the North Carolina Supreme Court's decision in *Stanback v. Stanback*, 254 S.E.2d 611 (N.C. 1979). This is one of my favorite opinions to use in my legal writing classes at the University of Houston Law Center, in part because the opinion is well reasoned, but also because it illustrates so much about the common law system. Notice how the law evolves right before your eyes. It also discusses some fundamental damage concepts which you will discuss in your first-year contracts class.

As you read *Stanback*, identify the rules the court creates and then applies. Ask yourself whether the North Carolina rule is any better than the rules from the other states, or whether the rule is better than (or even different from) North Carolina's prior common law rule. Notice how the court applies the doctrine of precedent, distinguishes cases, and limits others. Finally, notice how the court *applies* the law to the facts (at the very end of the opinion). Following the opinion, there are some questions for you to answer, so read the opinion slowly and take notes.

Stanback v. Stanback
254 S.E.2d 611 (N.C. 1979)

Plaintiff-wife brought this action seeking to recover . . . damages from defendant-husband for breach of contract . . . .

The complaint alleges that defendant-husband breached a part of their separation agreement, a supplementary letter-agreement given in consideration of the formal separation agreement's provision allocating the burden of payment of plaintiff-wife's attorneys' fees to her and increasing four of defendant's periodic payments to her by 25% of the wife's attorneys' fees as set by the court. The supplementary agreement was an agreement between the parties' attorneys, and reads in part as follows:

> "We agree that if Vanita Stanback is unable to deduct the fees she is required to pay you during 1968 that Fred Stanback will pay to her through you the difference in the federal and state income tax that she is required to pay by virtue of being unable to make this deduction for attorneys' fees.

> It is understood that a valid effort will be made by Mrs. Stanback to claim such deduction and that the tax returns for 1968, both federal and state, will be prepared under the supervision of one of you."

Plaintiff's complaint in Count Number 1 alleges: That plaintiff paid her attorneys $31,000.00, the fee set by the court, and claimed both federal and state income tax deductions in that amount; that the I.R.S. audited her 1968 tax return and disallowed $28,500.00 of the

$31,000.00 deduction; that the North Carolina Department of Revenue also audited plaintiff's 1968 tax return and disallowed $28,500.00 of the $31,000.00 deduction; that defendant, upon demand, refused to pay her tax deficiency; that as a result of this failure to honor their agreement, plaintiff was unable to pay her tax deficiency, and the United States subsequently filed a lien against her property; that in 1974 plaintiff borrowed $18,099.51, secured by a deed of trust on her home, to pay off her deficiency to the I.R.S. thus avoiding the sale of her home by the United States to satisfy the tax deficiency; that she has been unable to pay off the loan, and the lender is in the process of foreclosing on her home; that the State of North Carolina, as a means of collecting her State income tax deficiency, issued a garnishment against the defendant and, as a result of the garnishment, the defendant paid $2,989.00 plus interest to the State "using funds which he had agreed under the deed of separation between the parties to pay to the [plaintiff] for support and maintenance."

Plaintiff requested that the court award her $16,357.30 plus interest from December 31, 1968 as actual general damages. She also requested $250,000.00 consequential damages as compensation for mental anguish and loss of reputation in the community . . . . Plaintiff was allowed to amend her complaint to allege specifically that the consequential mental anguish damages were within the contemplation of the parties at the time they entered into the agreement.

The defendant moved . . . to dismiss . . . . The trial court . . . granted the . . . motion to dismiss . . . with the exception of that part of plaintiff's Count Number I requesting actual general damages for breach of the agreement.

From this order of the court, plaintiff appealed to the Court of Appeals, which affirmed the dismissals by the trial court. We granted plaintiff-appellant's petition for discretionary review of the decision of the Court of Appeals.

The motion to dismiss . . . tests the legal sufficiency of the complaint. *Sutton v. Duke*, 277 N.C. 94, 176 S.E.2d 161 (1970). In ruling on the motion the allegations of the complaint must be viewed as admitted, and on that basis the court must determine as a matter of law whether the allegations state a claim for which relief may be granted. . . . . As a general rule, "a complaint should not be dismissed for insufficiency unless it appears to a certainty that plaintiff is entitled to no relief under any state of facts which could be proved in support of the claim." The motion to dismiss the claims in Count Number I in this case was directed to the absence of any law to support the requests for relief. We therefor are required to examine the various requests for relief set forth in the claims in Count Number I and determine whether or not the law of this jurisdiction offers support for the requests made.

Count Number I-Breach of Contract

    e.   Actual Damages

Plaintiff's request for actual general damages was not dismissed by the trial court, and the sufficiency of that part of the claim is not before us.

Count Number I-Breach of Contract

    f.   Consequential Damages

In addition to her request for actual general damages under Count Number I, plaintiff requested that the court award her $250,000.00 in consequential damages as compensation for the "great mental anguish and anxiety [she suffered] as a result of the failure of the defendant to comply with his agreement." In support of this request plaintiff alleged: That she had insufficient resources to pay the deficiency assessed when the I.R.S. disallowed the major portion of her attempted deduction of the total amount paid to her attorneys; that upon her failure to pay, the I.R.S. filed a tax lien against her home, which became a matter of public record;

> that subsequently the I.R.S. came to her home and seized the property, posting a formal notice of seizure on the front door, visible to her neighbors and the public; that the I.R.S. subsequently levied on the property and published notice of sale of her home at public auction; that all the foregoing actions taken by the I.R.S. were given publicity in the local media thereby causing her to suffer great embarrassment, humiliation, and degradation in the eyes of her friends and the public in that "this information has been interpreted by the members of the public as indicating that she has failed to pay taxes which were justly due the Internal Revenue Service and indicating a lack of public responsibility and personal integrity"; that she was forced to borrow the sum needed to pay the deficiency, and because she is unable to pay off that loan, the

private lender is in the process of foreclosing on a deed of trust given on her home to secure the loan.

The trial court's action in granting defendant's motion to dismiss this request for relief raises the following issue on appeal: In an action based on an alleged breach of a tax deficiency indemnification agreement supplementing a general marital separation agreement is the plaintiff entitled to recover damages for mental anguish suffered as a result of the defendant's alleged breach?

When an action for breach of contract is brought, the damages recoverable are those which may reasonably be supposed to have been in the contemplation of the parties at the time they contracted. This limitation on the recovery of damages for breach of contract was first enunciated in the famous English case of *Hadley v. Baxendale*, 9 Exch. 341, 156 Eng.-Rep. 145 (1854). In applying this test we have often relied on the following declaration of it in the Restatement of the Law of Contracts:

> "Foreseeability of harm as a Requisite for Recovery. In awarding damages, compensation is given for only those injuries that the defendant had reason to foresee as a probable result of his breach when the contract was made. If the injury is one that follows the breach in the usual course of events, there is sufficient reason for the defendant to foresee it; otherwise, it must be shown specifically that the defendant had reason to know the facts and to foresee the injury."

Damages for injury that follows the breach in the usual course of events are always recoverable provided the plaintiff proves that such injury actually occurred as a result of the breach. Whether damages are recoverable for injury that does not follow breach of a particular contract in the usual course of events (special damages) depends upon the information communicated to or the knowledge of the breaching party at the time of contracting. *Troitino v. Goodman, supra; Iron Works Co. v. Cotton Oil Co.*, 192 N.C. 442, 135 S.E. 343 (1926). The test is generally described as one of foreseeability. In the first instance the damages recoverable are foreseeable because they are such that will follow in the ordinary course of events from breach of the particular kind of contract. In the second instance the damages recoverable are foreseeable because the party contracting had knowledge at the time he entered into the particular contract of the special circumstances giving rise to special damages upon breach, *i.e.,* damages that would not be expected to follow in the ordinary course of events from breach of the contract. This test of foreseeability generally achieves its purpose, *i.e.,* providing a workable method of imposing limitations on contractual liability, when strictly commercial contracts are involved and only damages for pecuniary loss are sought.

When recovery is sought for mental anguish suffered as the result of breach of contract, however, the rule has proven to be less than adequate, and courts as a general rule have denied recovery on policy grounds of limiting contractual risk with or without formal application of the *Hadley v. Baxendale* test. *See, e.g., Hall v. Encyclopedia Britannica, Inc.*, 325 Mich. 35, 37 N.W.2d 702 (1949); *Seidenbach's Inc. v. Williams*, Okl., 361 P.2d 185 (1961).

It is generally acknowledged that financial loss inflicted on an individual by breach of contract may often cause the party to suffer disappointment and mental anguish. McCormick on Damages, *supra*, at 145, pp. 592-93. Despite the probability of such mental anguish damages, recovery for them has been routinely denied in contract actions, generally on the stated grounds that mental anguish damages are too remote to have been in the contemplation of the parties to the contract. *E.g., Brunson v. Ranks Army Store*, 161 Neb. 519, 73 N.W.2d 803 (1955). This judicial reluctance to award damages for mental anguish in contract actions is reflected in the Restatement of the Law of Contracts, 341, p. 559:

> "In actions for breach of contract, damages will not be given as compensation for mental suffering, except where the breach was wanton or reckless and caused bodily harm and where it was the wanton or reckless breach of a contract to render a performance of such a character that the defendant had reason to know when the contract was made that the breach would cause mental suffering for reasons other than mere pecuniary loss."

The rule set forth in this section of the Restatement incorporates most of the exceptions which courts have created to the general rule against recovery of mental anguish damages in a breach of contract action. The earliest exceptions to the general rule came in cases involving breach of contract to convey a telegraph message. *SoRelle v. Western Union Telegraph Co.*, 55 Tex. 308 (1881), the first case in the United

States to hold that mental anguish damages were recoverable for breach of contract, involved the defendant's failure to transmit a message to plaintiff announcing his mother's death, which prevented him from attending her funeral. This Court adopted this limited exception for cases involving failure to transmit messages concerned with death or illness in *Young v. Telegraph Co.*, 107 N.C. 370, 11 S.E. 1044 (1890) and applied it in subsequent decisions. *Russ v. Telegraph Co.*, 222 N.C. 504, 23 S.E.2d 681 (1943); *Betts v. Telegraph Co.*, 167 N.C. 75, 83 S.E. 164 (1914); *Cashion v. Telegraph Co.*, 123 N.C. 267, 31 S.E. 493 (1898). Recovery in those cases was not limited by a requirement that the plaintiff suffer bodily harm as well as mental anguish. *Young v. Telegraph Co., supra.*

Other exceptions to the general rule against mental anguish damages in contract actions have been created. In *Allen v. Baker*, 86 N.C. 91 (1882), this Court held that such damages may be recovered for breach of contract to marry. Courts of other jurisdictions have allowed recovery of mental anguish damages when the breach amounts in substance to a wilful or independent tort. *E.g., Wall v. St. Louis & S. F. RR.*, 184 Mo.App. 127, 168 S.W. 257 (1914); and when the breach of contract involves the duty of an innkeeper or common carrier. *E.g., Southeastern Greyhound Corp. v. Graham*, 69 Ga.App. 621, 26 S.E.2d 371 (1943); *Milner Hotels Inc. v. Brent*, 207 Miss. 892, 43 So.2d 654 (1949). As the number of exceptions to the general rule has grown, some courts have attempted to formulate a rule to encompass them and provide a standard for determining whether a claim for mental anguish damage may be made in a contract action. In his treatise on remedies, Professor Dobbs notes this trend:

> Another group of cases have tried to formulate a broader doctrine, allowing recovery for mental distress resulting from breach of contract in a wide range of non-tortious breach situations. The formula for expressing the broader rule of recovery probably has not reached its ultimate form and it is expressed in various ways. The essential idea seems to be that some contracts clearly have what might be called personal rather than pecuniary purposes in view, and that the purpose of such contracts is utterly frustrated until mental damages are awarded for the breach." Dobbs, supra, at 12.4, p. 819.

Professor Dobbs correctly points out that in an attempt to formulate a rule to encompass the various exceptions courts have gone beyond the mere creation of isolated exceptions to the general rule and by doing so have formulated a principle that has the potential of allowing recovery for mental anguish in a wider range of cases. *See Crisci v. Security Ins. Co. of New Haven, Conn.*, 66 Cal.2d 425, 58 Cal.Rptr. 13, 426 P.2d 173 (1967); *Westervelt v. McCullough*, 68 Cal.App. 198, 228 P. 734 (1924).

The case of *Lamm v. Shingleton*, 231 N.C. 10, 55 S.E.2d 810 (1949) represents this Court's formulation of a flexible rule to encompass the various exceptions to the general rule against allowing mental anguish damages in a contract action. *Lamm* involved breach of a burial contract. Several months after defendant had performed his contract to bury plaintiff's husband, the vault in which plaintiff's husband's casket had been buried arose above the level of the ground during a very rainy spell of weather. Upon being informed of this, defendant took steps to reinter the body. The plaintiff was present at the time defendant raised the vault and it was discovered that the locks on the vault had either not been fastened or had broken and the vault had filled with water and mud, wetting the casket. Plaintiff sought damages for the shock and resulting nervous condition she alleged she had suffered as a result of viewing the damage to the casket. This Court held that the plaintiff's action was for breach of the contract made with defendant to bury plaintiff's husband and not an action in tort. The Court first took note of the general rule against mental anguish damages in contract actions stating:

> "[C]ontracts are usually commercial in nature and relate to property or to services to be rendered in connection with business or professional operations. Pecuniary interest is dominant. Therefore, as a general rule, damages for mental anguish suffered by reason of the breach thereof are not recoverable. Some type of mental anguish, anxiety, or distress is apt to result from the breach of any contract which causes pecuniary loss. Yet damages therefor are deemed to be too remote to have been in the contemplation of the parties at the time the contract was entered into to be considered as an element of compensatory damages." *Id.* at 14, 55 S.E.2d at 813.

Taking note of the various isolated exceptions to this general rule this Court in *Lamm* adopted what it described as "a definite exception" to the general rule, indicating that this formulation of the exception was sufficient to encompass the various isolated exceptions to the general rule and allow plaintiff to maintain her action for mental anguish damages:

> "Where the contract is personal in nature and the contractual duty or obligation is so coupled with matters of mental concern or solicitude, or with the sensibilities of the party to whom the duty is owed, that a breach of that duty will necessarily or reasonably result in mental anguish or suffering, and it should be known to the parties from the nature of the contract that such suffering will result from its breach, compensatory damages therefore may be recovered. 15 A.J. 600; McCormick on Damages 592; *Warner v. Allen*, 34 A.L.R. 1348. In such case the party sought to be charged is presumed to have contracted with reference to the payment of damages of that character in the event such damages should accrue on account of his breach of the contract." (Emphasis added.) *Id.* at 14-15, 55 S.E.2d at 813.

Applying this formulation of the exception to the alleged breach of the burial contract plaintiff had made with defendant, the Court in *Lamm* observed:

> "The tenderest feelings of the human heart center around the remains of the dead. When the defendants contracted with plaintiff to inter the body of the deceased husband in a workmanlike manner they did so with the knowledge that she was the widow and would naturally and probably suffer mental anguish if they failed to fulfill their contractual obligation in the manner here charged. The contract was predominantly personal in nature and no substantial pecuniary loss would follow its breach. Her mental concern, her sensibilities, and her solicitude were the prime considerations for the contract, and the contract itself was such as to put the defendants on notice that a failure on their part to inter the body properly would probably produce mental suffering on her part. It cannot be said, therefore, that such damages were not within the contemplation of the parties at the time the contract was made." (Emphasis added.) *Id.* at 15, 55 S.E.2d at 813-14.

In *Stewart v. Rudner,* 349 Mich. 459, 84 N.W.2d 816 (1957), the Michigan Supreme Court formulated an exception to the general rule against mental anguish damages in contract actions similar to that adopted in Lamm v. Shingleton, supra. Stewart involved an alleged breach of an agreement by defendant doctor to perform a Caesarian section delivery of plaintiff's child which failure resulted in the stillbirth of the child. Finding that plaintiff's complaint did indeed state a cause of action for mental anguish damages the Court in Stewart observed:

> "Few areas of our law, however, are more shrouded in mists of history and of doubt than this area of recovery for mental distress, for grief, anxiety, or sorrow. . . . We have come to realize, slowly it is true, that the law protects interests of personality, as well as the physical integrity of the person, and that emotional damage is just as real (and as compensable) as physical damages. . . ."

> . . . .

> "It is true, in the ordinary commercial contract, damages are not recoverable for disappointment, even amounting to alleged anguish, because of breach. Such damages are, in the words of defendant's requested charge, 'too remote.' But these are contracts entered into for the accomplishment of a commercial purpose.

> Pecuniary interests are paramount. In such cases breach of contract may cause worry and anxiety varying in degree and kind from contract to contract, depending upon the urgencies thereof, the state of mind of the contracting parties, and other elements, but is has long been settled that recovery therefor was not contemplated by the parties as the 'natural and probable' result of the breach. *Hadley v. Baxendale,* (9 Ex. 341, 156 Eng.Rep. 145, 5 Eng.Rul.Cas. 502); *Clark v. Moore,* 3 Mich. 55; *Miholevich v. Mid-West Mutual Auto Insurance Co.,* 261 Mich. 495, 246 N.W. 202, (86 A.L.R. 633); *Frederick v. Hillebrand,* 199 Mich. 333, 165 N.W. 810.

> "Yet not all contracts are purely commercial in their nature. Some involve rights we cherish, dignities we respect, emotions recognized by all as both sacred and personal. In

such cases the award of damages for mental distress and suffering is a commonplace, even in actions ex contractu . . . ."

. . . .

"When we have a contract concerned not with trade and commerce but with life and death, not with profit but with elements of personality, not with pecuniary aggrandizement but with matters of mental concern and solicitude, then a breach of duty with respect to such contracts will inevitably and necessarily result in mental anguish, pain and suffering. In such cases the parties may reasonably be said to have contracted with reference to the payment of damages therefor in event of breach. Far from being outside the contemplation of the parties they are an integral and inseparable part of it." (Emphasis added.) *Id*. at 465-71, 84 N.W.2d at 821-24.

The Alabama Supreme Court has also enunciated a rule intended to encompass the various exceptions to the general rule. In the case of *F. Becker Asphaltum Co. v. Murphy*, 224 Ala. 655, 141 So. 630 (1932) it was stated thusly:

"Yet where the contractual duty or obligation is so coupled with matters of mental concern or solicitude, or with the feelings of the party to whom the duty is owed, that a breach of that duty will necessarily or reasonably result in mental anguish or suffering, it is just that damages therefor be taken into consideration and awarded." *Id*. at 657, 141 So. at 631.

See also Hill v. Sereneck, 355 So.2d 1129 (Ala.Civ.App.1978).

There is a line of cases in California allowing recovery for mental anguish damages in contract actions. One of the earliest of these was *Westervelt v. McCullough*, 68 Cal.App. 198, 228 P. 734 (1924), wherein the plaintiff was allowed to recover for injuries she suffered as a result of defendant's breach of promise to provide plaintiff a home for the duration of plaintiff's life. Although the case involved physical suffering and illness resulting from mental anguish rather than mental anguish alone, the California court relied predominantly on contract cases from other jurisdictions in which recovery for mental anguish alone was allowed to hold:

> "Whenever the terms of a contract relate to matters which concern directly the comfort, happiness, or personal welfare of one of the parties, or the subject matter of which is such as directly to affect or move the affection, self-esteem, or tender feelings of that party, he may recover damages for physical suffering or illness proximately caused by its breach." *Id.* at 208-09, 228 P. at 738.

Subsequent California cases have applied this principle to recovery of damages in a contract action for mental anguish damages. *See Windeler v. Scheers Jewelers*, 8 Cal.App.3d 844, 88 Cal.Rptr. 39 (1970).

The standard for recovery adopted by the California courts appears to be the broadest in this area of the law. We think it is overly broad and imposes too great a burden on parties to a contract.

Having reexamined our own holding in *Lamm v. Shingleton, supra*, and cases from other jurisdictions in the same vein, we hold that a claim for mental anguish damages resulting from breach of contract is stated only when the plaintiff's complaint reveals the following. First, that the contract was not one concerned with trade and commerce with concomitant elements of profit involved. Second, that the contract was one in which the benefits contracted for were other than pecuniary, *i.e.*, one in which pecuniary interests were not the dominant motivating factor in the decision to contract. And third, the contract must be one in which the benefits contracted for relate directly to matters of dignity, mental concern or solicitude, or the sensibilities of the party to whom the duty is owed, and which directly involves interests and emotions recognized by all as involving great probability of resulting mental anguish if not respected.

Upon breach of contract of the nature just described, the mental anguish suffered will in almost every case result from other than pecuniary loss. And when a contract of such nature is involved, mental anguish damages are a natural and probable consequence of breach, and it can reasonably be said that such damages were within the contemplation of the parties at the time they contracted. In such an event, it is presumed that they contracted with reference to the payment of such damages in the event of breach. *Lamm v. Shingleton, supra*, at 14-15, 55 S.E.2d at 813; McCormick on Damages, supra, 595, p. 592.

Applying the foregoing principles to the present case, we affirm the opinion of the Court of Appeals holding that the trial court properly granted defendant's . . . motion to dismiss plaintiff's claim for mental anguish consequential damages. Although plaintiff's complaint reveals the contract she made with defendant husband was clearly not one concerned with trade and commerce and elements of profit, it also clearly reveals pecuniary interest was the motivating factor in the decision to enter into the contract. The agreement was one for the payment of money in the event plaintiff was unable to deduct fees she had paid to her attorneys and consequently assessed a deficiency on her income tax return for the year 1968. That plaintiff may also have sought to protect herself from the mental anguish which might or might not have resulted in the event of breach of such an agreement was a subordinate factor in her decision to enter into such a contract, if indeed a factor at all. *See Farmers Ins. Exchange v. Henderson*, 82 Ariz. 335, 313 P.2d 404 (1957); *Bolden v. John Hancock Mut. Life Ins. Co.*, 422 F. Supp. 28 (E.D.Mich. 1976). *But see Crisci v. Security Ins. Co. of New Haven, Conn., supra*.

Moreover, plaintiff's complaint clearly fails to show that the agreement was one in which the benefits she contracted for were directly related in any way to matters of mental concern or solicitude or her sensibilities, and that it directly involved interests and emotions recognized by all as involving great probability of resulting mental anguish if not respected. The agreement she made was for the payment of money to protect her from the economic loss she would suffer in the event her attempted deduction of the fees paid to her attorneys was disallowed. The contract is clearly distinguishable from those for breach of which mental anguish damages are recoverable, such as burial contracts, *Lamm v. Shingleton, supra*, contracts to marry, *Allen v. Baker, supra*, contracts to perform funeral services, *Meyer v. Nottger*, Iowa, 241 N.W.2d 911 (1976), and contracts to perform certain medical services, *Stewart v. Rudner, supra*. The trial court was correct in dismissing, and the Court of Appeals was correct in affirming the dismissal of plaintiff's claim for consequential mental anguish damages contained in Count Number I of her complaint. Accordingly we affirm the Court of Appeals upon this aspect of the case.

* * *

Things to think about:

1.   Write out "the rule" from *Stanback*, and the tests for each of its subparts, in outline form. Quote it or use language as close to the court's as you can.

ANSWER: *Stanback* typifies common law rules: there is a general rule (no mental anguish damages) with an exception (mental anguish damages if . . .):

Mental anguish damages are not recoverable for breach of contract unless the plaintiff's complaint reveals all of the following:

(1) the contract was not one concerned with trade and commerce with concomitant elements of profit involved;

(2) the contract was one in which the benefits contracted for were other than pecuniary, *i.e.*, one in which pecuniary interests were not the dominant motivating factor in the decision to contract; and

(3) the contract must be one in which the benefits contracted for relate directly to matters of dignity, mental concern or solicitude, or the sensibilities of the party to whom the duty is owned, and which directly involves interests and emotions recognized by all as involving great probability of resulting mental anguish if not respected.

2.   Suppose your client comes to you and says he has a breach of contract claim against the caterer of his daughter's wedding reception in North Carolina. He tells you that without any reason the caterer, right in the middle of the reception, gathered up all the food and drink, leaving his daughter embarrassed in front of 200 guests. What would you tell him regarding the likelihood of his recovering damages for mental anguish under *Stanback*? How would the *Stanback* test apply to those facts?

ANSWER: You would go through each part of the *Stanback* test and *apply* it to your client's facts by *comparing* the facts to those in *Stanback*. So, you might write:

Even though mental anguish damages are generally not recoverable for breach of contract, our client probably will be able to recover mental anguish damages under the three-part exception from *Stanback v. Stanback*, 254 S.E.2d 611 (N.C. 1979). First, the contract for catering of a wedding reception probably is "not one concerned with trade and commerce with concomitant elements of profit involved." *Stanback*, 254 S.E.2d at 617. The *Stanback* court held that a contract, made in connection with a divorce, for the husband to pay the wife money if certain income tax deductions were denied to the wife was not concerned with trade and commerce. *Id.* Thus, a court would probably hold that a contract to cater a wedding is also not concerned with trade and commerce.

Second, a court would likely hold that the catering contract, at least from our client's perspective, was "one in which the benefits contracted for were other than pecuniary, *i.e.*, one in which pecuniary interests were not the dominant motivating factor in the decision to contract." *Id.* In *Stanback*, the agreement was merely supplementary to a divorce agreement to pay money if a tax deduction was not allowed, and so the court held pecuniary interests were the dominating factor and so denied recovery of mental anguish damages. *Id.* Here, from our client's perspective, the contract is to receive personal services for an important public event. Therefore, a court would likely find that pecuniary interest was not the dominant factor.

The third requirement presents the greatest difficulty to our client. To recover mental anguish damages, "the contract must be one in which the benefits contracted for relate directly to matters of dignity, mental concern or solicitude, or the sensibilities of the party to whom the duty is owned, and which directly involves interests and emotions recognized by all as involving great probability of resulting mental anguish if not respected." *Id.* The *Stanback* court recognized that the contract there was "for the payment of money to protect her from economic loss . . . ." *Id.* This contract was not for economic protection, but it is unclear whether a wedding reception is a "matter of dignity" or whether catering directly relates to "the sensibilities" of our client. *Id.* As the *Stanback* court emphasized, most cases awarding mental anguish damages involved burials, but here . . . .

3. Is this a fair statement of what *Stanback* stands for: mental anguish damages are not recoverable for breach of any contract made in connection with a divorce. Why, or why not? Is that statement too broad? Or, is it too narrow? What language from the *Stanback* case best states the limited nature of its holding?

ANSWER: *Stanback* does not stand for the proposition that mental anguish damages are not recoverable for breach of every contract in connection with a divorce. As the *Stanback* court stated, the agreement at issue "was one for the payment of money in the event plaintiff was unable to deduct fees she had paid to her attorneys . . . ." *Stanback*, 254 S.E.2d at 621. Only similar agreements made in connection with a divorce are thus within *Stanback*.

4.   (a) Where does the "application" of the rule to the facts occur in *Stanback*? (b) What elements of the exception did the plaintiff win on?

ANSWER: (a) The last two paragraphs of the decision contain the court's application of the law to the facts before it. (Notice the words "*Applying the foregoing principles* . . . ." When courts apply the law, they often begin that part of their opinions with phrases like "applying," "here," "under these principles," or "in the case at bar.")

(b) The plaintiff in *Stanback* alleged that the contract was "clearly not one concerned with trade and commerce and elements of profit," but failed to allege that the contract "clearly reveals pecuniary interest was the motivating factor in the decision to enter into the contract." The *Stanback* court held that it was not enough that "plaintiff may *also* have sought to protect herself from the mental anguish" because it "was a subordinate factor . . . if indeed a factor at all." Finally, the plaintiff failed to allege facts which showed that the contract clearly was not "one in which the benefits she contracted for were directly related in any way to matters of mental concern . . . [or one that] directly involved interest and emotions recognized by all as involving great probability of resulting mental anguish if not respected." The *Stanback* court reasoned that the "agreement she made was for the payment of money."

D.   Statutory Interpretation.

In the common law system, the court's role is more or less the same when "interpreting" statutes or constitutions as when applying purely court-developed rules. Although some issues arise when analyzing statutes that do not come up when applying judge-made rules (*e.g.*, when applying an ambiguous statute, the courts look to legislative history as to what the legislators or Congressmen said during the debate on the law—there is no "legislative history" to judge-made rules) the process is strikingly similar. Once a court interprets a statute, that opinion will be precedent on later courts analyzing the same statute. *See generally, Easter Seal Society for Crippled Children and Adults of Louisiana, Inc. v. Playboy Enterprises*, 815 F.2d 323, 325 (5th Cir. 1987) (interpreting an undefined term in a federal statute, court recognized that "a substantial body of cases developed as courts worked out the definitions backwards in the usual manner of the common law").[17] Most often, of course, courts are forced to interpret statutes which are ambiguous, silent on the particular issue, and which have no legislative history. These courts usually then reason by looking at the other sections of the statute, and by trying to achieve the purpose of the statute. *See, e.g., Miles v. City Council of Augusta*, 551 F. Supp. 349 (S.D. Ga. 1982) ("Although the ordinance does not provide for the licensing of a talking cat, section 2 of the ordinance does require any 'Agent or Agency not specifically mentioned ...' to pay a $50.00 tax"), *aff'd*, 710 F.2d 1542 (11th Cir. 1983).

---

[17] Wonder how the Easter Seals Society for Crippled Children ever crossed paths with Playboy? Playboy had been a producer or distributer of a porno flick entitled "Candy the Stripper" which contained footage from a Mardi Gras parade put on by people belonging to the Easter Seals Society. 815 F.2d at 324-25. The film was shown on cable television in New Orleans, and "[o]ne or more viewers recognized themselves in the field footage now apart of 'Candy.'" Consequently, the Easter Seals Society sought an injunction against further use of the footage. 815 F.2d at 324.

The humor created by the style of the case was not lost on Judge Gee, who wrote:

> Thus, this most delightful of case names: *Easter Seal Society for Crippled Children v. Playboy Enterprises*; seriously rivaled, in our judgment, only by *United States v. 111/4 Dozen Packages of Article Labeled in Part Mrs. Moffat's Shoo Fly Powders for Drunkenness*, 40 F. Supp. 208 (W.D.N.Y. 1941)... and *United States ex rel. Mayo v. Satan and his Staff*, 54 F.R.D. 282 (W.D. Pa. 1971).

815 F.2d at 325 n.1. There are plenty of other funny case names. *E.g., Jordache Enterprises, Inc. v. Hogg Wyld, Ltd. and Oink, Inc.*, 828 F.2d 1482 (10th Cir. 1987) (analyzing whether blue jeans for fat women with pig logo and labelled "Lardashe" would be confused with Jordache jeans); *People versus PORN v. Nixon*, 465 F.Supp. 340 (N.D. Cal. 1978) (group called "People versus Profit of Richard Nixon" sought order requiring President Nixon to return all profits from Watergate to the federal government); *We've Carried the Rich for 200 Years, Let's Get Them Off Our Backs—July 4th Coalition v. City of Philadelphia*, 414 F. Supp. 611 (E.D. Pa. 1976).

The Common Law Reasoning Process

1. Hypotheticals.

Though they appear direct and simple, statutes are often subject to wide-ranging interpretation by judges when applied to particular sets of facts. The reasoning process is no different in applying a statute than it is under the general common law methods.

For example, suppose a state legislature or the Congress enacts a statute which says, "Abortion is illegal unless the mother's life is in danger." Under the statute, a woman who wants an abortion must prove to a court that her life would be "in danger" without one. What does "in danger" mean?

The rule could develop as follows. First, a case arises where the doctor testifies that the woman would be 100% certain to die during childbirth. It seems likely that a court faced with those facts would write an opinion stating that those facts constitute "in danger" in terms of the statute.

Another case could arise where the doctor testifies that there is a 50% chance she could die; the next case, 25%; then 10%. Eventually, a rule develops whereby women and doctors can predict the legality of their behavior: at some point the interpretation will develop that 25% is "in danger" but 24% is not.

Then, however, the rule will develop further when someone comes along at 20%, but the doctor testifies that even if she doesn't die, she will be paralyzed, and so the court will focus on what "mother's *life*" means. At that point, the court may carve out an exception to the 25% rule, and publish an opinion setting forth this new rule which will then become applied, adapted, changed, and disagreed with or limited by later courts.

That is a simple hypothetical example of how courts interpret statutes by applying their language to the facts of cases. It is also how the common law develops; instead of a statute saying "no abortion unless the mother's life is in danger," a court could have so held under the state's common law or the federal constitution. The same process would then ensue.

2. Real Examples of Statutory Interpretations.

What follows are three court opinions interpreting *real* statutes. You can see the common law reasoning process at work, even though they are statutes.

Once again pay attention to how I write about the cases. That is part of what you should be doing—getting familiar with legal writing, with how lawyers write about the law.

a. Rocky the Fighting Tortoise. After you have read the first example, ask yourself what part of the court's language is *dicta*: is it whether Rocky is an "animal," or whether he's a "fighting" animal. Which did it have to decide in order to resolve the case? Why did it bother resolving both? Why, a cynical person might ask, did it bother at all?

In *Jett v. Municipal Court*, 223 Cal. Rptr. 111, 112 (Cal. Ct. App. 1986), the defendant had been convicted of subjecting an animal, namely "Rocky, a/k/a J.P., a 50-year-old aldabra tortoise," to needless suffering and permitting Rocky to be on a street without adequate care or attention. *Id.* The trial court had fined Jett and ordered him to turn Rocky over to Mesa College, which apparently had cared for it after Jett had been arrested. *Id.* Jett then sought a writ of mandate for return of the tortoise, arguing that the statute did not give the court authority to take Rocky away. *Id.* at 113.

On appeal, the court noted that California's statute on the issue—Section 599aa—permitted only "fighting birds or animals" to be taken away from their owners. *Id.* at 114. Stating that a tortoise was not a "bird,"[18] the question for the court became whether Rocky the aldabra tortoise was a "fighting animal" in terms of California Penal Code § 599aa. *Id.* Interpreting that statute, the court reasoned:

> The People, nevertheless, seriously contend the forfeiture of fighting animals provided for in section 599aa authorized the court to award Rocky to Mesa College. This argument fails. Rocky is not a fighting animal. He is a reptile of the order Testudinata and of the genus Testudo, characterized as long-lived, slow-moving and herbivorous.
>
> It is true for some purposes, a tortoise is deemed an animal. Thus, a motion picture exhibiting the intentional killing of, or cruelty to an animal may be enjoined as a nuisance. For these purposes, the word 'animal' means any amphibian, bird, mammal or reptile, but not a fish[19] or insect. "Animal" in its broadest sense includes any organism

---

18   The conclusion that a tortoise is not a "bird" seems obvious. However, in *Regina v. Ojibway*, 8 Crim. L. Q. 137 (Canada 1965), the court held that a statute which prohibited killing small birds applied to the killing of a horse. Apparently, horses are "birds," but tortoises are not. Can a tortoise be both a "bird" and an "animal?" Is the statement that tortoises are not birds *dicta*? *See also* the next footnote.

19   [Court's footnote:]

Shakespeare, however, considered a tortoise a kind of fish:

"I do remember an apothecary, —
And hereabouts he dwells,—which late I noted
In tatter'd weeds, with overwhelming brows

of the animal kingdom, one of the three divisions into which natural objects are divided, the others being mineral and plant. We conclude the word "animal" as used in these Penal Code sections means a mammal as distinguished from a bird, reptile or other non-mammal.

> This slow-moving, grass-grazing giant tortoise is not a fighting animal. To say Rocky belongs in the ring is worthy of Mr. Bumble's observation in Charles Dickens' Oliver Twist: "if the law supposes that, ... the law is a ass, a idiot."

223 Cal. Rptr. at 114-15 (citations omitted).[20] The concurring judge noted that the argument was probably moot because Jett's conviction had been reversed, but he wrote that he hoped that "our decision will forestall the same problem should we be faced with Rocky II." *Id.* at 115 (Work, J., concurring).

Suppose the next dispute involves a *snapping* turtle. What result? Why? Suppose it involved a cat that had been trained to fight? What about a bull which had been in a bullfight? Are bulls and cats which are trained to fight "fighting animals" in terms of the statute? What's "fighting" really mean?

These are the kinds of issues which your professors will raise in class to illustrate legal reasoning. This is the sort of analysis which the common law requires.

b. **Animal Kingdom.** Here is a second example of a court interpreting a statute (in the form of a federal regulation promulgated by a federal agency under its congressional authority). In *United States v. Sproed,* 628 F. Supp. 1234 (D. Or. 1986), Mr. Sproed was cited by a park ranger because he and his young son had allegedly been unlawfully catching butterflies. The park ranger who had written the citation could find no law which they had broken, even

---

> Culling simples; meager were his looks,
> Sharp misery had worn him to the bones:
> And in his needy shop a tortoise hung,
> An alligator stuff'd, and other skins
> Of ill-shaped fishes .....

(Shakespeare, Romeo and Juliet, act IV, sc. v.)

20   The court also rejected, understandably with less discussion, the state's argument that "Rocky should be equated with a child" and so "Jett's rights to Rocky should be terminated as parental rights must yield when necessary to protect the child's best interest." 223 Cal. Rptr. at 115.

though he had spent "30 minutes on his C.B. and looking through his book...." 628 F. Supp. at 1237. Ultimately, the ranger relied on 36 C.F.R. § 2.1(a)(1),[21] which prohibited "[p]ossessing, destroying, injuring, removing, digging, or disturbing" any living or dead "wildlife," which was defined as "any member of the animal kingdom." 628 F. Supp. at 1236.

Thus, the court was squarely faced with determining whether a butterfly was "any member of the animal kingdom" in terms of this important federal regulation. Quoting poetry and relying on a Bloom County comic strip, the court affirmed the magistrate's order dismissing the citation and held that a butterfly was not a "member of the animal kingdom."[22]

What are butterflies, if not "wildlife?" Are they plants? Suppose a later dispute arises where a commercial butterfly breeding company sends thousands of paid employees into our national parks to gather every butterfly they can find to sell on the open market. How do you argue that the court should reach a different result than *Sproed*? Do you limit *Sproed* to cases involving non-commercial catchings? How does the Code of Federal Regulations recognize that distinction? Does it? Has the *Sproed* decision opened the possibility for the commercial exploitation of all our butterflies?

c.   Vessels in Navigation. Another interesting example of statutory interpretation occurred in *McClendon v. OMI Offshore Marine Service*, 807 F. Supp. 1266 (E.D. Tex. 1992). In that case, Mr. McClendon had been cooking a potato in the oven in the galley of a ship called the Galveston. "The potato was laced with mercury instead of the more traditional condiments." 807 F. Supp. at

---

21   "C.F.R." is Bluebook for "Code of Federal Regulations," the name for the hundreds of volumes of federal rules and regulations put out by the various federal agencies. These regulations often have about the same effect as a federal law enacted by Congress.

22   For other interesting cases involving statutes, see, for example, *The Eliza*, 4 U.S. (4 Dall.) 37, 39 (1800) (analyzing whether the French are an "enemy" in terms of a statute); *Mackensworth v. American Trading Transp. Co.*, 367 F. Supp. 373 (E.D. Penn. 1973) (analyzing, in rhyming verse, Pennsylvania's long-arm statute and constitutional due process).

One statute, which has yet to be interpreted by the courts, outlaws "thrashing" pecan trees, which is defined as beating or striking a pecan tree with a stick or other object. Tex. Rev. Civ. Stat. art. 6143.1 (Vernon Supp. 1994). Thrashers could be imprisoned for up to three months. *Id.* In 1971, the Texas legislature saw fit to allow people to thrash their own pecan trees. *See id.*

1267. Apparently, he was cooking the potato with mercury in it "in an effort to retrieve gold." *Id.* "Not surprisingly, McClendon sustained injuries while breathing mercury vapors escaping from the very hot oven containing the mercury-laden Idaho potato." *Id.*

The plaintiff brought suit under the Jones Act, which is a federal statute that only allows lawsuits where the injury occurs while the person is employed upon a "vessel in navigation." The court noted that the legal rule for determining whether a ship is considered to be "in navigation" is "whether or not the vessel was in drydock, the nature and extent of repair operations and who controls them." *Id.* The court held that the vessel was not "in navigation," reasoning:

> In this instance, McClendon was acting as a caretaker when injured aboard the GALVESTON at a time when it was in drydock, minus captain and crew, without any power of her own, and undergoing extensive repairs by contract workers which would eventually take 77 days to complete and over $25 million to pay for. Its bottom had been substantially removed. She was utterly incapable of navigation. Plaintiff admitted at oral argument that, had the chalks been pulled out from under her at the time he was injured, she would have slid from her birth into the water and down to the bottom of the river. In light of these undisputed facts, the court finds that reasonable persons could not conclude that the plaintiff was employed on a "vessel in navigation"; consequently, McClendon was not a Jones Act seamen and so cannot bring a Jones Act suit.

807 F. Supp. at 1267-68.[23]

---

23   In addition, the court noted that a plaintiff trying to recover under the Jones Act also had to establish that he was working in the "course of his employment" within the meaning of the Jones Act, which is limited to activities which are related to the furtherance of the vessel. 807 F. Supp. at 1268. "The court cannot find, nor does plaintiff supply, any case law to support the proposition that the practice of alchemy is within the duties of a seamen who is acting as a caretaker aboard a bottomless vessel under the Jones Act, even if that practice is shared by the Captain of a nearby port." 807 F. Supp. at 1268. In addition, the court held that the plaintiff's negligence was the entire cause of his injury because "the plaintiff admitted that he was well aware of the dangers of combining fire, mercury, and Idaho potatoes in enclosed, unventilated space." *Id.*

Suppose you have a case where the boat was about to sink, was taking on lots of water, and no doubt would have sunk in ten minutes. So, the defendant put the boat in drydock to keep it from sinking. Before a single repair had been made, however, someone was injured. How do you argue to a judge that even under *McClendon* the vessel was "in navigation?"

d.   Which Cow Did It?   As a final example of opinions where the judge interpreted a statute, we turn to the district court opinion in *Durst v. Newby*, 685 F. Supp. 250 (S.D. Ga. 1988). In *Durst*, Mr. Durst was driving a tractor-trailer on a Georgia highway to deliver his load of gasoline. His truck collided with a cow standing in the middle of the roadway—described by the court as a "pensive all-black heifer oblivious to its fate," 685 F. Supp. at 250—and he lost control of his truck, which overturned into a ditch and exploded. Though seriously injured, the plaintiff "was able to escape from the tractor-trailer before it was consumed in flames. The pensive Angus was less fortunate." 685 F. Supp. at 250.

The issue for the court was whether the plaintiff had sufficient evidence to show that the defendant actually owned the cow: the cow had no markings, and it was not the practice of either the defendant—who was sued because he owned pasture adjacent to the point in the road where the collision occurred, and he had owned about 32 black heifers at the time the accident occurred—or any of his neighbors to mark or otherwise identify their cows in any way. 685 F. Supp. at 251.

Despite the inability to positively identify whose cow it was, the plaintiff alleged that the defendant owned and controlled her. The plaintiff based this allegation on the opinions of the defendant's neighbors, who had testified in depositions that the defendant's cows had strayed beyond his land several times. The court was faced with the question of whether the neighbors' testimony as to the general wanderings of the defendant's cows was admissible evidence.

The legal rule governing this question comes from a statute: Federal Rule of Evidence 404 generally prohibits admission of "evidence of a person's character." Thus, the court had to determine whether Rule 404 prohibited consideration of the testimony as to the cow's character of wandering around the neighborhood. The court reasoned:

> Both parties have discussed the admissibility of evidence regarding prior wanderings of defendant Newby's cows. The defendant contends this evidence is inadmissible character evidence, mistakenly relying on a Georgia statute analogous to Fed. R. Evid. 404. The plaintiff asserts the admissibility of such evidence as an exception within the scope of Rule 404(b). Only the opinion of one neighbor, Henry Strother, is primarily based on prior cattle escapes, however, and the plaintiff has

sufficiently established the existence of a genuine issue of material fact without Mr. Strother's deposition. Therefore, this question need not be decided here. The Court notes, however, that evidence regarding a cow's character is probably not rendered inadmissible by Rule 404 because the rule refers to "evidence of a *person's* character." Rather, the wanderlust of cows is simply a relevant fact not relating to the character of a party or witness.

685 F. Supp. at 252 n.2 (emphasis in original).

There are two points to be made with *Newby*. The first is that the parties should have paid more attention to the language of the statute; the language of the statute answered the question. The second point is humorous: we know that (for some legal purpose) dogs lie somewhere between "people" and "things." How would a court, faced with admissibility of evidence concerning the wanderings of dogs, deal with the holding of *Newby*?

E.   Conclusion.

Let's leave these examples of common law and statutory analysis and get back to the *concepts*.

You should be seeing that, regardless of whether the source of the rule is judge-made or legislatively enacted, the rules are applied by later courts to disputes involving different parties and different, but similar, facts. Comparing the earlier opinions to the new disputes is part of the "doctrine of precedent." If there is a later dispute with similar facts, the later court will apply the same rule the courts applied in the earlier opinion and reach the same result unless there is a *distinction* between the present case and the earlier one.

Read the following explanation from Justice Cardozo slowly, and see if it makes sense to you at this point. If it does, you've taken a big first step toward being a step ahead at law school:

The common law consists of an evolving collection of "rules."

Stare decisis [strict precedent] is at least the everyday working rule of our law.... [T]he work of deciding cases in accordance with precedents that plainly fit them is similar to deciding cases in accordance with a statute. It is a process of search, comparison and little more.... The sample nearest in shade supplies the rule. But, of course, ... no judge of a high court, worthy of his office, views the function of his place so narrowly .... It is when ... there is no decisive precedent, that the serious business of the judge begins. He must then fashion the law for the litigants before him. In fashioning it for them, he will be fashioning it for others.

B.N. Cardozo, *The Nature of the Judicial Process* 20-21 (1932).[24]
Precedent, in the form of prior written opinions, contains the "rules" from which lawyers may analyze or argue their clients' cases: if the result in the earlier opinion favors his client's position, the lawyer will argue that the same result reached in the earlier opinion should be reached in his client's case; if the earlier opinion is against the client's position, the lawyer will argue that a different result is called for, because of *distinctions* between the *facts* of the earlier opinion and his client's dispute. (The lawyer may also argue that the rule of the earlier opinion should be applied only to particular facts or, rarely, that the rule should be abandoned as unjust or unwise.)

Law school prepares you to be a lawyer. Your job as a lawyer will be to determine whether the facts in your client's dispute "fit" within the earlier opinion (if favorable); or if the earlier opinion reached an unfavorable result, that the presence or absence of certain *facts* in your client's dispute which were not present in the first opinion mandates a different result, or the application of a different rule, or even the creation of a new one.

Legal argument and reasoning involves analyzing whether a dispute is like the prior opinions with "good" results, or whether it is like the prior opinions with "bad" results. You will learn during law school how to analyze cases for factual similarities and distinctions which are legally significant. This is not easy to do:

> If justice requires that like cases be decided alike, this implies equality before the law. Yet no more than two men's finger-prints are identical, are all the facts of two legal proceedings. The law itself selects—either by general rules or by the individuation of equity—what facts are relevant to exclude precedent. J. Stone comments: *"Unfortunately, as lawyers have come to see, the question whether an earlier case is a 'precedent' for the present situation depends on an assessment of 'essential similarities' and 'differences' between the two."*

3 *Dictionary of the History of Ideas* 28 (1973) (emphasis added).
Read that passage again.

---

24 Everyone quotes Cardozo. He was a very good judge who wrote very colorfully. If I can, I'll work in Learned Hand, too. Learned Hand was a very good judge who wrote very well, and he had a great name. His brother, Augustus N. Hand, was probably just as smart, but—lacking a great name—he is not as well known today. Other great judge names include: Minor Wisdom, Judge Justice, and Judge Gee ("gee, Judge Gee").

This passage underscores a critical point. The *result* reached by a court when deciding a dispute is almost always *fact*-driven. "Policy" comes up only secondarily. This is a tremendous shock for law students. Most students believe they will be writing political science papers and focusing on the broad implications of the court's decisions. This, for the most part, is not the correct approach.

The focus in law primarily is whether the *facts* of a later dispute are so different in meaningful ways from the earlier opinion that logic, reason and justice require a different *result*. There may be a policy justification for recognizing that a factual distinction is significant enough to warrant a different result, but most often the policy is equity and fairness. Pure policy arguments come up primarily when (a) advocating for or against a rule in an area of the law where your jurisdiction has not ruled yet; (b) advocating that the old rule should be limited to particular facts because that limitation serves a policy purpose (or serves justice); or (c) advocating that the earlier rule should be either rejected or overruled. When working in the common law, lawyers deal in fact, not policy.

This is why the focus in law school is on distinctions of fact, not policy arguments. The initial and critical question which lawyers face is whether the facts of their clients' dispute are enough like the prior opinions that the same result from those opinions will be reached. In law school, you must identify *factual* distinctions which should cause a different result—perhaps because there is a policy which would be served by reaching a different result. (Or that the same result should be reached *despite* meaningful factual distinctions.) The critical inquiry will be whether the *result* of the prior opinions must be applied to the new dispute, despite the factual differences.

Let's go over this again, with slightly different terminology. In the common law process the facts of a case are compared to the facts of the prior opinions to determine whether the present case is sufficiently similar to the earlier case to warrant being treated as if it were the same. As you can imagine, because there are usually many opinions on each point, complex fact comparisons are often necessary in order to determine on which side of the line the later dispute should fall.

Stare decisis makes the common law process very slow to, and very cautious toward, change. The basic principle is: the law must be followed. If a case has already laid down a rule in a particular area, a judge must be persuaded that there is a *factual* distinction between your case and the earlier opinion before he will reach a different result from the earlier case. For this reason, the common law changes very slowly. As one famous commentator analogized:

> The dynamics of the common law and the development of one of the most important technical rules of baseball, although on the surface completely different in outlook and philosophy, share significant

elements. Both have been essentially conservative, changing only as often as a need for change is perceived, and then only to the extent necessary to remove the need for further change. Although problems are solved very slowly when this attitude prevails, the solutions that are adopted do not create many new difficulties. If the process reaps few rewards, it also runs few risks.

The Common Law Origins of the Infield Fly Rule, 123 U. Penn. L. Rev. 1474, 1480-81 (1975).

However, the law does change. As one court noted, in overruling earlier cases courts should not "feel compelled to sacrifice their sense of reason and justice upon the altar of the Golden Calf of precedent." *Lorence v. Hospital Board of Morgan County,* 320 So.2d 631, 634 (Ala. 1975).[25]

Law school teaches you the skills to become part of this slow evolution of the law.

---

[25]   The *Lorence* court went on to quote *sixty-eight* lines of "quaint poetic lines of Sam Walter Foss" to show why precedent should not be followed when it "can no longer be supported by reason and justice...." 320 So.2d at 634. The poem contains such memorable stanzas as:

> For thus such reverence is lent
> To well-established precedent.
> A moral lesson this might teach,
> Were I ordained to preach.

320 So.2d at 635, citing Stevenson, *The Home Book of Verse,* p. 1896 (7th ed. 1940).

V. Why Law School Is Structured Like It Is

One goal of this book is to make law school easier. If you understand the *process* of law school, you will do better at it. It helps to draw away from the trees and get a view of the forest. This book has been looking on the forest level, and we are now about to look at the continental level. In law school, you will be studying bark, not even trees, and no one will help you to see the trees, let alone the forest.

Long after law school was over, I had a revelation. The operation of the common law system and doctrine of precedent explain why law school is structured as it is. (During your first year, you will probably spend much time wondering if there is any structure to it.) The discussion which follows will help you get perspective on this point, and this insight will help you do better and get more out of law school, too.

I often tell my law students at the University of Houston Law Center that "law school is backwards." By that I mean that we learn the law backwards, or seemingly so: the casebooks that law students take to class each day are not just compendiums of rules, laid out in logical order, but instead, they are just case after case after case after case after case . . . (though the cases are arranged in a general legal-logical order).

You would think that if law school was designed as are most undergraduate courses—to *explain* the *subject matter* to you—then law school would be organized and taught in a logical, rule-based fashion. When you take an English composition class, the professor explains rules of grammar, sentence structure, and what not. When you take an astronomy class, the professor explains the stellar spectra, she shows you the visible light spectrum, and tells you that it goes from red, to orange, to yellow, to green, to blue, to violet (more or less—hey, it's been a while). Your professors tell you the "rules" or subject matter.

Instead, law school seems backwards because you are not told the rules. They do not just explain that, for there to be a cause of action for negligence, there must be duty, breach of duty, causation, and damages. Instead, you will be made to read a bunch of cases, and reason from the facts and the courts' statements of the law, what the "rules" are. Law school will not explain to you, in black-letter rules, what must take place in order for there to be an enforceable contract. Your law professors will not simply give you an outline of what the law defines to be "consideration," or a substitute for consideration, to support a contract.

Your professors and your law books do not list the rules; instead, they "explain" them through cases, which has to be one of the most opaque ways to learn something. Indeed, most law students buy commercial outlines (remember "outlines" from the first chapter?) to get *precisely* the sort of information you would think law school would be designed to provide.

What makes the whole process of legal education seem even more backwards is how law students prepare for finals. Toward the end of the semester—or throughout it, depending on your style—you will make "outlines" for each class. As explained in the first chapter, outlines are logically structured statements of the rules, in outline form (hence the name), from all of the cases you have read for each particular class.

For instance, for your torts class, you will probably cover intentional torts (usually battery and assault), negligence, and strict liability. So you will have one big section of your outline based on "intentional torts," such as assault and battery. You will have it divided in to parts according to the elements of each cause of action: put more concretely, in order to allege a "cause of action" for, say, battery—that is, to state a claim for which a court can properly award money damages from the defendant to the plaintiff—the plaintiff must claim that the defendant (a) intentionally touched the plaintiff (b) in a harmful or offensive way, and that (c) it caused foreseeable damage to the plaintiff.

Your law school outline might look something like this:

1. **Battery**: there must be (a) intentional (b) harmful or offensive contact (c) causing foreseeable damages. *Smith v. Paul.*

    a. **Intentional acts**: an act which is not volitional is not intentional. *Smith v. Paul.*

        (1) Person who struck someone while experiencing his first epileptic fit did not act intentionally. *Smith v. Paul.*

        (2) Person with history of epilepsy who drove car acted with intent. *Jones v. Illinois.*

    b. **Harmful or offensive**: an act which a reasonable person would view as harmful or offensive is sufficient. *Smith v. Paul.*

        (1) No reason for there to be any actual injury—harmful or offensive touching is enough. *Fred v. Barney.*

(2)   Does not matter if defendant meant the touching in kindness or as a joke. *Bill v. John.*

c.   **Damages**: must be foreseeable *etc., etc., etc.*

Thus, as part of preparing for finals, you sit down and create outlines for each course which essentially consist of all of the rules from each case in a logical, useful order—yet that is exactly what you would think you would have been *reading* the whole semester, and instead they make *you write* it! (Again, copies of portions of some of my outlines from law school are in the appendices. This is a good time to take another look at them.)

Then, you go into your final, and you read a hypothetical set of facts written by the professor, and under all kinds of time pressure, you go through your outline to "spot the issues" and write your answer, which consists of "applying" those "rules" from your own outline to the facts presented in the hypothetical by comparing the facts and outcomes of the cases in your outline with the facts described in the hypothetical.

For example, the professor might present a hypothetical in which a child (who, he tells you, is too young to really know right from wrong) pulls a chair out from underneath his mother's friend, just before she was going to sit down. So she falls on her butt. (Trust me: you will see this fact pattern early in law school in your torts class.)

You read the facts, and realize that these facts sound like battery, and maybe negligence. So you go through your outline, and analyze for your professor whether the mother's friend could make a successful battery claim against the child. (Your mind probably races off on whether the parent can be liable for the child's acts [the kid has no money, so why sue him, you think] and in a panic you realize you do not know the answer, and begin to wonder whether it matters.)

You try to sketch out an answer by "spotting the issues." You write down the general rule for battery: there must be intentional harmful contact causing foreseeable damages. You cite *Smith v. Paul.*

Was there an intent—that is the first sub-issue. Your mind races: here is a little boy who does not *know* right from wrong, and he certainly did not *intend* to hurt her. Does that matter? How does it compare to the epilepsy cases, and to the results those courts reached: maybe it was not intent *to hurt* someone, but intent *to do* the act which caused the harm??? The boy obviously intended to pull out the chair—it was not like an epileptic, who does not intend to flail around. Hmmm.... You notice that everyone else is furiously writing out what, you are certain, are Nobel-prize winning answers that Justice Cardozo himself would fawn over. (He's dead, though.)

You scrawl out something which you fully believe to be incoherent and wrong, but, you think, "hey, everyone is in the same boat." You write down that the plaintiff will argue that the boy intended to do the act—he intended to pull the chair—and there is no proof the little boy had pulled chairs repeatedly, so it is unlike the *Jones* case. But, you write, the defendant would argue that the little boy clearly knew she would fall down. You write that a court would probably conclude there was intent to do the act which caused the harm.

You write down the next sub-issue and think: was there touching? He did not touch her at all. Does that matter? Her butt touched the ground, which he must have realized would happen, and that is the harmful contact, but he did not actually do it by touching *her*....

You look at your watch. Yikes! You write the rules about touching, apply them to your hypothetical by comparing the facts and results of the earlier cases which analyzed the "harmful contact" issue, and then move on to damages, which looks pretty easy . . . and it is, until you read that the hypothetical plaintiff had osteoporosis and had died from hitting the ground. So the plaintiff's estate is seeking damages for 30 years of lost wages.

The little boy could not have foreseen that she would die, could he?

You read your outline trying to find out whether the defendant has to foresee the kind and degree of the harm (death), or whether it is enough if he can foresee that the general type of damages (butt hitting ground) will occur.

You write furiously.

Your head aches.

You think about other careers.

You remember that you are actually *paying* for this experience.

You wonder, for the seventy-sixth time since Thanksgiving break, why you are doing this.

You look at your watch.

You look around the room at everyone else's bowed, assured head.

You move on to the next hypothetical.

"Hey, everyone is in the same boat."

Why is law school structured this way? Why do you have to read through all these cases in order to write your *own* set of rules, which you put in your *own* outline (which, in theory, are the same set of rules everyone else should come up with)? Why didn't they just give you the rules the first time around? What the heck is this whole process for anyway?

It is all backwards ... or so it seems.

Now, why is it backwards? Is it backwards at all? Perhaps there is something to all of this.

It's not really backwards. It just seems that way because you have to learn the common law process that way: law school is not designed, and it could not function, as a way to explain to you what the rules are in a certain "area" of law

The reason your professors do not try to teach you *all* the rules for each subject matter or area of practice (like labor, entertainment, patent, whatever) is simple: there are just too many discrete areas of the law to teach every "rule" for every "area." More importantly, even the most narrow area of the law is extremely broad, and the rules are always evolving and being changed by courts. There is no way law school could teach you everything you need to know.

Faced with this reality, law school trains you to be a lawyer by giving you the skills necessary to read the opinions and statutes on any particular subject and to figure out what the "rules" are. In large measure, the "subject matter" of law school is the case *method*, not the *substance* of each case. At most, the substance you learn will help you only to spot the general issues and to be aware of general legal principles.

For these reasons, while law school classes certainly do give you the "rules" in the areas you will choose to study, those rules are provided to you in the context of cases, not just outlines. Therefore, most law school classes are designed to teach you how to *read* cases and figure out, by reading those cases, what the rules are and how they apply to differing fact patterns. Then, once you figure out those rules, you can apply them to your client's facts and explain them to your client, your boss, or the judge.

In your regular classes (*i.e.,* torts, civil procedure, contracts, *etc.*), your professor will call on you to recite a case and then he will ask you to apply the "rule" from that case to slightly different fact patterns: through that process, you will begin to realize that the "rule" from the case really depends on—indeed, is defined by—its facts. That is how the common law system works. That is why you have to read the cases before you can figure out the rule, because *there are no "rules" outside of the cases themselves.* That is why law school is not backwards. You are learning how to *reason* under the common law system.

In legal writing class, which is the most important class in law school, you learn how to communicate the content of the law in a logical, structured manner. You will do the same thing in your legal writing class as you will do on your finals. Hence, the stronger your effort at learning to write clearly, the better your grades will be. Also keep in mind that potential employers will want a writing sample: the better you do, the more effort you put in, the better off you will be. Legal writing is also what you will do in your summer jobs.

It is what you will do as a lawyer.

VI. Time Out

During law school, you will find yourself facing a very hectic schedule and incredible demands on your time, abilities, and sanity. During my first semester, one of my classmates committed suicide, the pressures were so great. Those pressures will remain with you during your legal career; suicide and depression are very common among lawyers, who on average are an unhappy lot.

One way to combat these pressures is with humor. Another way is to not take yourself too seriously, even though the work that you will be doing both in school and as a lawyer is very serious. Keep it all in perspective. The world will not end if your client does not win. (You may not be able to eat, but the world will not end.)

These pressures were recognized by a district judge in a major antitrust case, which ultimately went all the way to the United States Supreme Court. At the end of a 90-page opinion, the judge published his "time out rule." *Zenith Radio Corp. v. Matsushita Elec. Indus. Co.*, 478 F. Supp. 889, 959 (E.D. Pa. 1979). Facing an enormously complex suit with major discovery disputes and voluminous amounts of documents and legal issues, the judge issued the following order:

"Time Out" Rule

A. *Statement of Rule*

For no good cause shown* each side will be entitled to three (3) time outs between now and the date of trial. A time out is defined as a one week period in which no discovery can be served, all deadlines are postponed and counsel can generally goof off.

1. The procedure for calling a time out will be as follows:

Both plaintiffs and defendants will designate one individual as the official time out persons (hereinafter referred to as the "Designated Whistler"). The designated whistler will be issued a whistle from the case liaison logistics committee which will be strung around his, her or its neck. When a time out is desired, the designated whistler will go to the offices of opposing lead counsel (see ¶ XVI.E.) and blow the whistle three (3) times. Thereafter there will be a one (1) week time out.

2. As stated above, each side is entitled to three time outs. However during the period of the two month warning (see ¶ B below) each side will be entitled to only one time out, providing that side still has remaining at least one time out.

3. Time outs must not be called on two consecutive one week periods. That is there must be an intervening week between time out periods. This rule is designed to prevent counsel from spending more than one week of their time with their family, friends, partners and associates.

4. As stated above, each side will be entitled to only three time outs. Any attempt by any side to exceed this three time out limit will be regarded by the Court as a serious infraction of the rules (hereinafter "illegal use of whistle"). The sanction for illegal use of whistle will be that such counsel attempting to exceed the three time outs will have his, her or its desk moved five yards (in the event of a non-flagrant violation) or fifteen yards (in the event of a flagrant infraction) further from the jury box at trial.

B. *Two Month Warning*

As stated above, there will be a two month warning. Such a two month warning will be called by the Court two months prior to trial. At this point, there will be a three day stoppage of the clock in which all counsel will be required to get their personal affairs in order. Personal affairs will include such items as Last Will and Testament, final instructions to spouse and family, arrangements for publication of memoirs and other less important details. During the two month warning, the clock will run continuously except for time outs described in paragraph A above.

*No good cause shown is defined as family events, such as anniversaries, birthdays, sporting events involving siblings, laziness, genuine ennui (pronounced NUE); drunkenness, firm events, such as annual dinner dance or outing; and anything else which helps attorneys to keep their sanity during the course of these proceedings.

478 F. Supp. at 959-960.

Time Out

Every once in a while during law school, call yourself a "time out." Walk away from it all. Go see a movie, walk around the campus, go dancing, or get away from it however you like. You will lose a couple of hours of study time, but the regeneration that you will gain and the renewed perspective that you will receive will provide you with far more than you will have lost during those two hours. Don't feel guilty or anxious about doing so: you are helping your studies, not hindering them.

VII. The Legal Research Process

Now, we switch gears. For the rest of the book, we focus more on legal writing and research. However, both legal writing and research are closely related to legal reasoning and the common law process. You will learn more about these issues in the remainder of this book.

I have taught legal research and writing at the University of Houston Law Center for four years. My students' most common complaint has been that they did not feel comfortable with legal research because no one ever explained to them *why* they were doing certain things, such as "Shepardizing" cases. The next section of this book addresses legal writing and research.

Law schools typically teach legal research during the first semester of legal writing class. You will probably do "canned" legal research exercises where you will be asked to find opinions, law review articles, and statutes which discuss certain specified topics. You will probably have mixed feelings about these legal research exercises. My students always complain about them. I did, too.

To be fair, it is hard to teach legal research because it is best learned by doing, not hearing, and it is understood only through repetition. No matter how long you do it, you will continue to get more efficient at finding the law, and more comfortable at determining when you have found "all" of the opinions. In addition, by its nature, the common law does not lend itself very well to finding answers to questions raised by hypothetical fact patterns. At best, legal research can lead only to law which will give you the basis for an informed and educated guess as to how a court would rule on a particular issue under the peculiar set of facts, because, almost without a doubt, no court has ever faced exactly the same facts you are analyzing.

The next few pages will give you an overview of legal research, and then the following few pages are chock-full of hints to help you get more efficient at and more comfortable with finding the law. The focus is on researching case law—the prior opinions—as opposed to finding a statute or law review article on a particular subject. Reading this section now will get you used to how the case law is organized.

There are lots of textbooks which explain the *details* of the legal research process, and you will probably be forced to pay $30 or $40 for one during your first year. You may never read it. (I didn't.) This section is intended to give you the broader view of legal research, to explain *why* you will be doing certain things. Once again, the goal is to help you see the forest, not any specific tree. There are countless trees in the legal forest.

A.   Law Reporters.

That's right: after mentioning them repeatedly for half the book, I am now finally going to tell you about reporters. You will see why this subject fits here once you're done with this chapter.

All opinions can be printed in one or more of the "reporters" (if the court wants its opinion to be published, a decision which is entirely up to it). After an appeal or trial, the court may choose to order that its opinion be published in a reporter. The primary source of legal authority is these "reporters." They report mostly the state and federal supreme and appellate court decisions, but they also include decisions rendered by federal trial courts.

There are two primary kinds of reporters: federal and state. The federal reporters contain the opinions written by federal courts; the state reporters publish opinions by state courts. In addition, many specialized reporters report cases concerning certain narrow subject matters, such as the Bankruptcy Reporter, labor law reporters, the Federal Rules Decisions, the United States Patent Quarterly, antitrust reporters, and so on. These specialized reporters sometimes publish cases which are not printed in the primary reporters and reprint many of the same cases as published in the state or federal reporters. Some cases are not reported in written form anywhere, but are available only on Westlaw and Lexis, the computerized legal databases. However, most are reported in at least the state or federal reporters, and many cases are reported in more than one reporter.

The federal reporters are divided into three. They correspond to the three levels of the federal judicial pyramid: (a) at the top are the "United States Reports" (and the Supreme Court and Lawyers Edition Reporters), (b) in the middle are the "Federal Reporters," and (c) at the bottom are the "Federal Supplements." The U.S. Reports contain only United States Supreme Court opinions. The most current series of Federal Reporters are the "Federal Reporter, Second Series," ("F.2d"), commonly called "F-seconds." The F-seconds contain the decisions from the federal appellate courts (also called the "circuit courts"). (The F-seconds were originally just called the Federal Case Reporters. Then they started F.2d's, and we hit the F.3d's at the end of 1993, after volume 999 of the F.2d's was published.) The "F-Supps" report opinions from the federal district courts, bankruptcy courts, and some other lower court decisions. Thus, the federal case law reporters correspond with the federal judicial pyramid.

In contrast, the state reporters compile cases by geographic regions, not according to the state judicial pyramid. For example, cases from the appellate courts of California, Arizona, Nevada, New Mexico, Colorado, and Utah are in the "Pacific" reporter series. The other names of regional reporters include "Northwest, Northeast, Southwest, Southern, Pacific," and others. Just as with the F.2d's, these geographic reporters are now into their second series. So you have, for instance, "P.2d" for "Pacific Reporter, Second Series," and "S.W.2d" for "Southwestern Reporter, Second Series."

Besides having their cases published in the regional reporters, some states, such as California and New York, have their own state reporters which publish only one state's opinions. There is no state court version of the F-Supps, and so state trial court opinions are generally not reported.

Thus, the three federal case reporters correspond to the three levels of the federal judicial pyramid—Supreme Court Reporter on top; F.2d's and F.3d's (with the appellate court opinions) in the middle; and the F.Supp.'s (with the district court decisions) on bottom. The state court reporters, however, are published according to the geographic location of the state. If the state is in the south, for example, all of its published opinions appear in the Southern Reporters.

1. The West Publishing Company's Headnote System.

I wrote earlier that this discussion about reporters belongs here—in the legal research chapter—not above, in the discussion of the common law. This next section will show you why the reporter systems are best understood here.

A copy of *WNS, Inc. v. Farrow*, 884 F.2d 200 (5th Cir. 1988) is reproduced in Appendix D. Look at the opinion as you read this section. (See if you can figure out why I picked it!)

The first part of the opinion is the "style" or "caption." This tells you the names of the parties and their posture both in the trial court (*e.g.*, plaintiff or defendant) and on appeal (*e.g.*, appellant (loser below) or appellee (winner below)).

The first paragraph after the date of the opinion is the "synopsis." The synopsis is useful because it gives you a short overview of the facts and result, so you can initially determine whether the case is factually and legally similar and whether the court came out your way on the relevant issue. However, the first paragraph is only a synopsis. The synopsis is prepared by West Publishing, *not* the court. In fact, you must keep in mind that nothing between the date of the opinion and the names of the judges on the panel was written by the court. Therefore, it is *not* law; do not cite it, do not quote it, and do not rely on its accuracy. You should also keep in mind that West makes mistakes; if you trust what the headnotes say, and it is wrong, your grades will suffer. (In the real world, your opponent will make you look very foolish.) Do not do it. You must read *the case*. (The dangers of relying on West's headnotes are described below.)

Following the synopsis are the "headnotes." Headnotes are helpful on two levels. Within the case you are reading they help you locate which paragraph of the opinion relates to the topic you are researching. For example, if the issue you are researching is who has the burden of proof, you can quickly determine that the relevant discussion is in the paragraph in the opinion which begins with "[3]." (Do you see why? Look at how the *opinion*—not the headnotes, but the text of the actual opinion—is numbered with bracketed numbers. Find paragraph "[3]" in the opinion.) *WNS, Inc. v. Farrow* is a fairly short opinion. When you are faced with lengthy opinions, or opinions which discuss many separate issues, the headnotes can be even more helpful in locating information within an opinion. (Again, however, even though the real opinions have these headnote numbers, your casebook cases will not.)

Headnotes are useful for conducting research beyond the opinion you are reading. You can go to the state or federal digests, for example, and read only headnotes under the specific topic you are interested in. Those cases will tend to discuss similar factual and legal issues. You can also use Westlaw to search all descriptions listed under that particular headnote. Both kinds of research are very helpful. Thus, the headnotes are useful for legal research.

The cases in your classroom casebooks will *not* have any synopsis or headnotes. The casebooks will contain edited versions of only the actual court opinions next discussed. It takes more time to read opinions without headnotes.

The rest of the opinion following the judges' names is called—the "opinion." That is where you will find the law and facts. That is the critical part. It is the only part which was written by the court; it is the only part which has the force of law.

B. Finding the Law.

As shown above, the common law system relies on a process in which *facts* of cases are compared by judges and lawyers to determine whether the present dispute is *sufficiently* similar to the earlier opinion to warrant being treated as if it were *exactly the same*. Because there are usually many cases on each point, complex fact comparisons are often necessary in order to determine on which side of the line the dispute should fall. Accordingly, your research should be geared toward locating the cases which apply the relevant legal rule and which are *factually* closest to the fact pattern of your dispute. Thus, "finding the law" means finding the prior opinions which analyzed the legal issue you are interested in under similar or analogous facts.

There are essentially two-and-a-half steps to finding the law: (1) getting your initial hook into the law; and (2a) finding all of the law you can and (2b) making sure that the law you found and intend to rely on is good law. The first step probably demands the most creativity and requires the most thinking. The second step-and-a-half is the most tedious and can be the most frustrating because you never know when you have found "all the law there is"—you must make a *judgment* about it. As you are about to see, the last half-step is important, and probably the easiest, thanks to services designed specifically for that purpose, including Shepard's, Westlaw, and Lexis.

1. Step One: How to Find the Law. You need to figure out how courts "look" at the issue facing you to figure out which cases are *legally* relevant. The issue will seldom be how your professor characterizes it, and virtually never the way a client phrases it. In the real world, no lawyer will ever ask you, "Please research whether I can argue that a promisor's performance is excused if a house that the promisor had agreed to sell to the promisee was destroyed before the time for my performance had come due." Instead, you are going to be told: "My client has been sued because he didn't sell the house that he had agreed to sell because it burned down the night before they were going to close. This jerk is suing for $20,000 for breach of contract. How do I get my client out of this mess? I want an answer tomorrow morning."

You need to determine what legal rules the courts in the controlling jurisdiction have applied when they have faced fact patterns like the one you've been assigned to research. Case law—opinions—has always been organized by category. The "big" categories are contracts, torts, and property. (There are many "big" categories which are created by statute, such as civil procedure, secured transactions, and federal securities law.) There are hundreds and thousands of sub-categories within each of these big categories, many of which also overlap. We already looked at some cases which tried to categorize according to terms in statutes. E.g., *McClendon v. OMI Offshore Marine Serv.*, 807 F. Supp. 1266 (E.D. Tex. 1992) (holding that a ship in drydock with no engine or bottom, which would have sunk to the bottom of the river if put in the water, was not a "vessel in navigation"); *Durst v. Newby*, 685 F. Supp. 250, 252 n. 2 (S.D. Ga. 1988) (analyzing whether a cow is a "person" in terms of a rule of evidence). In *Nix v. Hedden*, 13 S.Ct. 881, 882 (1893), the United States Supreme Court held that tomatoes were "vegetables" in terms of certain federal statutes. You need to find out what "box" the courts which have faced facts like your client's have used before.

This first step in finding out how to find the law requires that you be creative and imagine how a court facing facts similar to your client's problem would characterize the issue. It is also a dangerous time, in that you need to be certain that you are looking at the right *legal* issue. Let's return to the example of the house burning down. You were asked to determine whether the seller could be liable to the buyer for breach of contract. Where houses have burned down, there have been suits brought against the realtor, the bank, the insurance company and the escrow company; there have been suits brought by the buyer as well as the seller; and there have been suits brought by the buyer against the seller for causes of action other than breach of contract (such as, for example, negligence or even fraud). If you start researching the wrong legal issue, you will get into the wrong headnotes or digest topics. Unless you realize it, you may research a whole line of cases which have no *legal* relevance to the problem. Be careful during this first step.

You have a variety of resources to help you get your hooks into the law. You have many "secondary authorities." "Secondary authorities" is a term that lawyers use to describe all legal authority other than cases and statutes. They are called "secondary" because they do not have the force of law: what is written in law review articles or the "hornbooks"—such as AmJur, C.J.S., ALR, Wright & Miller, or Prosser & Keeton on Torts—is *not* "the law." It is just someone's summary of the way he or she says the law is or ought to be. Some courts may find their opinion authoritative enough to follow, but they don't have to. Secondary authority is never controlling precedent.

There are many secondary authorities. For example, you have law reviews, which have articles on many, many topics, though often at a theoretical level. Even so, they can give you different perspectives on the issue you're researching. The best thing about law reviews is that they usually have a billion footnotes with cites to cajillions of cases, and so are a good way to find the case law.[26] As one judge commented, "to one digging into the bowels of the law, a fat footnote is a mother lode, a vein of purest gold." Fuld, *A Judge Looks at the Law Review,* 28 N.Y.U.L. Rev. 915, 919 (1953).

You also can find out how to find the law by reading treatises, which collect the cases on various topics, and which also can be cited to a court as potentially persuasive authority. Treatises include Prosser & Keeton on Torts, Corbin on Contracts, Wigmore on Evidence, and many others. You have the general law tomes, such as AmJur, CJS, and others, which summarize the law by topic and collect the cases. Although not many lawyers or courts will be

---

[26] *See, e.g.,* David Hricik, *The Allocation of the Risk of Infringement c Intellectual Property Rights Under Article 2 of the Uniform Commercial Code* 20 Am. Intel. Prop. L.Q.J. 71 (1992); David Hricik, *The United States Coppe Industry in the World Market: Running Hard Yet Losing Ground,* 8 Nw. J. Int' L. & Bus. 686 (1988). *But cf. State v. Hricik,* 490 N.E.2d 941 (Ohio App. 1985 (acquitting John R. Hricik of charges from driving an overweight truck).

persuaded by what these books say the law is, they often do a great job of collecting case cites for you.

"Secondary" sources which may be persuasive authority include the *Restatements of the Law*. There are *Restatements* on the law of property, torts, contracts, and others (even a forthcoming *Restatement of the Law Governing Lawyers*). Each multi-volume set was designed to be a summary (or "restatement") of the common law rules for each of these broad areas. Think of them as an attempt to make a civil law style codification of the common law. You can use the index of the relevant *Restatement* to find the *Restatement's* rule for your issue. Then you can check the cases listed following the rule to see if that particular section has been cited in the state whose laws apply to your issue.

Perhaps the most important tool you have for finding the law are the indices and tables of content for these different secondary materials. By reading the indices, you can find out how the law characterizes the issue you are researching. For example, you are trying to figure out whether the seller is excused from performing his contract because the house he was supposed to sell next week burned to the ground last night. You look through indices and tables of contents for the *Restatement (Second) of Contracts*, the various treatises on contract law, and the digests, and see listed topics such as "Frustration of Contract," "Impossibility of Performance," and "Excuse of Performance." These sound like they might relate to your question. By then reading those sections or headnotes, you might find case law discussing similar fact patterns, or at least determine which legal issues are not relevant to your question, and thus narrow the scope of your research by process of elimination.

Finally, as a way to find the law, you have Westlaw and Lexis.[27] Lexis and Westlaw are computerized databases which contain virtually every case ever decided in the United States, as well as every state's statutes, federal laws, and gobs and gobs of other neat stuff. You can use a computer to search through all or part of the computerized documents for specific words or combinations of words. For example, you can search for all cases with the words "nuclear sabotage" in the same sentence as "trillion." If you do, you will find *Windsor v. Pan Am. Airways*, 744 F.2d 1187 (5th Cir. 1984). There, the Fifth Circuit affirmed the dismissal of plaintiff's complaint, which sought $400 trillion in damages arising from the crash of a commercial jetliner. Plaintiff alleged that Pan American Airways conspired with the family of President Kennedy and President Carter to cause the crash . . . ." 744 F.2d at 1188. "Inexplicably, Presidents Johnson and Nixon were implicitly exonerated from this presidential

---

27 Lexis is not a car; Lexus is. *See Mead Data Control, Inc. v. Toyota Motor Sales, U.S.A., Inc.*, 875 F.2d 1026 (2d Cir. 1989). Don't get them confused.

miscreancy." *Id.* The Fifth Circuit commended the district court for "[d]emonstrating remarkable restraint" by carefully reviewing the complaint before dismissing it, even though the plaintiff had also sought the arrest and detention of the widow of Martin Luther King, Jr. *Id.*

You will have Lexis and Westlaw training during your legal writing course. The advantage of Lexis and Westlaw is that you can search *facts* in order to find the law. For example, you can search for the word "house" in the same sentence as "burned" or "destroyed" and in the same sentence as "contract" or "agreement" in the same sentence as "seller" to see if you can find any controlling precedent where courts analyzed the precise fact pattern facing your client. Suppose your law professor asks what the rule should be where the house is not damaged, but has been infested with ghosts. You can run the same search, but substitute "ghosts" or "poltergeists" for "burned" and "destroyed." You will find the relevant opinion. *See Stambovsky v. Ackley*, 572 N.Y.S.2d 672 (N.Y. App. 1991) (allowing buyer to rescind contract to buy house allegedly infested with poltergeists). You cannot search narrow fact patterns anywhere else as easily as you can on Westlaw and Lexis.

Having said that, however, the use of Lexis and Westlaw, especially by baby lawyers and law students, presents its own problems and dangers. Although using a computerized data base such as Lexis and Westlaw can be an easy way to find some law, if you do not "hit the books" you will miss some potentially highly relevant cases, because courts will analyze the issue you are researching using words that you won't manage to use in your searches. For example, a "building" or "warehouse"—not a house—may have burned down. In addition, by reading the entire opinions, you will see slightly different arguments that will not appear on the computer screen, and those arguments could lead you to other issues or topics. It is also very hard to understand an opinion from what appears on a single computer screen. Despite these shortcomings, computerized legal research presents a quick (but very expensive)[28] way to get your hooks into the law. Its best use may be to get a start on finding the cases, but then to follow up by hitting the books. Use computer-based research, but keep its shortcomings in mind.

Headnotes are also useful in conducting research beyond the opinion you are reading. (Headnotes are discussed above, concerning the *WNS, Inc. v Farrow* opinion.) Once you find a case which is legally on-point, you can go to

---

28   Westlaw and Lexis usually provide law schools with free training and free research time, so that the students get familiar with and reliant upon computerized legal research services. Be forewarned, however, that in the real world many clients balk at the cost, and expect very little use of these technologies, even if they may be more cost-effective overall.

the state or federal *digests* and read only headnotes under the specific "key number" topics you are interested in. Those cases will tend to discuss similar factual and legal issues. You can also use Westlaw (but not Lexis) to search all descriptions listed under that particular headnote. Both kinds of research are very helpful. You can even begin the research process by reading the digest indices to find relevant headnotes. For instance, the digests (like Illinois Digest, the decennial digests, and the federal practice digests) collect various topics by headnotes. Once you find the headnotes which discuss your topic, you can scan through them to find cases which sound like they analyze your issue. Thus, the headnotes are useful for legal *research*.

2. Step Two: Finding the Rest of the Law. Once you determine which categories are relevant to your issue (and also which digest headnotes, which Restatement sections, and which treatise topics), you need to locate all of the law on those topics within your jurisdiction. There are two steps to finding the rest of the law.

a. Find the Rest of the Legally or Factually Analogous Cases.

The first step is to go diligently through as many treatises, digests, law reviews and other materials that you can find to locate all of the relevant cases, meaning all the controlling cases which are legally on-point and factually similar or analogous. Once you feel as though you keep seeing the same cases over and over, you've probably found all that you're going to find using this method.

The second part of the process of finding the rest of the legally or factually relevant cases is really tedious, but crucial. You must take the cases you have identified as being relevant and then go *first* backward and *then* forward to find any additional law.

That's right, go backward, then go forward. Backward in time, then forward in time.

Let me explain.

When a court is writing an opinion, it will locate the relevant opinions on the issues it is addressing. Its opinion may cite to those earlier opinions, explaining how those earlier opinions either control or are distinguishable from the case the court has before it.

You go *backward* by reading the opinions you intend to use in your work to see if they cite any earlier cases which also seem to be relevant to your issue. If so, you need to read them. If those older cases are relevant, then you need to repeat the process with those cases: you need to read them to see if they cite older cases which look relevant (and if so, check them to see if they need to be addressed). (For each older case you find, you also need to look at its future for relevant cases.)

You go *forward* by using Shepard's (or its equivalents on Westlaw or Lexis) to see if any later courts have cited the opinions you have found. Shepard's is a series of books which list every time an opinion is cited in another opinion. You will learn how to "Shepardize" cases during your legal research course. You check the Shepard's books (book*s*, not book) to see if any subsequent opinion has ever cited *the relevant headnote* of your opinion. If so, you read that opinion to see if it really has anything to do with your issue. If so, then you add that opinion to the pile of opinions you may need to write about, and you read it to see if *it* cites any *earlier* opinions which you haven't found, and then you Shepardize that opinion to see if any *later* opinion has cited it on the relevant headnotes, and so on and so on and so on.

It is tedious, but crucial.

It is also critical to Shepardize every opinion because a later court—either one up the judicial pyramid or even the same court which decided the opinion—may have overruled or limited the opinion you are reading. For example, you could be researching the issue of whether a party may recover damages for emotional distress where the body of their pet dog was not returned to them for burial, and the first opinion you find is *Smith v. Palace Transportation Co., Inc.*, 253 N.Y.S. 87 (N.Y. Mun. Ct. 1931), which holds that mental anguish damages are not recoverable because a dog is merely an item of personal property, and you did not Shepardize that case, then you would not find *Corso v. Crawford Dog and Cat Hospital, Inc.*, 415 N.Y.S. 2d 182 (N.Y. City Ct. 1979). In that case, the "plaintiff had arranged for an elaborate funeral for the dog, including a headstone, an epitaph, and attendance by plaintiff's two sisters and a friend. A casket was delivered to the funeral which, upon opening the casket, instead of the dog's body, the plaintiff found the body of a dead cat." 415 N.Y.S. 2d at 183. The court overruled *Smith v. Palace Transportation Co.*, holding "that a pet is not just a thing, but occupies a special place somewhere in between a person and a piece of personal property." *Id.* The court reasoned:

> This decision is not to be construed to include an award for the loss of a family heirloom which would also cause great mental anguish. An heirloom, while it might be the source of good feelings is merely an inanimate object and is not capable of returning love and affection. It does not respond to human stimulation; it has no brain capable of displaying emotion which in turn causes a human response. Losing the right to memorialize a pet rock, or a pet tree, or losing a family picture album is not actionable. But a dog—that is something else. To say it is a piece of personal property and no more is a repudiation of our humaneness. This I cannot accept.

Id.[29] It is important to Shepardize your cases.

Everyone asks, "how do I know when I've found all the law?" The answer is: you don't. A slightly less frustrating answer is that, with experience, you'll have a better idea of when you have. Deciding when to stop "is a complex judgment based on many factors that are weighted differently in various situations . . . ." Christina L. Kunz, *Terminating Research*, Perspectives, 2, 3 (Fall 1993).

You might get more comfort from the following rule of thumb: if you start seeing the same opinions over and over, and nothing new which is more relevant, you're probably close to finding as many opinions as you are going to find. Take some time to read what you've found to see if maybe you've missed a way to look at it, and if not, pack it in and don't worry about it.

Although at first you will find it difficult to get used to, you will rarely find "an answer" to something you're researching by spending hours and hours digging through the law. Every opinion you find will be different from the facts of your hypothetical, and you will be convinced that a more analogous or similar opinion lies somewhere in the next volume. The law is seldom so clear that the one opinion that you didn't find will hold the answer to everything you had set out to find. You are also not going to *know* you have found all the opinions. At some point, you will have to stop. As you gain experience, your level of comfort with that judgment will increase.

b. Making Sure the Law You Found is Still Good Law.

The final step is really a part of the second step, but I separate it to underscore its importance. You need to make sure the cases you intend to discuss in your memorandum or brief have not been reversed on appeal, overruled by a later court, or limited to certain facts. Remember the judicial pyramids? You need to make sure that the opinion you found was not later overruled by a court further up the pyramid. Or, maybe other courts—on any level of the pyramid—have limited, distinguished or otherwise criticized the opinion. It is critical not to rely on an opinion which is no longer good law. There's this little thing called embarrassment, another little thing called humiliation, and a final not-so-little thing called malpractice. If the other side shows that you relied on bad law, your credibility with the judge (and your boss and your client) will be damaged. *See, e.g., United States v. Collins*, 920 F.2d

---

29   Query: Suppose a pet fish has been improperly disposed of prior to funeral. Under *Corso*, could someone recover mental anguish damages? Is a fish "capable of returning love and affection"? Does it "respond to human stimulation"?

619 (10th Cir. 1990) (lawyer violated ethical rule by citing a case in his appellate brief which he should have known had been overruled). Verify that your cases are good law.

You do this with Shepard's or its Westlaw or Lexis equivalents. Shepard's has a one- or two-letter code which it notes every time a later opinion distinguishes or criticizes an earlier opinion. It also notes if a later court up the pyramid took an appeal of that very case. It also notes when a later court overrules a decision. So it is important to Shepardize your opinions as one step in finding all the law.

C.   Which Cases Are "Relevant"?

Until now, we have not undiscussed how to determine when a case is "relevant" enough that you need to include it in your research (or mention it in your memo or brief). This issue of relevance relates to both aspects of legal research—finding the law and finding the rest of the law—and to the doctrine of precedent.

As a rule of thumb, when you are finding the law, it is best to cast a wide net. When finding the rest of the law, narrow your scope slightly. When writing, use a slightly narrower scope and rely on only the most factually similar or analogous opinions which are legally on-point.

There are two levels of relevance in this context: factual and legal. The best opinion would be one that involved the *same* legal issues under *similar* facts. Again, for example, an ideal case in the burned-down-house hypothetical would be one where the opinion analyzed under the controlling state's law a suit for breach of a written contract by the potential buyer against the potential seller of a house that was supposed to have been sold, but that had burned down.

If you can't find a factually almost-identical opinion, then find one that analyzes *analogous* facts: for example, a boat burned down, not a house; or an earthquake occurred instead of a fire. If you can't find anything even close to the facts, look in other jurisdictions (*i.e.*, see if a court in another state has analyzed the precise fact pattern). If you can't find the exact legal issue, then you will have to look for analogous legal issues. Usually you can find cases which are legally relevant, but it is much harder to find the factually similar opinions.

1. Legal Relevance.

Because most legal issues are distinct and have been analyzed, if the *legal issue* is different in the earlier opinion from the legal issue in your dispute, then the opinion is probably not legally relevant. Always be sure that the opinion is legally on-point.

You must read the opinions carefully to determine legal relevance. Is it applying the relevant jurisdiction's law? Is it the same legal question? If the case is not discussing the same legal point as your dispute implicates, it is not legally relevant.

For example, if you are trying to determine whether the seller is liable for breach of *contract*, opinions which analyze whether he can be liable for having committed a *tort* are not on-point. You may want to cite them in your memorandum[30] so that your professor (or client) will know that tort liability does or doesn't exist, but those opinions are not legally relevant. They are not *legally* "on-point."

2. Factual Relevance.

The basic tests for *factual* relevance involve common sense. Does the opinion involve the *same* fact pattern? Does it involve an *analogous* one? If not, then the opinion is probably irrelevant or not very persuasive. Here's what one commentator had to say about how to tell whether an opinion is factually similar enough to be "precedential":

> The more similarities you find between your problem's facts and those of a decided case, the more likely that the decided case will determine your problem's outcome. Conversely, the more factual distinctions, the less likely that the decided case will control.

> Whether you feel the facts of a particular court decision are analogous to your problem's will often depend on *the level of generalization at which you operate* and the degree of insight and creativity you bring to your research and analysis of the holdings of decided cases ....

---

30 You would probably use "*see also*" and then list one or two of the more recent or more analogous cases. "*See also*" is a Bluebook "signal" which is discussed below.

This technique of using analogy to evaluate the applicability of existing court decisions to new sets of facts lies at the core of the analytical process involved in lawyering. It is a creative process that makes lawyering more an art than a science, and, as with any art, it requires practice to achieve mastery. As you work with this technique, simply *keep firmly in mind that your goal is to find as many analogies and distinctions as possible, on as many levels of generalization as possible, between your immediate research problem and the court decisions you feel may bear on its resolution.*

Wren & Wren, *The Legal Research Manual,* 80-81 (2d ed. 1986) (emphasis added).

For example, if one of the opinions involves a fact pattern in which the owner had deliberately burned the house down so he could get insurance instead of the sales price (because the insurance was higher), that opinion and the legal rule that it applies probably have little to do with your case. A court would probably recognize that the seller's intentional wrong-doing requires that the seller be liable: that rule makes sense in that context. But if you have other opinions where the seller didn't burn the house down and the seller wasn't liable, those cases are more factually analogous, and thus more relevant. That's not to say that you might not want to cite that opinion, for instance as an example of when a seller can be liable for breach of contract when the house burns down, but at best it is on the edge of factual relevance.

One of the most frustrating things you'll ever run into is an opinion which examined the fact pattern you are analyzing but never made an explicit comment about the fact that is key to you: it just didn't matter to those parties or to that court like it does to you. An opinion which has the same facts but does not analyze whether those facts are important is of dubious precedential value. The opinion must *discuss the issue* "enough" so that it is clear that the court *decided* the issue in light of those facts. Likewise, the opinion must have enough facts so that you can *compare* the facts of the case with your facts. *See generally,* Arrigo, *Analogization: Lost Art or Teachable Skill?,* Perspectives, Teaching Legal Research and Writing, p. 36 (Jan. 1993).

3. Conclusion.

Make sure that any opinions actually decide the same legal issues which you are analyzing. A common problem my students have is to cite a factually similar case which has no legal relevance. For example, they will be analyzing a sexual harassment fact pattern, and the legal question will be whether the employee, if she proved sexual harassment, is entitled to mental anguish damages. The students too often cite cases with very similar fact patterns, but which say nothing about the recoverability of mental anguish damages, or which award such damages without any analysis.

In sum, the case must address both the *legal* and *factual* issues before you, or it is not "on-point." The reason? Under the doctrine of *stare decisis,* a "case is precedent only if it involves the same issue as does the client's case and has similar enough facts to be analogizable." Arrigo, *Analogization: Lost Art or Teachable Skill?*, at 38. You will have to recognize analogies in the prior decisions to your facts; you will also have to recognize distinctions. There is a lot of *judgment* required to decide which cases are on-point and which are irrelevant.

That is what you will be paid to do as a lawyer.

IX. The Step Between Research and Writing: Reading and Thinking

Once you believe you have found all the opinions, then read them and *think* about what they say. It is important to read the opinions in chronological order. You will see how the law developed and understand the evolution of the legal rules. You will see that distinctions were drawn by the courts that you may be able to use: maybe one court incorrectly interpreted an earlier opinion (that happens a lot). Only by reading the opinions carefully can you discern such things, which may be important.

Moreover, it is crucial to read the whole opinion, not just the portion which discusses your issue. The facts are usually given by the court at the beginning of each opinion. The facts must be analogous to your own for the case to be relevant. Perhaps just a paragraph or two away from the discussion of your point the court said something that either makes the opinion extremely helpful or virtually irrelevant. You *must* understand the facts of the opinion to fully understand its meaning.

The next step is to think. Which opinions involve facts that are most like your fact pattern? Do those opinions have favorable results? If unfavorable, what *factual distinctions* are there which you could use to argue that there should be a different result in your client's dispute? Is the law consistent? Where are the inconsistencies? Can they be reconciled in a way which leads to a favorable result in your client's dispute? Are there policy reasons driving the cases which, in light of your facts, can be used? You need to determine which opinions with good results are most like your fact pattern, and which opinions with bad results are most like yours, and figure out how you can argue that your case is like the cases with good results, and distinguishable from the cases with bad results.

Remember: legal reasoning involves deciding on which side of the line your client's dispute falls. Is it more similar to the opinions where the courts found that a contract existed, or opinions where the courts found that the parties had only agreed to try to negotiate a contract? Does it fall into the box where mental damages are recoverable, or into the box where they are not?

Finally, before you actually begin to write, consider this insightful and accurate analogy by a critic of legal writing:

> Picture the following as vividly as you can. You are a lawyer. You arrived at the office in New York at 6:30 a.m. . . . [and] have worked straight through to 9:00 p.m. You have redeemed your car from the parking lot and have fought the traffic and the incipient inclement weather up into Connecticut. You approach a toll booth. The sign says "40¢—Exact Change Left Lane." You . . . come up with a nickel, a dime, and a quarter—all the change you have. You enter the Exact Change lane. In front of you is a shining red light, but no barrier; to the left of you, the hopper. . . . You heave the change at the hopper. The quarter drops in; the dime drops in; but the nickel hits the rim and bounces out. What do you do? Do you put the car in park, get out, and grovel in the gravel for your nickel? Do you put the car in reverse and change to another lane where a human being can make change for your dollar bill? No. You go through the red light.
>
> You go through the red light, I would argue, because of a misconception of the purpose of tolls. At this anxious moment you are not feeling that before you continue on that road the government must receive from you 40¢, with which it will keep the roads in good repair and pay the toll booth operators. Instead you believe that before continuing on that road you must be dispossessed of 40¢. You have been dispossessed of 40¢ It is therefore moral, if a bit risky, for you to plunge further into the Connecticut darkness.
>
> That is the misconception lawyers . . . have concerning the writing task. So much work has preceded the actual writing . . . . The thinking is done; now you have only to *write* it. You cast all of your knowledge on the subject out of your mind onto the paper, not caring if the audience will actually receive your 40¢ worth of wisdom, but caring only that you unburden yourself of it. It's all out there—on the paper, in the gravel—and that is what matters.

George D. Gopen, *The State of Legal Writing: Res Ipsa Loquitur*, 86 Mich. L. Rev. 333, 342-43 (1987).

Don't leave your thoughts on the gravel. Put 'em in the hopper.

X. Legal Writing: How Lawyers Write about Cases

As the discussion of the common law process and the doctrine of precedent should have made clear, legal reasoning tends to be very linear and categorized. Legal rules are designed to be applied to facts in order to put the facts into one "box" or another. Often there are "tests" which courts "apply" to the facts before them in order to reach a legal conclusion on an issue. Because legal reasoning is linear, so too is legal writing. Creative writers, stream of consciousness writers, and English majors generally have the hardest time with legal writing.

For instance, whether someone has been negligent depends upon whether (a) there was a duty owed by the defendant to the plaintiff (b) which was breached (c) and that breach was a proximate cause of (d) damages to the plaintiff. If the plaintiff's lawyer cannot fit the facts of his client's case into *each* box, he loses. Whether someone has been "negligent" depends on whether *each* element is shown. In turn, each element has its own tests, its own sub-categories. For instance, the first element of negligence—whether someone owes someone else a duty— depends on whether that person (1) did some affirmative act, or (2) created a dangerous situation, or (3) has some special relationship with the other person. When lawyers write or think, they go through each element in order, apply each element's "test" to the facts before them, and then reach a conclusion, *i.e.*, here, whether the defendant did or did not owe a duty to the plaintiff. *This means you should outline your writings*, even if you normally do not outline when you write. Trust me, it will help you a ton at the start.

A. CRPAW: Conclusion-Rule-Proof of Rule-Application-Wrap-Up.

The linear approach to legal reasoning is apparent from one of its more commonly taught methodologies for legal writing: CRPAW which stands for Conclusion/Rule/Proof of Rule/Application/Wrap-up. CRPAW is not a rule about legal writing which always works. Instead, it is a valuable tool to help you structure your writing. It will produce the type of writing which professors want to see.

The "conclusion" is a topic sentence which makes the point of your analysis. The "rule" is a statement of the legal rule. The "proof of rule" may be a case cite, a cite to a statute, or a lengthy discussion of the case law, depending on how much support you need in order to show that your statement of the "rule" is correct. The "application" is a section in which you apply the rule to the facts of your dispute. It can be a very long section. The "wrap-up" is a sentence or two which wraps up the analysis by stating the "conclusion" in terms of your facts.

What follows are three examples of CRPAW analysis. Read each of the sentences labeled "a," and then those labeled "b," and then those labeled "c." Then look at the groups of sentences— the sentences which are "conclusions," then those which are "proofs of rules"—so you can see what each step in the C-R-P-A-W analysis requires. You will essentially read three complete analyses. This should give you some idea of the structure of legal writing. You should be able to see how cases are used, when to write about the facts of the cases, and how to support rules with legal authority.

Conclusion:

a. Sears is entitled to summary judgment because it did not owe plaintiff any legal duty.

b. The court should remand the case to state court because Barnett's petition for removal was untimely.

c. The court will probably hold that the ship was not a "vessel in navigation" because it was in dry-dock, had no bottom, and would have slid to the bottom of the river had it been in the water.

Rule:

a. A store owner owes a duty to provide security in the common areas of a shopping center only when the plaintiff proves that "substantial, significant similar criminal acts have occurred in the precise area where the alleged incident occurred."

b. Removal is untimely where "it is not filed right away."

c. The factors determining whether a ship was a "vessel in navigation" include "whether or not the vessel was in dry dock, the nature and extent of repair operations and who controls them."

Proof of Rule:

   a.   *Workman v. Fiesta Mart of Am. Inc.,* 666 S.W.2d 555, 523 (Tex. App. —Houston [14th Dist.] 1993, writ ref'd n.r.e.) (affirming summary judgment for defendant). For example, in *Workman,* the court granted summary judgment....

   b.   28 U.S.C. 1441(a). *See Noble v. Bradford Marine, Inc.,* 789 F. Supp. 395 (S.D. Fla. 1992) (remanding for untimely removal).

   c.   *McClendon v. OMI Offshore Marine Serv., Inc.,* 807 F. Supp. 1266 (E.D. Tex. 1992). For example, in *McClendon,* the court held that the ship was not a "vessel in navigation" because (a) it was in dry dock (b) without crew (c) undergoing $25 million in repairs which would take 77 days to complete and (d) had no bottom, and so would have slid to the bottom of the river had it not been in dry dock.

Application:

   a.   Here, there is no competent summary judgment evidence that Sears had any prior knowledge of purse snatchings in the Baybrook Mall parking lot. Instead, plaintiff's own expert admitted that there had been no purse snatching in the six months prior to plaintiff's alleged incident.....

   b.   In the case at bar, Barnett's petition for removal was not filed within 30 days of service on the first defendant, but instead was filed exactly 76 days after the first defendant had been served with process, as is shown by Exhibit A.

   c.   In this case, (a) the ship was in dry dock (b) without crew (c) undergoing $5 million in repairs which were expected to take at least 30 days and (d) plaintiff's own expert has testified that the ship was "not navigable, and probably would have sunk to the bottom if it had been in the water." Blather depo. at 982.

Wrap-up:

   a.   Because no competent summary judgment evidence shows that Sears had any prior knowledge of *any* prior crime in the parking lot—let alone "substantial, significant, similar crime"—Sears did not owe plaintiff any duty. Accordingly, and as in *Workman,* Sears is entitled to summary judgment.

b. As in *Noble,* Barnett's removal "is untimely and is a defect deemed 'way' improvident." *Noble,* 789 F. Supp. at 397. His "most bogus attempt at removal is 'not worthy' and the Defendants must 'party on' in state court." *Id.*

c. Although the facts are not as strong as in *McClendon,* in substance it cannot be meaningfully distinguished. For that reason, a court would probably hold that the ship involved here was not a "vessel in navigation." Accordingly, Boat Company should be able to obtain summary judgment on that issue.

CRPAW is a *concept* which *guides* legal writing: it is not a rigid structure. But its beauty is that it works most of the time. For example, suppose your analysis shows that there are three reasons why you should win. You could use CRPAW and begin by stating "Defendant is entitled to summary judgment for three reasons. First, . . . Second, . . . Third, ..." Then, you would go through each point, and separately use CRPAW for each point (as shown below, in an example).

B. An Example of Legal Analysis.

This section contains two examples of legal analysis. The first is hypothetical, the second is real. They are patterned after the other dominant legal writing methodology: IRAC. The "issue" corresponds to the "conclusion" of CRPAW; the "rule" corresponds to the "rule" and "proof of rule" of CRPAW; the "application" corresponds to the "application" of CRPAW; and the "conclusion" corresponds to the "wrap-up" of CRPAW.

Arnold Schwarzenegger is walking in Chicago along Lake Michigan, near Oak Street Beach, and sees a woman drowning. Arnold, who is a great swimmer, does nothing. Woman's husband sues Arnold, claiming Arnold was negligent for not rescuing his wife, though he could have. He seeks damages for wrongful death.

Was Arnold negligent? Your torts exam might look something like this:

To state a cause of action for negligence under Illinois law, a plaintiff must show (a) duty, (b) breach of duty, (c) causation, and (d) damages. *Fred v. Barney,* 522 N.W.2d 422, 427 (Ill. 1987). Even though plaintiff has stated facts which show breach, causation, and damages, he has failed to show that there was a legal duty owed by the defendant to the woman. Therefore, plaintiff has failed to state a cause of action for negligence.

(a)   <u>Duty</u>. Arnold did not owe a duty to the woman. Whether someone owes a duty to another person depends on whether they (1) did some affirmative act, or (2) created a dangerous situation, or (3) has some special relationship with the other person.   Defendant Schwarzenegger did nothing which caused the woman to go into the water, nor is it alleged that he created a dangerous condition. He was a witness to a drowning. Therefore, unless Arnold had some special relationship with the woman, there is no duty.

It is well settled that "there is no general duty to rescue." *Tim v. Bob*, 622 N.W.2d 332, 339 (Ill. App. 1989). Unless the defendant is related to the victim, or the victim is a child, he does not have a "special relationship" and thus has no duty to attempt rescue. *Tim v. Bob*, 622 N.W.2d at 340. No such special relationship is even alleged between Arnold and the woman. Therefore, plaintiff has failed to state a claim for negligence.

(b)   <u>Breach</u>. If there were a duty, however, plaintiff clearly has plead facts which show a breach of duty. In general, the test for whether a defendant has breached a duty is whether he failed to exercise ordinary care. *Sam v. Bill*, 521 N.W.2d 340, 347 (Ill. 1978). Here, the plaintiff alleges that Arnold saw the woman, but did nothing, and claims Arnold could have saved the woman, as he was a good swimmer. This would appear to establish breach.

(c)   <u>Causation</u>. Likewise, if there were a duty, the plaintiff would have established causation. In general, causation is established when the resulting harm was reasonably foreseeable to the defendant. *Susie v. Beverly*, 127 N.W.2d 197, 201 (Ill. 1937). It seems clear that it was foreseeable to Arnold that, if he did not rescue the woman, she would drown. Therefore, causation is alleged sufficiently.

(d)   <u>Damages</u>. In general, all damages which are proximately caused by the defendant's negligence are recoverable. *Elise v. Carolyn*, 801 N.W.2d 874, 874 (Ill. 1993). Here the wrongful death damages are clearly recoverable.

Therefore, even though all of the other elements of a negligence case seem present, because plaintiff has failed to allege any facts which establish any duty from Arnold to the woman, plaintiff has not stated a cause of action for negligence.

Notice the organizational pattern of each lettered paragraph: the first sentence states the *issue*; the second the *rule* (along with a case cite as proof of that rule); the third *applies* that rule to the facts "here"; the fourth reaches a *conclusion*. This is the basic pattern of legal writing.

Usually what your legal research will reveal is this: several cases have been decided which apply a general rule to generally similar fact patterns. Suppose, for instance, that you have the same facts as in the Arnold hypothetical, but the drowning occurred in Indiana, so Indiana law applies. Under Indiana law, you discover that someone who has a "special relationship" with the decedent must have a duty to rescue. Your research shows that several Indiana cases have analyzed whether a "special relationship" (in terms of whether there is a duty to rescue) can exist between people who are not related by blood or marriage. Suppose the rule as stated in these cases is all the same (as it usually is): whether a "special relationship" exists depends on the "totality of the circumstances surrounding the relationship between the plaintiff and defendant." The cases also all say that this is a question for the judge, not the jury, to decide.

But each case comes to a different result: in two cases no special relationship was found because the plaintiff and defendant were complete strangers. In a third case, the plaintiff and defendant had met once at a bar. In a fourth case, the court held that there was a "special relationship" because, though not married, the plaintiff and defendant had been living together at the time of the incident. This is the usual result of legal research: of the legally relevant cases, some are clearly on one side or the other of your fact pattern—and thus deserve little discussion—but one or two cases are the most similar, and thus require some discussion of the facts.

Your facts are that she knew who Arnold was, and in fact she was a huge fan of his. She had even met him once, received his autograph, and had written him fan letters on his birthday for the past five years.

If you are writing about this, *do not* go through four separate paragraphs (one for each of the earlier cases on-point) and lay out the facts of each case, comparing them to yours. Instead, get rid of the cases that are factually furthest from your case (on both ends of the question) with a short sentence. (First, of course, state the rule—"the existence of a 'special relationship' depends on the totality of the facts [cite case].") For example:

> The Indiana courts which have applied this "totality of the facts" test to determine whether a special relationship exists have found no special relationship where the parties have never met. *See Smith v. Jones*, 5 N.W.2d 8, 10 (Ind. 1984); *Bob v. Fred*, 10 N.W.2d 1, 2 (Ind. Ct. App. 1992). On the other hand, where the parties have been living together, courts have found a special relationship. *See Tim v. Bill*, 5 N.W.2d 1,

3 (Ind. 1987); *Tom v. Harry*, 9 N.W.2d 7, 51 (Ind. Ct. App. 1975). Obviously, the facts here are between those two extremes.

A case with similar facts is *Frank v. Susie*, 9 N.W.2d 100, 105 (Ind. 1987), where the court analyzed whether a special relationship existed where the parties had met once at a bar. Although finding no special relationship, the court stated that it was "a close question." 9 N.W.2d at 104.

Here, the facts seem stronger than in *Frank*. Arnold met our client once, and she corresponded with him regularly. Moreover, the court may be influenced by his general notoriety. On the other hand, the court may be hesitant to impose a duty to rescue on every celebrity who happens to sign an autograph and receive fan mail, which will be how the defendant characterizes that position.

For these reasons, it is unclear whether a court would find that a special relationship existed. Therefore, discovery should be targeted toward finding out whether Arnold answered his mail, whether he encouraged people to believe in this integrity, and similar topics.

Notice the structure. Notice the transitions. Notice that there is a conclusion (or "wrap up") which applies the law to our facts and reaches a conclusion ("it is unclear . . . .").

C.   Fallacies in Logic.

Because legal reasoning must be logical, here are some basic logical fallacies to avoid.

1.   Hasty Generalizations involve conclusions based on too few or atypical examples. For example, "In the *Stanback* case, the court held mental anguish damages could not be recovered for a breach of contract involving divorce. Therefore, our clients cannot recover them in their case, because it is a divorce case, too."

2.   Oversimplification occurs by saying something was caused by a single event, when in fact it actually may have complex causes. For example, "The court denied recovery of mental anguish damages in *Stanback* because it was a divorce case."

3.   Mistaken Causal Relation. There are at least two kinds of mistaken causal relationships. First, *confusing sequence with cause and effect*, erroneously concluding that B was caused by A because B came after A. Maybe B just happened to occur after A, with no causal link. Second, *the fallacy of common cause and effect.* For example, suppose you notice that every conscientious, rich lawyer owns at least two BMWs, but those who own none are deceitful and poor. If you confuse sequence with cause and effect, you would advocate giving a BMW to every lawyer who had none, to make him ethical and rich.

4. Faulty Analogy occurs by reasoning that because two cases are similar in some ways, they are also similar in other ways. Analogies are dangerous. The two cases being compared should not differ in any respect essential to the purpose of the analogy. For example, in *Stambovsky v. Ackley*, 572 N.Y.S.2d 672 (N.Y. App. 1991), the court analogized the failure of a seller of a house to warn that he had bragged that it was infested with poltergeists with the failure of a seller to disclose that there was industrial waste on land allegedly used only as a farm—ignoring the obvious difference that ghosts are not real, but industrial waste is.

5. Non-Sequiturs ("it does not follow"). Leaping to a conclusion not supported by what has been stated before. For example: "In *Stanback*, the court held that mental anguish damages may not be recovered for breach of any contracts relating to divorce. Therefore, plaintiff is not entitled to mental anguish damages for breach of the catering contract."

6. Begging the Question Assuming the truth of a proposition which needs proof. For example, simply stating that it is stupid to put mercury in a potato and then bake it in an enclosed space to create gold. This assumes that it is inarguably stupid to do so; yet people have done so. *McClendon v. OMI Offshore Marine Serv.*, 807 F. Supp. 1266, 1267 (E.D. Tex. 1992).

7. The Logical Consequences Problem (proving too much). People will often make arguments or reach conclusions which have logical consequences which cannot be true. For example, reasoning that *Stanback* applies to *all* divorce contracts necessarily means that mental anguish damages could not be recovered for breach of a contract to pay child support or alimony. That cannot be the law, but it is a logical consequence of Stanback's holding.

8. Ignoring the Question. Relying on irrelevant but inflammatory facts to ignore the issue which must be addressed.

9. The Ultimate Test. The fundamental test, often overlooked by lawyers as well as law students, remains the "smile" test. If you can't make the argument without smiling at it, you probably ought not to make it to a judge. Likewise, make sure your position passes the "smell" test. Keep common sense and good judgment in mind.

Sometimes, however, the cases simply reach results which cannot be reconciled. For example, compare *Peek v. Ciccone,* 288 F. Supp. 329, 334 (W.D. Mo. 1968) (upholding prisoner's right to write to the Pope to "share the good news" that the prisoner was "Christ reincarnated") and *Collins v. Henman,* 676 F. Supp. 175 (S.D. Ill. 1987) (where prisoner claimed he was "not Raymond Collins but the 'Prophet Mohammed,'" court stated that it was "not the place of the court to decide... who is a true prophet") (*dicta*), with *Gordon v. Secretary of State of New Jersey,* 460 F. Supp. 1026 (D. N.J. 1978) (prisoner claimed he was denied the office of the Presidency of the United States because of his illegal incarceration). Query: is the rule in federal court that it is not frivolous to claim you are a son of a god, but it is to claim that you should have been president? Are our priorities backward? Maybe logic can't explain everything.

Each of these logical fallacies can be used against you, but you can also use them to test arguments made against you.

D. Legal Writing Class.

1. Introduction.

Legal writing class has two primary goals: (1) to teach you how to *find* the law and (2) to teach you how to *explain* the law in both (a) informative and (b) persuasive fashions. Accordingly, this section of the book will preview the work you will do to achieve those goals. Typically, the first several weeks of your first semester will focus entirely on finding the law. The rest of the year continues that learning process, but most of the legal writing class is devoted to what you do *after* you complete your research.

This section is intended to teach you how to write "like a lawyer." I want to tell you what most law schools do *not* mean by "writing like a lawyer": They do not mean long sentences with lots of legal mumbo jumbo. They do *not* mean opaque analysis. They do not mean quoting the rules from the case without any thought to what the facts were. They *do* mean well-structured, well-organized, crisp writing that gets to the point and moves on.

The purpose of legal writing is to explain what the present state of the law is in a particular area and either *predict* (in a memo) how a court would apply these existing rules to your client's fact pattern, or *persuade* (in a brief or motion) that the court should extend or limit the existing rules based upon some factual similarities or distinctions between existing case law and your client's facts. These different purposes have a major impact on how to write and characterize the law and facts.

One thing you must remember in writing either memoranda or briefs is this: *Sergeant Schultz is reading your paper.* What is he famous for saying?

"I know nothing."

Your reader *knows nothing* about the *facts* or the *law*.

You have to tell the reader things in a logical fashion, which usually means the facts are given first, so the reader has context for the legal discussion. You should present the facts in chronological order, being careful to identify the important actors by name. Don't assume familiarity with the facts or the law.

2.   The Purpose of a Memorandum.

Write as if the professor (or lawyer) you are writing for does *not* know anything about the particular law you are explaining. You have to *explain* the law to him. Do that by explaining what the rules are, and how those rules would likely be applied to the facts presented. Explain the rules by quoting or paraphrasing them from the relevant cases. Predict how a court would likely rule by comparing the facts of your client's case with the facts and results of the cases you found which had the most similar facts.

There are several steps to writing a memorandum.

First, do the research.

Second, read the opinions. Do not rely on the headnotes or the synopsis. Headnotes are "not authority; rather [they are] a publisher's interpretation of what the particular court stated." *Tyson v. Jones & Laughlin Steel Corp.*, 958 F.2d 756, 763 (7th Cir. 1992) (imposing monetary sanctions on the party which quoted headnotes in his brief). *See Lewis v. East Feliciana Parish Board*, 635 F. Supp. 296, 299 n.8 (M.D. La. 1986) (headnotes form no part of the opinion), *aff'd*, 820 F.2d 143 (5th Cir. 1987).

The opinions are best read in chronological order. That way you will both see the development of the rule and be able to understand how later courts have interpreted the earlier opinions. Make sure you read the facts so that you understand what the precise factual and legal issues were before the court in each case. Often, if you read only the few paragraphs which explicitly address your issue, you will not get a full appreciation (or, worse, an inaccurate understanding) of what the case actually stands for. Understand the facts of the opinion: diagram them on the opinion if necessary (I often do).

Third, after you have read all the opinions, outline the "rule" and its exceptions. Nine times out of ten, the law consists of a "test" or a rule and an exception. For example, in *Stanback*, the court created a three-part test, which can be outlined as follows:

A claim for mental anguish damages resulting from breach of contract is stated only when the plaintiff's complaint reveals the following:

(1)   the contract was not one concerned with trade and commerce with concomitant elements of profit involved;

(2)   the contract was one in which the benefits contracted for were other than pecuniary, *i.e.*, one in which pecuniary interests were not the dominant motivating factor in the decision to contract; and

(3)   the contract must be one in which the benefits contracted for relate directly to matters of dignity, mental concern or solicitude, or the sensibilities of the party to whom the duty is owned, and which directly involves interests and emotions recognized by all as involving great probability of resulting mental anguish if not respected.

Stanback can also be viewed as creating a general rule (no damages for emotional distress) with an exception, for which it created a three-part test. General rules with exceptions are the most common forms of legal "rules."

The content of the legal rule will directly control the structure of your writing. If there is a three-part test, you will have to write about all three parts. For example, look back at the first Arnold Schwarzennager example (concerning duty-breach-causation-damages). Notice how the four-part rule is set out in the first paragraph, and then each lettered paragraph analyzes each sub-part of the rule.

Fourth, determine the structure of your memorandum. Outline it if you can. The global structure is dictated by the question(s) you are addressing. The structure within each question presented is usually determined by the "rules" and exceptions from the cases.

Fifth, decide which opinions should be discussed under each point of the outline. This is a crucial step. Determine which opinions must be cited to set out the legal rules, which need to be discussed at length because they have similar facts, and which are only so tangentially related that they need be discussed, if at all, only by being cited, and perhaps then only in a footnote.

You will do this by determining which opinions are factually most similar to yours. Some opinions will be clearly "better" than your facts and others will be far "worse." Put another way, there will be some opinions where the court had faced a fact pattern that was far weaker than your own and the court reached a bad result. In other opinions, the court will have faced far better facts than yours and reached a good result. Nine times out of ten some opinions will have reached different results while facing only *slightly* different fact patterns.

Those opinions, the ones with facts closest to yours but with inconsistent results, are the ones that you probably will have to discuss. They have similar facts but reached different results. How are those opinions similar, or analogous to your dispute? How are they different, or distinguishable? Again, only *rarely* will you discuss in a memo the facts of an opinion at length, but these are questions you must ask to figure out which opinions need to be discussed.

Sixth, write. Try to write one draft all the way through instead of "revising as you go," trying to get each sentence exactly right the first time through. The writing process will help you understand the law better if you write it through once without worrying about Bluebook rules, spelling, grammar, and the like.

Seventh, revise. Do at least one more draft.

Eighth, wait. Revise again after you let it sit for a day. Time and fresh eyes will permit you to see many things you did not see before.

Ninth, edit. Shorten the sentences. Use labels. Check for consistency. Bluebook it. Make it simpler. Put in headings and road-map sentences.

Tenth, hand it in.

Eleventh, celebrate by taking a "Time Out." You deserve it. Then, with clear conscience and happy heart, go study more. Congratulations!

3. The Structure of a Memorandum.

As with all things legal, memoranda have evolved into standardized forms. While there is some variation, most law firms and law schools expect memoranda to be done in the following format:

I.   Facts
II.   Question Presented
III.   Short Answer
IV.   Analysis
V.   Conclusion

I.   <u>Facts.</u>

The facts should state only those, but all, facts necessary to analyze the question presented. For instance, if your memorandum analyzes whether running a stop sign constitutes negligence per se, you do not need to include any information about how fast the car was going when it hit the other car, or whether it was day or night (unless, of course, those facts are relevant to your analysis of the stop sign issue).

II.   <u>Question Presented.</u>

The question presented is usually, but not always, phrased in the form of a "Whether . ...." For instance: "Whether running a stop sign constitutes negligence per se under Illinois law." I often phrase the question presented in more of a statement form: "This memorandum analyzes whether running a stop sign constitutes negligence per se under Illinois law."

Note that you can have more than one question presented in a memorandum. For example, it could be

a.   "Whether running a stop sign constitutes negligence per se."

b.   "Whether evidence of any other negligence is required in order to find liability".

III.   Short Answer.

The short answer is usually one word followed by a one sentence explanation. For instance: "No. Although the Illinois Supreme Court has never decided the issue, numerous courts of appeal have held that running a stop sign is not negligence per se."

Note that for *each question* presented, there should be *one answer*. It is easier for the reader if you lay out the questions presented by number or letter, and then precede each short answer with the respective number. Also organize your analysis section using the same numbering system.

IV.   Analysis.

By far, the bulk of the writing should be included in the "analysis" section. When you are writing the memorandum, you must assume that the lawyer has only minimal familiarity with the opinions. Your job in writing a memorandum is to explain the law to the reader. The simple, though enormously effective, systems for doing that are "IRAC" and "CRPAW," which we discussed earlier.

You will spend a lot of time discussing the concepts underlying IRAC, particularly the "application" section. The application section is where you will compare the facts of the earlier cases to our facts, as done in the Arnold hypo above.

My point here is only to briefly introduce you to the concepts, and to give you a practical example of reasoning rules from the cases. I want to emphasize that IRAC and CRPAW are not the only ways to analyze the law, but they are easy ways to do it when you are starting out, and they are also effective at persuading judges that you are right. It works, judges are used to it, and you will see it in the opinions you read for class. More importantly, your professors may give you better grades because they are used to it, and your summer employers will also expect you to do it.

Here is an example of some cases applying a rule and how to write about them. (This hypothetical has no attachment to the real world. Do not think that it analyzes battery correctly; it does not.)

The facts of your law school hypothetical are: someone came at your client with a knife, so your client punched the man, killing him. You have found three opinions, all from the Florida Supreme Court, the state where the incident occurred, all legally on point:

<u>Oldest Case:</u>	A man punched someone for no reason.
<u>Result:</u>	Battery.
<u>Middle Case:</u>	A woman shot someone because he shot at her.
<u>Result:</u>	Self-defense, as a matter of law, so her battery was excused or justified.
<u>New Case:</u>	A man shot someone who was much bigger than he, and who was threatening him and who was crazed on drugs.
<u>Result:</u>	Citing Oldest Case and Middle Case, the court held that whether the man had a defense to battery depends on whether his fear of bodily harm was reasonable. If so, then it was self-defense; if not, then it was battery. The Supreme Court remanded for the jury to decide because under these facts it could not say that, as a matter of law, it was self-defense.

The issue is whether it is self-defense for your client to have punched a man who came at him with a knife. (More precisely, the issue is whether there is an "excuse" for what is clearly battery [punching someone].) The rule from the opinion decided by the Supreme Court is that, where you cause someone physical injury, it is battery unless the defendant can show self-defense, which depends upon whether it was reasonable for him to fear bodily harm. Those parts are easy. (Actually, there is a lot contained in that rule. For instance, it says that "unless the defendant can show" which seems to suggest that it is the defendant's burden to prove it. Note also that most rules are really a rule and an exception. Here, it is "if you hit someone it is a battery unless you can show self-defense.")

Note, however, that the "rule" has absolutely no meaning. You must then use the facts of each case to give meaning to what the rule says. (This is done in the application section, discussed next.) It is important to understand this: the facts in the opinion give the legal rules their meaning. Focus on what the facts were and what the opinion says about those facts. A rule means nothing when it is considered outside the context of the facts of the opinion.

A lawyer needs practical, *fact-based* distinctions and *analogies* between the facts of your case and the facts of the reported opinions. Is a knife "like" a gun? Is it "like" a big crazed man on drugs? Why? Why not? Does it matter whether there was a weapon? This highlights what we discussed earlier: policy arguments are secondary to factual distinctions. Arguing that "the policy of redressing wrongs against innocent victims will be aided by judgment in my client's favor" will get you nowhere. Judges seldom decide cases on the basis of policy; their goal is to move their docket and to avoid being reversed on appeal. They want to know what the law is and how it applies to your facts, not what grandiose policies might be served should they rule for your client in the dispute.

You will have to make judgments in applying the opinions. There will never be an opinion which squarely answers a question under your facts—because there will always be distinctions—so you will have to make judgments about whether there is a sufficient distinction between your facts and the facts of the opinion such that a court would come to a different result. Don't be timid in making those judgments, but be sure to indicate when you are hypothesizing about the future or predicting what a court would likely do. For instance, you might say "While a court may conclude that waving a knife is akin to firing a gun, a gun is clearly a more dangerous weapon than a knife . . .." You must reason through the law and apply it to the facts. Don't be afraid to make conclusions or predictions—it is what your professors want you to do, and what clients will be paying you to do!

V. Conclusion.

The conclusion of a memorandum does not need to rehash the analysis, and it should be extremely short and concise. It is also a place where you can make comments about strategy for handling the case in light of your research.

4. A Memorandum by a First-Year Law Student.

MEMORANDUM

TO: David Hricik
FROM: Patrick Stellitano
RE: Claim for mental anguish damages for breach of contract in *Peggy Johnson v. The Magic Catering Company*

I. Facts.

Our client, Magic Catering, made two contracts with plaintiff, Mrs. Johnson, and breached them both. Under the first contract, Mrs. Johnson paid $1,000 for Magic Catering to provide a magician at her seventeenth anniversary party. On his way to the party, the magician, Mark Stelter, was in a car accident caused by another driver. Our client's owner and manager, Victoria Lazar, could not find a substitute and she reimbursed Mrs. Johnson. She also apologized and paid her $100 for the inconvenience.

Mrs. Johnson testified during her deposition that she told Magic Catering prior to negotiating the contract that magic was not important to her. She thought her guests might like it, though.

Mrs. Johnson claims $100,000 in damages for mental anguish caused by our client's failure to perform magic. She says she will be reminded of this embarrassment every anniversary for the rest of her life.

Our client also made a contract to provide food and beverages for the party for which Mrs. Johnson paid $8,000. After Ms. Lazar reimbursed Mrs. Johnson for the magic contract, she suddenly ordered her employees to pack up the food and beverages. She shouted to the guests, "Nothin's been paid for, so stop eatin' right now."

The employees grabbed food and drink—some of it from the hands of guests. Ms. Lazar loudly called Mrs. Johnson "a cheapskate, who was trying to rip off Magic Catering." Mrs. Johnson and her guests were appalled, outraged and astonished to see this. Ms. Lazar testified at her deposition that she did all of this "because I was in a bad mood."

Mrs. Johnson claims $175,000 for mental distress and shock caused by the lack of food and beverages, as well as Ms. Lazar's language and behavior. She also wants her $8,000 back.

Both contracts provide that if Magic Catering fails to perform, Mrs. Johnson is entitled to a full refund without exceptions. We have admitted that our client failed to perform.

II.   Question Presented.

Can Mrs. Johnson recover mental anguish damages solely for a claim of breach of contract under either contract?

III.   Short Answer.

To recover mental anguish damages, Mrs. Johnson must show that the breach of either contract was intentional or that the contract was of such a personal nature that mental anguish was a foreseeable result of a breach. She cannot recover mental anguish damages for breach of the magic contract. This breach was not intentional. Nor was it foreseeable that she would suffer from mental anguish if magic was not performed. She can recover under the catering contract. The breach was intentional and without legal excuse or justification.

IV. Analysis.

Damages for mental suffering due to pecuniary loss following a breach of contract are generally not recoverable under Colorado law. *Adams v. Frontier Airlines Federal Credit Union*, 691 P.2d 352, 355 (Colo. App. 1984). However, if mental anguish is the natural and proximate consequence of a willful and wanton breach, then damages can be recovered. *Trimble v. City & County of Denver*, 697 P.2d 716, 731 (Colo. 1985). Second, mental anguish damages may be recovered if the contract is of such a personal nature that the parties could foresee that a breach would result in severe emotional distress. *Id.*

a. Willful Breach.

A willful (or wanton) breach of contract is a breach committed intentionally without justification or legal excuse. *Smith v. Hoyer*, 697 P.2d 761, 764 (Colo. App. 1984). Recovery may not be had for a mere passive breach. *Id.* The breach need not, however, be accompanied by outrageous conduct. *Denver Publishing Co. v. Kirk*, 729 P.2d 1004, 1008 (Colo. App. 1986). Whether conduct is willful is a question of fact for the jury. *Id.* If there is a mere scintilla of evidence or no evidence at all of willfulness, then the court is justified in taking the issue from the jury. *Lutz Farms v. Asgrow Seed Co.*, 948 P.2d 638, 647 (10th Cir. 1991) (applying Colorado law).

Mrs. Johnson has shown no evidence that Ms. Lazar's failure to provide magic was intentional. Rather, Ms. Lazar's efforts to perform were thwarted by circumstances beyond her control; namely, the car accident. Therefore, no genuine issue of fact exists and summary judgment should be granted on the issue of willful breach of the magic contract as a matter of law.

However, a motion for summary judgement would probably not be granted on the issue of willful breach of the catering contract. Ms. Lazar intentionally took away the beverages and food. Whether Ms. Johnson's mental anguish is a natural consequence of this breach is also a question of fact for the jury. *Lutz Farms v. Asgrow Seed Co.*, *supra*.

b. Personal Contracts.

The second possible basis for recovering mental anguish damages under Colorado law depends on whether either contract could be considered to be of such a personal nature that a breach would foreseeably result in mental anguish, then proof of willful conduct is not required. *Trimble*, 697 P.2d at 731. Plaintiff has the burden of proving that the contract falls within this exception. *See id.*

The precise contours of this exception are unclear. However, recovery of mental anguish damages under this theory has been explicitly rejected in cases involving breach of funeral contracts, where the casket has been breached and the remains of the decedent revealed to the surviving family members. *Kimelman v. City of Colorado Springs*, 775 P.2d 51, 53 (Colo. App. 1988).

Here, it seems likely that a court would grant summary judgment in favor of Magic Catering for breach of the magic contract. Ms. Johnson stated that magic was not an important part of the party. Summary judgment should be granted on this issue.

As for the catering contract, however, the answer is less clear. Magic Catering can argue that the failure to provide food at a wedding anniversary is far less distressing than watching a departed loved one fall headlong into the grave. Because mental anguish damages may not be covered in the case of funeral contracts, because they are not of a "personal" nature, so too they should be denied in a suit for breach of a catering contract regardless of the importance of food to Ms. Johnson. Magic Catering might be able to obtain summary judgment on this issue.

V. Conclusion.

Magic Catering should move for summary judgment on the issue of breach of the magic contract: there is no evidence that the breach was willful, nor was the contract of such a personal nature that would foreseeably have caused Ms. Johnson mental anguish. On the other hand, it is a closer question as to whether Magic Catering should move for summary judgment motion on the catering contract. Even if the catering contract was not a "personal contract," there is enough evidence of an intentional breach to submit this question to the jury.

5. Memoranda Are Not Briefs.

You will write two kinds of legal documents during your first year: memoranda and briefs. Memoranda and briefs differ completely in their purpose: memoranda are designed to be relatively neutral analyses of the law which *predict* what the court might do or how opposing parties might argue the law, but briefs are *persuasive*, not just informative. Memoranda discuss the weak points fairly and dispassionately; briefs deal with the weak points, but aggressively and persuasively.

Memoranda should objectively analyze both sides of the issue. For example, note the structure in this analysis, which lays out both sides of the argument:

As to whether running a stop sign constitutes negligence *per se*, each side has reasonable arguments. Plaintiff will rely on the one case which stated that this is the rule in Nevada. *See, e.g., Bob v. Bill*, 578 P.2d 221, 227 (Nev. 1978). On the other hand, defendant can show that in *Bob* the court was not faced with the issue of whether running a stop sign must always constitute negligence because there the jury had found the defendant negligent, and the issue was solely one of damages. *See Bob*, 578 P.2d at 226 ("We address only the award of compensatory damages, defendant having waived all other points.") Thus, the language from *Bob* is *dicta*, and several courts from other jurisdictions have held that running a stop sign is merely evidence of negligence, but is not negligence per se. *See Mary Jane v. Ruth*, 197 N.E.2d 501, 505 (N.D. 1954). For this reason, both sides have reasonable arguments, but a court would probably hold that it is not negligence *per se*.

You can use "on the one hand/on the other hand" or "defendant will argue/plaintiff will argue" to accomplish the purpose of analyzing both sides. Be sure to argue the best you can for the opposing party. Better to do it in an internal memo than to have the arguments shredded in open court by opposing counsel.

a.   Briefs: Persuade, Persuade, Persuade.

The sole purpose of a brief is to persuade.

Remember that in writing a brief you are making an argument. A brief exists to persuade. Every sentence should be written to persuade. Its primary purpose—if not its sole purpose—is to persuade. Persuade, persuade, and persuade.

Often, the goal of a brief is to make clear the equities, or fairness, of your client's position and why under the law your client should win. The brief should make the judge *want* to rule for your client and make him believe that the law is such that he *has* to rule for your client. A judge who is not persuaded on both levels—the equities and the law—is less likely to side with your client.

There are two major components to a brief: the facts and the law. Both should be written as persuasively as possible. The only fundamental limit on advocacy is this: truth in fact and accuracy in law. The most damaging thing a lawyer can do to his case is get caught stretching the facts too far or misstating the law. The judge will hate you. Deal with the facts and the law as they are, not as you would like them to be.

That does not mean you cannot "color" the facts, that you cannot put a "spin" on them.

Each sentence in a brief should be as accurate as it can be, but as persuasive as it can be without making it inaccurate. You will develop judgment about what is overreaching and what is advocacy.

Overreaching on the facts will make you lose credibility with the judge. There are countless examples where overreaching on the facts lost the case. For example, in *Searight v. State of New Jersey,* 412 F. Supp. 413 (D. N.J. 1976), a prisoner claimed that his civil rights had been violated when the defendants injected a radium electric beam into his eye. The exaggeration: the plaintiff claimed that someone now talks to him from inside his head, through some sort of radio beam connection. The court was not sympathetic to this exaggeration: it dismissed his suit, offering only the suggestion that he block the broadcast to the antenna in his brain by using a paperclip chain, extending down the leg of his trousers to the floor, so as to ground out the antenna. 412 F. Supp. at 415.

Exaggeration has caused many plaintiffs to lose their day in court. For example, in *Jackson v. Carpenter,* 921 F.2d 68 (5th Cir. 1991), a prisoner claimed that the sheriff had unlawfully removed from his head a silver dollar worth $126 million. The Fifth Circuit affirmed the dismissal of the complaint and the imposition of sanctions of $30 on the prisoner, stating that his "patently meritless arguments and accompanying illustrations try even the most patient members of this court." 921 F.2d at 69. Had Mr. Jackson not so tremendously exaggerated the value of the silver dollar, he might have had his day in court.

Such was also the fate of the plaintiff in *Franklin v. Oregon,* 563 F. Supp. 1310 (D. Or. 1983). There the judge dismissed all sixty-four cases which the plaintiff had filed that the judge had been able to find. 563 F. Supp. at 1317 & n. 3. Clearly, the plaintiff's weaker arguments—for example, that the prison guards wore "clopping heels on their boots, which causes plaintiff to feel he's in a Natsy [sic] prison camp" and that a Portland TV station had caused him $3 million in mental anguish damages by misidentifying a "14 wheeler tractor and trailer rig" as an "18 wheeler"—detracted from his ostensibly stronger arguments (for example, that his constitutional rights were violated because the prison's lawns were overwatered).

Tell a good factual story. You write facts persuasively by asking how the facts are best told from your client's perspective. What is your "theory of the case?" What is his, her or its *story*? Why is what happened to them wrong or unfair? From the defense standpoint, why is the suit aimed at the wrong party? Was this whole thing the plaintiff's fault? Someone else's? Or, is it that the defendant did everything right, and yet still got sued by some yahoo lawyer? Was the defendant at fault, but the damages sought are plainly ridiculous? These fundamental themes must come through in telling the facts.

A typical factual story will have two or three parts. The first part is a wonderful tale of perfect happiness. The plaintiff is fine, happy, and minding his own business. Life is good. Then suddenly and without warning the defendant did whatever she did, ruining the plaintiff's life forever. The only thing that will help now is money. Or, from the defendant's perspective, it could be the same thing. Defendant was doing everything she was supposed to be doing, when suddenly an accident occurred which was caused by, if anyone, the plaintiff. But, just a few days later, plaintiff had the gall to sue her for something that was plaintiff's own fault. What an outrage!

Think about those two or three major components before you write your statement of facts.

This is from the story from the case of *Wile E. Coyote v. Acme Co.*, No. B19294 (S.W. Dist. Az).[31] While it is not the fact section of a brief, with slight editing, it could be:

Mr. Coyote states that on occasions too numerous to list in this document he has suffered mishaps with explosives purchased of Defendant: the Acme "Little Giant" Firecracker, the Acme Self-Guided Aerial Bomb, etc.... Indeed, it is safe to say that not once has an explosive purchased of Defendant by Mr. Coyote performed in an expected manner. To cite just one example: at the expense of much time and personal effort, Mr. Coyote constructed around the outer rim of a butte a wooden trough beginning at the top of the butte and spiralling downward around it to some few feet above a black X painted on the desert floor. The trough was designed in such a way that a spherical explosive of the type sold by Defendant would roll easily and swiftly down to the point of detonation indicated by the X. Mr. Coyote placed a generous pile of birdseed directly on the X, and then, carrying the spherical Acme Bomb (Catalogue #78-832), climbed to the top of the butte. Mr. Coyote's prey, seeing the birdseed, approached, and Mr. Coyote proceeded to light the fuse. In an instant, the fuse burned down to the stem, causing the bomb to detonate.

In addition to reducing all Mr. Coyote's careful preparations to naught, the premature detonation of Defendant's product resulted in the following disfigurements to Mr. Coyote:

1. Severe singeing of the hair on the head, neck, and muzzle.
2. Sooty discoloration.
3. Fracture of the left ear at the stem, causing the ear to dangle in the aftershock with a creaking noise.

---

31   Ian Frazier, *Coyote v. Acme*, 20 Litigation, 64, 64 (July 1994).

4. Full or partial combustion of whiskers, producing kinking, frazzling, and ashy disintegration.
5. Radical widening of the eyes, due to brow and lid charring.

We come now to the Acme Spring-Powered Shoes, ...

Notice the themes: everything is going fine, plaintiff is *relying on defendant* to do its job right. Plaintiff was let down by the defendant. Someone's got to pay for this, and that someone is the defendant, who caused all these injuries.

This idea—of telling a good story—is present in the following original petition from a real lawsuit.[32] Again, it could easily serve as the fact section for a brief (though it is quite detailed):

There was a public event in Houston denominated a "Annual Symphony Class Run" and also "the fun run event" managed, sponsored and organized by Defendants.... Plaintiff resides in an apartment complex on Memorial Drive, and on the day of the occurrence ... departed from there in her vehicle at 8:20 a.m., heading for work in the Post Oak area. Normally, because a median prevents left turns from Plaintiff's driveway, Plaintiff would have turned right, naturally, and then proceeded to the first intersection, Shepherd Drive, where Plaintiff would make a u-turn, and then take Memorial Drive west to the 610 feeder road. But Shepherd Drive had been barricaded on account of the Fun Run Event that morning, preventing Plaintiff from taking her normal route. Since there were no directions, Plaintiff then tried to exit Memorial at Waugh Drive, the next intersection, which had been barricaded also. Thus, Plaintiff had to continue on Memorial Drive and was led into downtown Houston, an area unfamiliar to her.

Because Plaintiff was expected for a staff meeting at work at 9:30 sharp, Plaintiff became, at this point, nervous and upset, not knowing quite where Plaintiff was or how to find a route to work. Plaintiff turned right at the first electric signal, hoping to find a familiar street name. Several blocks down, Plaintiff saw a sign reading "to Allen Parkway" and pointing to the right. Recognizing the name, Plaintiff turned right and proceeded about one-half block, only to be stopped by two barricades of which she had no advance notice. Directly on the other side of the

---

[32] Hevenstreit v. Beneke et. al, No. 91-052337; In the 152nd Judicial District Court in Harris County, Texas.

barricades was a patrol car, and inside, Plaintiff saw an officer, who indicated she should not proceed any further.

Late for work and unable to find a viable route, Plaintiff then stopped the car, got out, and walked between the barricades and over to the officer, who was about one car length away from her vehicle. Plaintiff explained to the officer what had happened, and he directed her to an alternative route. Turning to return to her car, Plaintiff tripped over one of the barricade's legs which somehow was disjointed and constituted a special defect as defined in Texas Civil Practices and Remedies code Section 101.060(c), and fell forward, landing on her right arm (her writing arm), and her right knee.... As a result, Plaintiff broke her arm, shattered some bones in her wrist, and bruised her knee....

Again, this is well written. It tells a sympathetic story *from the plaintiff's perspective*. Notice how all of the plaintiff's dilemma is caused by the defendants. Even her agitation and confusion is because she's been lost downtown and has a meeting she must attend—not because she didn't give herself enough time to get to work. Notice that the complaint takes advantage of stating what did *not* happen—it makes an issue out of facts which did not occur. For example, it notes that "she had no advance notice" of the barricades. Again, this can be highly persuasive, particularly in negligence cases where the allegation is that the damage was caused by an untaken precaution (failing to drive slowly in the rain; failing to render aid after the accident; failing to have the car inspected, *etc.*).

A very effective but often overlooked approach is to emphasize what *did not happen*. It is always useful to state what *didn't* happen, what was missing, or what should have been done but was not. These are "facts," too, and they are just as relevant and just as powerful as those facts which did occur or exist.

The second component of a brief is the legal argument. Take a chance when drafting your argument. Be creative. Write several different arguments or approaches to each argument, and then pick the ones that are your strongest and hone them further. Don't argue everything in the brief you turn in (to the teacher or the court). If you do, then your weak arguments will drag your strong ones down with them.

How do you make a legal *argument*, as opposed to merely *explaining* the law, as you do in a memorandum? (The following discussion applies to both opening and responsive briefs, but the special problems attendant to responsive briefs are discussed further below.)

First, read the cases. (I said at the beginning that this book repeats some points. This is one of those points.) You have to understand the law before you can write an argument. Don't read just the headnotes or just the "rule." Read the whole case, and understand its facts.

Second, *think* about the facts of the opinions and the facts in your case. What are the strengths and weaknesses of your client's facts when compared to those in the cases.

Third, make an outline. Even if you are not a fan of outlining or made do without outlining throughout college , make at least a rough "idea" outline. Especially for longer briefs, outlining will save a lot of time in the long run, and result in a better product and so a higher grade.

Writing a legal argument is structurally very similar to writing a legal memorandum. CRPAW and IRAC still work in persuasive writing.

For an example of CRPAW, suppose you are moving for summary judgment in the case in which the lady fell over the barricade after being forced to drive to downtown Houston. This might be your argument as a lawyer representing the defendant:

> *[Conclusion]* Defendant is entitled to summary judgment because it did not owe any legal duty to plaintiff. *[Rule]* Defendant did not owe a duty to plaintiff to warn plaintiff how to navigate the streets of downtown Houston. [Proof of rule] Numerous courts have granted summary judgment on claims like plaintiff's. For example, in *Smith v. Jones,* 888 S.W.2d 555, 585 (Tex. App. —Houston [14th Dist.] 1993, no writ), the court affirmed summary judgment on the plaintiff's claim that the defendant—which, like defendant here, was a sponsor of a road race—had a duty to post "directions" because it had barricaded certain roads. Other courts have reached similar results. *E.g., Bob v. Fred,* 889 S.W.2d 587, 593 (Tex. 1992) (affirming summary judgment against claim of failure to provide directions for merchant which had blocked off portion of shopping mall); *Garcia v. Ebenezer,* 988 S.W.2d 543, 559 (Tex. App. —Dallas 1989, writ ref'd n.r.e.) (same); *Elmer v. Jethro,* 567 S.W.2d 444, 454 (Tex. App. —San Antonio 1984, no writ) (defendant sponsor of road race owed duty to post directions solely because it had promised city in writing that no "unnecessary" disruption of traffic would occur).
>
> *[Application]* Here, plaintiff's sole claim is that because defendant had barricaded the road in order to permit a safe race, defendant had a duty to provide directions to anyone in the area as to how to go wherever he wanted to go. Not only is this legally incorrect under *Smith v. Jones,* it is ridiculous to impose a duty on the sponsor of a road race to predict where every person who might come across the barricade wanted to go instead.

> *[Wrap-up]* Plaintiff's effort to impose such a duty is thus factually misguided and legally unsupportable. Because defendant did not owe any duty to plaintiff, defendant is entitled to summary judgment.

Notice that this argument addresses the case law at different levels of generality. For example, the *Smith v. Jones* case, because it is factually the most pertinent, is discussed at some length, while the *Fred* and *Garcia* cases are given only a general introduction and a parenthetical insert. Adverse authority is addressed by citing to the *Elmer v. Jethro* case and distinguishing it on its facts. Your argument needs to address the law at these various levels—specific support, general support, and adverse authority.

A brief should address the law directly, even if it is not all favorable. For example, as the movant or appellant, the brief should take the steam away from the responsive brief by addressing unfavorable cases and distinguishing them. Be sure to distinguish the bad cases *on their facts*. Similarly, emphasize good case law by showing the *factual similarities* between the good cases and your case. This does not necessarily involve a long explication of what the facts and result were (it could, but usually it will not). Instead, it may require a general statement followed by citations with parenthetical explanations. For example, you could write something like: "Of course, other courts have reached different results when faced with fact patterns not raised here. *See, e.g.*, *Smith v. Jones*, 5 F.3d 222, 223 (5th Cir. 1993) (no negligence where plaintiff ran stop sign because driver needed to extinguish fire in back seat of car)." By addressing any adverse authority and explaining it away, you steal the thunder from the responsive brief and make responding that much harder.

You also meet your ethical obligation to cite and discuss adverse authority. You have an ethical duty to advise the court of controlling adverse authority. That's right: if you know of a *bad* case—even if the other side missed it—you have an ethical duty to tell the court about it. How do you know whether you *must* disclose the case? The "more unhappy a lawyer is that he found an adverse precedent, the clearer it is that he must reveal it." Hazard and Hodes, *The Law of Lawyering*, 3.3:206 (2d ed. 1990). Judges, especially at the appellate level, are taking this obligation more seriously.

You should, too. Moreover, the issue of whether you *must* disclose is distinct from whether you should discuss adverse authority in order to be an effective advocate: if the other side finds the bad opinion, they will make much of your failure to cite it. The best course is to cite and distinguish, however briefly, any highly relevant adverse opinion—not so much as a matter of ethics, but as a means of advocacy.

Your argument must be made with a different tone than is used in memoranda. Pay attention to your tone. Tone should match the subject matter and your own style. If you are representing a plaintiff in a personal injury case, use the emotional facts which may help you (but don't overdo it). If your company has been sued for discrimination, you may want to sound indignant (but avoid sounding whiny or self-righteous). The right tone is always achieved by balancing competing goals.

When revising, pay particular attention to your diction. Don't sound like a lawyer. Make it punchy. Vary the length of your sentences, using shorter sentences when needed, longer ones only when shorter ones will not due. Short sentences add emphasis. Short sentences are easier to comprehend.

Similarly, shorter paragraphs are better paragraphs. They are easier to look at, and the white space makes a brief less daunting to the eye.

Briefs are places where you should avoid "writing like a lawyer." Use *a* few fresh rhetorical flourishes. You can use slight overstatement and slight hyperbole when making your argument. *Cf. White v. Samsung Elec. America, Inc.,* 971 F.2d 1395, 1396 (9th Cir. 1992) ("Plaintiff Vanna White is the hostess of "Wheel of Fortune," *one of the most popular game shows in television history.*") (emphasis added). But do not make it sound like if your side loses, giant cracks would open in the earth, and huge lizards would emerge to eat us all. As one federal appellate court judge put it, "embellishment and exaggeration will not get a lawyer anywhere but in trouble." Joel F. Dubina, *Effective Appellate Advocacy*, 20 Litig. 3, 4 (Winter 1994).

Read it aloud to *hear* how it sounds. Or, imagine one of your law professors making the argument in front of your class, and hear his or her voice reading your work aloud. How does it sound? The judge reading your brief will hear her own little voice in her head reading your words aloud to her, and so if it sounds odd out loud to you, it will sound odd to that little voice in her head, too. Change it until it sounds *right*.

Likewise, *look* at it. Does it have lots of long paragraphs, which makes it look daunting and complex? If it looks hard to understand, it will seem hard to comprehend to the judge. Shorter paragraphs look easier. The way it looks can effect what meaning it conveys. Pay attention to appearances.

b. Responsive Briefs.

Responsive briefs present unique problems. Lawyers disagree about everything, including what is the best approach in a responsive brief. I believe that the best approach is to first make *your* argument—why you should win—and then show why the movant's (or appellant's) arguments are wrong. Write your argument using CRPAW or IRAC, and at the end of the proof of rule (or application) "section" address and dispose of the other side's argument. (Where it works best depends on the argument itself, and judgment and experience will indicate where is best.) You should discuss (in a sentence, paragraph, or footnote) and distinguish the movant's cases, or describe how the movant's approach relies on logical fallacies, would lead to incorrect results, ignores the operative facts, or would be contrary to existing law or common sense.

Other useful tactics are to undercut the movant's (or appellant's) argument, if you can, by noting that the opinions he relies on came out the wrong way: that is, those opinions have unfavorable results. This approach is powerful where the other side has cited cases for the "rule" that the case states, without paying attention to how that particular court ruled on that issue. When this happens, an effective responsive argument is something like: "That plaintiff's argument is wrong is proven by its own authority: in every case cited by plaintiff, the courts *denied* the very relief plaintiff now seeks." This approach can be very effective; devastatingly so where the court has broad discretion to decide the issue.

For this reason, be sure to read the cases cited by your opponent. You will not believe how often lawyers cite cases for their words, ignoring what *result* the court reached in the opinion. It makes it tough when a party has to distinguish *his own* cases.

Some arguments are just sure-fire losers, however. When your client is a schmuck, it might be better just to give up. *See, e.g., Schmuck v. United States,* 109 S.Ct. 1443 (1989) (affirming conviction of Wayne T. Schmuck, used car salesman, for mail fraud). Learning to tell the winners from the losers is not a science. *See Freeman v. First Court of Appeals*, 844 S.W.2d 223 (Tex. 1992) (the only appeal I've helped on where we lost).

A special word about the tone of responsive briefs is also in order. (Although these observations apply primarily to responsive writing, they also are relevant to opening briefs.) In writing responsive briefs, remember that the *other side* "argues, asserts, or alleges" the bad things. You should just state the favorable positions as facts or law. For example, don't write (if you're the plaintiff) "Plaintiff claims he was injured when . . . ." Instead, just say "Plaintiff was injured when . . . ." (But, if you're the defendant, you would say "Plaintiff claims he was supposedly injured when....") The *other side* "claims" and "asserts" the bad stuff.

Similarly, use adjectives to characterize the arguments, such as "plaintiff relies on the inapposite case of . . ." or "ignoring this controlling case, defendant erroneously contends . . ." or "ignoring the overwhelming weight of this recent authority, plaintiff dredges up . . . ." These sorts of sentences are very useful ways to address the movant's assertions as to the law: after your proof of rule or application "section," after setting out the law as you contend it is, then use this sort of sentence to dismiss the movant's discussion about the law. However, avoid *ad hominem* attacks and name calling, and never attribute improper motives to your opponent.

c. **Real Brief—Excerpts.**

What follows is the bulk of the argument from the brief Lee Kaplan and I wrote and filed in the Fifth Circuit in the *WNS, Inc. v. Farrow* case. The resulting opinion is attached in the appendix. Some of the brief has been omitted.[33]

VII.
STATEMENT OF THE CASE

(i) <u>Course of proceedings and disposition in the district court</u>.

This suit commenced on December 18, 1987, when WNS, Inc. ("WNS" or "Appellant") filed its original petition in the 270th Judicial District Court of Harris County, Texas. WNS asserted several causes of action, sounding in both tort and contract, arising from transactions relating to negotiations and agreements regarding the purchase and operation of a franchise.

Appellees, James Larry Farrow and Mary Dee Farrow, removed the case to the United States District Court for the Southern District of Texas, Houston Division. The Farrows answered, <u>inter alia</u>, by denying that they had engaged in business within the State of Texas. The Farrows moved to dismiss the suit for lack of personal jurisdiction on the grounds that they were not residents of Texas and had not engaged in business in Texas.

In its order dated September 26, 1988, the district court granted the Farrows' motion to dismiss for lack of personal jurisdiction. The district court clearly held that it lacked personal jurisdiction over either appellee. On October 24, 1988, WNS timely filed its notice of appeal to this Court.

(ii) <u>Statement of facts</u>.

This case arises from the Farrows' failure to fulfill their contractual obligations as WNS franchisees, their fraud in obtaining WNS' proprietary information under the guise of their desire to become WNS franchisees, and their misappropriation and misapplication of WNS' confidential information and proprietary marks in a competing store.

---

33 Obviously, this is a legal argument. The "facts" are only allegations Nothing in this brief should be taken as true. This is an academic exercise.

WNS is a Texas corporation. It licenses the Deck the Walls trade name and trade and service marks (collectively, "proprietary marks") and it franchises a comprehensive system for opening and operating a Deck the Walls store (the "system"). WNS is in the business of franchising its system and licensing its proprietary marks to persons who operate Deck the Walls stores. In short, WNS provides its franchisees with a complete program for operating a Deck the Walls retail outlet.

The Farrows are individuals and residents of the State of Georgia. They do not maintain a regular place of business, nor are they domiciled, in Texas.

The Farrows contacted WNS in March 1986 to apply to become Deck the Walls franchisees. WNS requires all serious Deck the Walls applicants to come to Houston for an extensive formal interview. On or about March 7, 1986, the Farrows voluntarily and purposefully traveled to Texas to meet with WNS employees for the formal interview required of all franchise applicants, to structure a franchise agreement, and to negotiate for the franchise. Also on that day, WNS received in Texas the Farrows' application for a Georgia franchise. During the course of that day-long meeting, the Farrows and WNS discussed all aspects of the terms of a Deck the Walls franchise agreement.

Also during that meeting in Houston, the Farrows were interviewed by a WNS officer for the purpose of presenting themselves for favorable consideration as franchisees. The officer evaluated the Farrows' credentials and, based upon this interview, decided to approve the Farrows' franchise application.

During that Houston meeting, the parties negotiated and agreed to all terms of three separate contracts. First, the Farrows negotiated and agreed on all terms of a "Franchise Agreement," agreeing to buy a franchise for $171,857.04 to operate a store in Georgia. The Franchise Agreement required the Farrows to pay WNS an up-front payment and, thereafter, a royalty. The Franchise Agreement provided that Texas law governed. Mrs. Farrow ultimately signed the Franchise Agreement.

Second, because the Farrows did not have permanent financing, the parties negotiated and agreed to all terms of an agreement entitled "Loan/Lease Agreement," to enable the Farrows to operate the store before permanent financing was in place. Third, the Farrows and WNS negotiated and agreed on all terms of a "Sublease Agreement" for a space in a shopping center in Georgia. These three agreements required the Farrows to make rental payments in Texas, and to submit various reports, proposed advertising, and other payments to WNS in Texas.

After the meeting in Houston, the Farrows returned to Georgia. Later, they mailed a cashier's check (listing both of the Farrows as remitters) as partial payment of the financial obligations due under the Franchise Agreement to WNS in Texas, where it was received on March 20, 1986. On the same day, WNS sent the Farrows a copy of the Franchise Agreement for their signatures. In April 1986, WNS' Houston headquarters received a second check (again listing both of the Farrows as remitters) as the second contractually required payment.

As part of the franchise arrangement with WNS, both Mr. and Mrs. Farrow signed up for the Deck the Walls training course which all franchisees must take to fulfill their franchise obligations. Although both Mr. and Mrs. Farrow enrolled in the course, only Mrs. Farrow returned to Texas for the week-long seminar. In Houston, Mrs. Farrow spent about four days learning to operate equipment and studying framing techniques. She also spent about a day studying the Deck the Walls Operations System, another day learning the Deck the Walls Merchandising System, and still another day learning the specialized Deck the Walls sales techniques. WNS' Houston personnel also instructed her on other matters necessary to operate the franchise. In addition, Mrs. Farrow learned about and considered other services provided by WNS, such as bookkeeping. Finally, while in Houston Mrs. Farrow received confidential materials from WNS, including the Deck the Walls training manual, which she took to Georgia.

Under the impression that both Mr. and Mrs. Farrow were to be franchisees, WNS prepared the Franchise Agreement. On May 13, 1986, Mrs. Farrow signed the Authorization to Occupy (and related agreements) which showed both Farrows as franchisees. The Farrows opened the store that same day. However, when WNS later received the Franchise Agreement in Texas, it bore only the signature of Mrs. Farrow.

At that time, the Farrows first informed WNS that only Mrs. Farrow was to be a franchisee. WNS, through its attorney, then informed the Farrows of what had been understood and agreed all along: that both appellees were applying to be franchisees. Mrs. Farrow continued to operate the franchise until the beginning of April 1987.

On April 2, 1987, WNS took possession of the Georgia store and terminated the sublease. After terminating the franchise, WNS discovered that the Farrows had operated a competing store in violation of the Franchise Agreement. Only then did WNS realize that after inducing WNS to license Deck the Walls proprietary marks and information to the Farrows for use in an authorized Deck the Walls outlet, the Farrows had fraudulently opened a competing store in order to exploit the Deck the Walls proprietary marks. WNS alleges that while both Mr. and Mrs. Farrow had come to Texas and presented themselves as bona fide franchise applicants, they misrepresented their intentions to apply for and operate a Deck the Walls franchise in good faith. Because of the Farrows' fraud and breach of contract, WNS was injured in Texas.

XIII.
ARGUMENT

A.   WNS need only make a prima facie showing of personal jurisdiction.

To avoid dismissal for lack of personal jurisdiction, WNS need only make a prima facie showing of personal jurisdiction:

> [T]he party who bears the burden need only present a prima facie case for personal jurisdiction; proof by a preponderance of the evidence is not required. Moreover, on a motion to dismiss for lack of jurisdiction, uncontroverted allegations in the plaintiff's complaint must be taken as true, and conflicts between the facts contained in the parties' affidavits must be resolved in the plaintiff's favor for purposes of determining whether a prima facie case for personal jurisdiction exists.

D.J. Investments, Inc. v. Metzeler Motorcycle Tire, Inc., 754 F.2d 542, 545-46 (5th Cir. 1985) (citations omitted) (emphasis added). Accord, Colwell Realty Investments, Inc. v. Triple T Inns of Arizona, Inc., 785 F.2d 1330, 1332-33 (5th Cir. 1986).

B.   The sole issue is whether subjecting either defendant to jurisdiction in Texas violates the due process clause of the fourteenth amendment.

"It is well-settled that a defendant is amenable to the personal jurisdiction of a federal court in a diversity case to the extent permitted a state court in the state where the federal court sits." DeMelo v. Toche Marine, Inc., 711

F.2d 1260, 1264 (5th Cir. 1983). Two inquiries determine whether a federal district court has personal jurisdiction: "First, the law of the forum state must provide for the assertion of such jurisdiction; and second, the exercise of jurisdiction under the state law must comport with the dictates of the fourteenth amendment due process clause." Smith v. DeWalt Products Corp., 743 F.2d 277, 278 (5th Cir. 1984).

Regarding the first inquiry, it has long been held that the Texas long-arm statute reaches to the full extent permitted by due process.[34] Therefore, only the second inquiry is relevant. Helicopteros Nacionales de Columbia, S.A. v. Hall, 466 U.S. 408, 413 (1984); InterFirst Bank Clifton v. Fernandez, 844 F.2d 279, 282 (5th Cir. 1988) opinion withdrawn, in part, and substituted, in part, 853 F.2d 292 (5th Cir. 1988); Stuart v. Spademan, 772 F.2d 1185, 1189 (5th Cir. 1985); Colwell Realty Investments, 785 F.2d at 1333; Kawasaki Steel Corp. v. Middleton, 699 S.W.2d 199, 200 (Tex. 1985). The sole issue is whether subjecting either defendant to personal jurisdiction in Texas would violate due process.

C.   WNS must show, in a specific jurisdiction case, that the cause of action is related to an intentional tort committed in part in Texas or to a contract having substantial connection with Texas.

In determining whether due process is violated, this Court analyzes two requirements. First, "the nonresident must have some minimum contact with the forum which results from an affirmative act on the part of the nonresident." Colwell Realty Investments, 785 F.2d at 1333. WNS is required only to present a prima facie case to show that the Farrows have minimum contacts with Texas. Colwell Realty Investments, 785 F.2d at 1333. Second, "it must be fair and reasonable to require the nonresident to defend the suit in the forum state." Colwell Realty Investments, 785 F.2d at 1333. If WNS shows prima facie minimum contacts based upon proposeful availment, then the Farrows must "present a compelling case that the presence of some other considerations would render jurisdiction unreasonable." Burger King Co. v. Rudzewicz, 471 U.S. 462, 477 (1985); InterFirst Bank Clifton v. Fernandez, 844 F.2d at 283. See infra, page 25.

---

[34]   The Texas long-arm statute and its predecessor "reach[] as far as the federal constitutional requirements of due process will permit." Kawasaki Steel Corp. v. Middleton, 699 S.W.2d 199, 200 (Tex. 1985), quoting U-Anchor Advertising, Inc. v. Burt, 553 S.W.2d 760 (Tex. 1977).

In a "specific" jurisdiction case such as this,[35] the "fair warning" requirement of due process is satisfied "if the defendant has 'purposefully directed' his activities at residents of the forum, and the litigation results from alleged injuries that arise out of or relate to those activities." Burger King, 471 U.S. at 472 (citations omitted). Accord, Colwell Realty Investments, 785 F.2d at 1333.[36] "[T]he constitutional touchstone remains whether the defendant purposefully established 'minimum contacts' in the forum state." Burger King, 471 U.S. at 474 (citations omitted). Accord, Colwell Realty Investments, 785 F.2d at 1333.

The cases uniformly hold that where a nonresident purposefully commits an intentional tort in part in the forum state or enters into a contract creating substantial connections between itself and the forum state, the nonresident is considered to have availed itself "of the privilege of conducting business there, and because his activities are shielded by 'the benefits and protections' of the forum's law it is presumptively not

---

[35] "'Specific' jurisdiction refers to a suit' arising out of or related to the defendant's contacts with the forum.' General jurisdiction refers to a suit which does not arise from the nonresident's contacts with the forum, and is asserted only over defendants who maintain 'continuous and systematic' contacts in a particular forum." Interfirst Bank Clifton v. Fernandez, 844 F.2d 279, 283 (5th Cir. 1988) (citations omitted). See Burger King, 471 U.S. at 473, n. 15.

WNS does not contend that the Farrows' numerous contacts with Texas are sufficient to constitute 'continuous and systematic' contacts. WNS argues solely that the facts show a prima facie case of specific personal jurisdiction. See, e.g., Keeton v. Hustler Magazine, Inc., 465 U.S. 770 (1984); Calder v. Jones, 465 U.S. 783 (1984); Burger King Co. v. Rudzewicz, 471 U.S. 462 (1985); Asahi Metal Industry Co. v. Superior Court of California, 480 U.S. 102 (1987); Interfirst Bank Clifton v. Fernandez, 844 F.2d 279 (5th Cir. 1988); Stuart v. Spademan, 772 F.2d 1185 (5th Cir. 1985); D.J. Investments v. Metzeler Motorcycle Tire Agent Gregg, Inc., 754 F.2d 542 (5th Cir. 1985)

[36] "This 'purposeful availment' requirement ensures that a defendant will not be haled into a jurisdiction solely as a result of 'random,' 'fortuitous,' or 'attenuated' contacts, or of the 'unilateral activity of another party or third person.'" Burger King, 471 U.S. at 475 (citations omitted). Clearly, it is not "random" that defendants purposefully came to Texas to negotiate with a Texas corporation. Likewise, there is no "unilateral activity" here. Cf. World-Wide Volkswagen Corp. v. Woodson, 444 U.S. 286 (1980).

unreasonable to require him to submit to the burdens of litigation in that forum as well." Burger King, 471 U.S. at 475-76. Accord, Asahi, 480 U.S. at 112.[37] WNS submits that it has made a prima facie showing that both appellees purposefully committed a tort, in part, in Texas and that both appellees established substantial contractual connections with Texas. If WNS makes a prima facie showing of minimum contacts under either theory, then the district court had personal jurisdiction.

1.   WNS made a prima facie showing of minimum contacts by showing that the Farrows committed fraud, in part, in Texas.

The Supreme Court has twice examined personal jurisdiction in cases involving intentional torts. In both Keeton v. Hustler Magazine, Inc., 465 U.S. 770 (1984), and Calder v. Jones, 465 U.S. 783 (1984), the Court held that personal jurisdiction was constitutional because the defendants' acts were purposefully directed at residents of the forum state. In the libel case of Calder v. Jones, 465 U.S. 783, 790 (1984), the Court stated that "[defendants] are primary participants in an alleged wrongdoing intentionally directed at a California resident, and jurisdiction over them is proper on that basis."[38]

---

[37]   In both Burger King and Asahi, the Supreme Court cites as examples of the "substantial connection" test both contract and intentional tort cases. See Burger King, 462 U.S. at 475; Asahi, 480 U.S. at 112. Specifically, the Supreme Court in Asahi stated "[t]he 'substantial connection' between the defendant and the forum State necessary for a finding of minimum contacts must come about by an action of the defendant purposefully directed toward the forum State." Asahi at 112 (emphasis in original). The Court cites Burger King, a contract case, and Keeton v. Hustler Magazine, Inc., 465 U.S. 770 (1984), an intentional tort case.

[38]   The Court's reasoning was that personal jurisdiction in California was proper because defendants'

intentional, and allegedly tortious, actions were expressly aimed at California. [Defendants wrote and] edited an article that they knew would have a devastating impact upon respondent. And they knew that the brunt of that injury would be felt by respondent in [California]. . . . An individual injured in California need not go to Florida to seek redress from persons who, though remaining in Florida, knowingly cause the injury in California.

This Court has repeatedly held that "a single purposeful contact is sufficient to satisfy the due process requirement of 'minimum contacts' when the cause of action arises from the contact." Thompson v. Chrysler Motors Corp., 755 F.2d 1162, 1172 (5th Cir. 1985). Accord, Brown v. Flowers Industries, Inc., 688 F.2d 328 (5th Cir. 1982), cert. denied, 460 U.S. 1023 (1982); D.J. Investments, Inc. v. Metzeler Motorcycle Tire Agent Gregg, Inc., 754 F.2d 542 (5th Cir. 1985). This Court has held personal jurisdiction proper under "contacts" far more attenuated than here. For example, in Brown v. Flowers Industries, due process permitted assertion of personal jurisdiction over a nonresident defendant whose only contact with the forum state was the making of a single defamatory phone call from without to within the state. See also Thompson v. Chrysler Motors Corp., supra.

Likewise, in Metzeler, supra, this Court held personal jurisdiction was proper where the alleged misrepresentations were made primarily by phone, but a defendant did come to Texas once and made alleged misrepresentations.

> Some of the tortious activity took place in the state and the injurious effect fell entirely within the forum state. . . . [T]he instant cause of action for . . . fraud is related directly to the tortious activities which appellant cites as contacts which give rise to personal jurisdiction.

Metzeler, 754 F.2d at 548. This Court held that these allegations constituted a prima facie case of personal jurisdiction because "defendants 'should reasonably have anticipated' that they might be haled into court in Texas." Metzeler, 754 F.2d at 548.

Here, WNS alleges that both appellees purposefully came to Texas in order to obtain proprietary information by misrepresenting that they were interested in becoming Deck the Walls franchisees. (R. 154-55.) WNS alleges that it relied in Texas on such misrepresentations and was thereby damaged in Texas. (See R. 154-55.) Clearly, this constitutes a prima facie showing that the Farrows established "minimum contacts" by committing fraud, in part, in Texas.[39] See Metzeler, 754 F.2d at 547 & n.5. Indeed, the facts presented

---

Calder v. Jones, 465 U.S. at 789-90.

[39] The district court recognized that commission of a tort, in part, in Texas as sufficient. See Tr. 20-21. However, the district court stated that WNS had made "just an allegation." Tr. 21, line 5. An allegation was all WNS was

here show far more compelling contacts than in <u>Metzeler</u>, <u>Brown</u>, or <u>Thompson</u>. Therefore, the district court erred in concluding it lacked minimum contacts.

2. <u>The Farrows negotiated and agreed to all terms, and both parties began performance, of three agreements having substantial connection to Texas; because WNS is suing for breach of those agreements, personal jurisdiction is proper.</u>

<u>Burger King</u> is the leading Supreme Court case analyzing whether a non-resident will be considered to have "substantial connection" with the forum by reason of contractual relations. In <u>Burger King</u>, the Court stressed that the contract itself is not what establishes minimum contacts. <u>Burger King</u>, 471 U.S. at 478.

> Instead, we have emphasized the need for a 'highly realistic' approach that recognizes that a 'contract' is 'ordinarily but an intermediate step serving to tie up prior business negotiations with future consequences which themselves are the real object of the business transaction.' <u>It is these factors—prior negotiations and contemplated future consequences, along with the terms of the contract and the parties' actual course of dealing—that must be evaluated</u> in determining whether the defendant purposefully established minimum contacts with the forum.

<u>Id.</u>, 471 U.S. at 479 (citation omitted) (emphasis added).

The prior negotiations of the parties to the contract in <u>Burger King</u> took place entirely outside of the forum: Rudzewicz had <u>no</u> physical ties to Florida, the forum state. <u>Id.</u>, 471 U.S. at 479. The contract was long-term franchise. <u>Id.</u> 471 U.S. at 480. The other factors emphasized in <u>Burger King</u> were: (1) the contract documents emphasized Burger King's operations were conducted and supervised from Miami; (2) all relevant notices and payments were required to be sent to Miami; (3) the agreements were made in and enforced from Miami; (4) the parties' actual course of dealing repeatedly confirmed that decision-making authority was vested in Miami; (5) the contract specified that Florida law governed. <u>See</u> <u>Id.</u>, 471 U.S. at 480-82. The Supreme Court held personal jurisdiction was constitutional because "the franchise dispute grew directly out of 'a contract which had <u>substanti</u>

<u>required to make.</u> Indeed, as WNS argued below, the Farrows' denial that the committed fraud cannot overcome WNS' <u>prima facie</u> case. (<u>See</u> Tr. 8.)

connection with that State.'" Id., quoting McGee v. International Life Insurance Co., 355 U.S. 220 (1957). "Rudzewicz most certainly knew that he was affiliating himself with an enterprise based primarily in Florida." Id., 471 U.S. at 480.

The case at bar is nearly indistinguishable from Burger King: (1) the contract documents emphasized that WNS operations were conducted from Houston; (2) all relevant notices and payments were required to be sent to Houston; (3) the agreements were negotiated in and enforced from Houston; (4) the parties' course of dealings evidences that decision-making authority was vested in Houston; and (5) the contract specifies that Texas law governs.

The case at bar is more compelling than Burger King because the Farrows came to Texas to negotiate the agreements and Mrs. Farrow performed in part in Texas by returning for the week-long training course. As in Burger King, a long-term franchise agreement with continuing contacts was contemplated. In short, personal jurisdiction is proper because the Farrows, like Rudzewicz, most certainly knew they were affiliating themselves with an enterprise based primarily in Texas and thus could be sued in Texas for breach of contract.

WNS has made prima facie allegations which demonstrate that both defendants are bound by the franchise agreement. If proven, the allegations show an enforceable agreement between WNS and Mrs. Farrow for two reasons. First, she signed it and is therefore bound by it. See generally Vick v. McPherson, 360 S.W.2d 866 (Tex. Civ. App.—Amarillo, 1963 writ ref'd n.r.e.); Dailey v. Transitron Overseas Corp., 349 F.Supp. 797, 800 (S.D. Tex. 1972), aff'd 475 F.2d 12 (5th Cir. 1973). Second, Mrs. Farrow is bound by the contract because WNS alleges that she partially performed by making contractually-required payments to WNS in Texas, by attending the contractually-required course in Texas, and by operating the store in Georgia. See generally Walker v. Lorehn, 355 S.W.2d 71 (Tex. Civ. App.—Houston 1962, writ ref'd n.r.e.); Oak Cliff Realty Corp. v. Mauzy, 354 S.W.2d 693, 695 (Tex. Civ. App.—Fort Worth 1962, writ ref'd n.r.e.). In addition, WNS has alleged facts that, if proven, would estop Mrs. Farrow from raising this issue. See generally Wynnewood State Bank v. Brigham, 434 S.W.2d 874, 878 (Tex. Civ. App.—Texarkana 1968, writ ref'd n.r.e.).

The facts as to Mr. Farrow's activities are disputed. The Farrows contend that Mr. Farrow had virtually nothing to do with the franchise itself or with any franchise negotiations between WNS and Mrs. Farrow. However, this contention is belied by these facts: (a) Mr. Farrow signed an acknowledg-ment of receipt of the franchise circular; and (b) his name appears as a remitter (along with that of Mrs. Farrow) on the two checks totalling $43,170, which the Farrows paid to WNS. Those three documents are undisputed. In addition, WNS alleges, but the Farrows deny, (c) that Mr. Farrow came to Houston to participate in franchise negotiations; (d) that he negotiated and agreed to all terms of the three agreements; and (e) that he partially performed those agreements by making payments, signing up for (but not attending) the contractually-required course, and operating the store in Georgia.

These allegations are sufficient to make a prima facie showing that binds Mr. Farrow to the contracts despite the absence of his signature. If true, these facts would estop Mr. Farrow from invoking the Statute of Frauds. In addition, the allegations fairly suggest that Mrs. Farrow had apparent authority to bind Mr. Farrow to the agreements.

"The quality of the contacts as demonstrating purposeful availment is the issue, not their number or their status as pre- or post-agreement communications." Stuart v. Spademan, 772 F.2d at 1195. Under this Court's analysis of the quality of contacts in contractual contexts, WNS' allegations constitute prima facie allegations that the Farrows 'purposefully availed' themselves to the laws of Texas. Indeed, the facts of this case present a far more compelling showing of minimum contacts than were present in Stuart v. Spademan, Holt Oil & Gas Corp. v. Harvey, 801 F.2d 773 (5th Cir. 1986), cert. denied, 481 U.S. 1015 (1987), or Hydrokinetics Inc. v. Alaska Mechanical, Inc., 700 F.2d 1026 (5th Cir. 1983), cert. denied, 466 U.S. 962 (1984).

First, the Franchise Agreement specifies that Texas law applies, which is significant in determining whether the Farrows were 'fairly warned' that their activities might lead to litigation in Texas. See Metzeler, 754 F.2d at 548; Stuart v. Spademan, 772 F.2d at 1195-1196; InterFirst Bank Clifton v. Fernandez, 844 F.2d at 283-84; Hydrokinetics v. Alaska Mechanical, 700 F.2d at 1029-1030.

Second, the fact that substantial contractually-required performance was required to take place, and did in fact take place, in Texas evidences significant contacts. See Holt Oil & Gas v. Harvey, 801 F.2d at 778; Stuart v. Spademan, 772 F.2d at 1192-94; Hydrokinetics v. Alaska Mechanical, 700 F.2d at 1028-31.

Finally, the fact that the contractual relationship contemplated by the Franchise Agreement is long-term, as opposed to a single isolated purchase and sale, demonstrates significant contacts. See Hydrokinetics v. Alaska Mechanical, 700 F.2d at 1029; Stuart v. Spademan, 772 F.2d at 1194. Because the Franchise Agreement provided that Texas law governed, required substantial performance by both parties in Texas, and contemplated establishment of a five-year (minimum) franchise arrangement, the Farrows purposefully availed themselves of the laws of Texas. Hence, there were minimum contacts between the Farrows and Texas, and personal jurisdiction for a suit based upon those contacts does not offend due process.

D. Asserting personal jurisdiction over the defendants comports with fair play and substantial justice.

"Once it has been decided that a defendant purposefully established minimum contacts within the forum State, these contacts may be considered in light of other factors to determine whether the assertion of personal jurisdiction would comport with 'fair play and substantial justice.'" Burger King, 471 U.S. at 476, quoting International Shoe Co. v. Washington, 326 U.S. 310 (1945). Where, as here, a defendant who has purposefully directed "his activities at forum residents seeks to defeat jurisdiction, he must present a compelling case that the presence of some other considerations would render jurisdiction unreasonable. Most such considerations usually may be accommodated through means short of finding jurisdiction unconstitutional." Burger King, 471 U.S. at 476 (emphasis added).

> [1] the burden on defendant, [2] the forum state's interest in adjudicating the dispute, [3] the plaintiff's interest in obtaining convenient and effective relief, [4] the interstate judicial system's interest in obtaining the most efficient resolution of controversies, and [5] the shared interest of the several States in furthering fundamental substantive social policies.

Id. 447 U.S. at 477.

The Farrows cannot sustain this burden. First, it is obvious that one party or the other is going to have to travel. WNS would be significantly more inconvenienced by a foreign forum than the Farrows for several reasons. First, in absolute numbers, the number of WNS personnel involved in the negotiation of the various agreements far exceeds the number of appellees involved. Further, several key individuals have left the employment of WNS and now work elsewhere in Houston. Consequently, if the case must be heard in Georgia, their testimony could be unavailable because they would be beyond the subpoena jurisdiction of a Georgia district court.

Second, it is "beyond dispute that [Texas] has a significant interest in redressing injuries that actually occur within the state." <u>Keeton v. Hustler Magazine</u>, 465 U.S. at 776. In <u>Keeton</u>, the Court held that the state's interest extended so far as to protect a <u>nonresident</u> injured by actions occurring in the state. Here, WNS, a <u>resident</u> of Texas, was injured in Texas by the Farrows. Clearly, the interest of Texas in this litigation is stronger than that of New Hampshire in <u>Keeton</u>. <u>See</u> <u>Interfirst Bank Clifton v. Fernandez</u>, 844 F.2d at 285.

Third, for the reasons set forth above, it would be far more convenient and efficient for WNS to bring this suit in Texas than in Georgia.

Finally, the district court's exercise of jurisdiction in this case is not inconsistent with Georgia's interests. Additionally, the parties (or at least WNS and Mrs. Farrow), under the Franchise Agreement, have already agreed that Texas law governs their dispute. Likewise, since the misrepresentations, reliance, and injury occurred in Texas, Texas law governs the tort claim as well. The federal courts of the state whose substantive law governs the rights of the parties can most appropriately interpret the laws of that state. <u>Odom v. Thomas</u>, 338 F. Supp. 877 (S.D. Tex. 1971).

For these reasons, it would not offend notions of fair play and substantial justice to subject the Farrows to jurisdiction in Texas. Therefore, it is not unconstitutional to do so.

IX.
CONCLUSION

Subjecting the Farrows to suit in Texas is reasonable, in accord with the precepts of due process, and promotes the orderly administration of laws. Therefore, the decision of the district court to dismiss for lack of personal jurisdiction should be reversed, and the case should be remanded to that court.

[The opinion which resulted from this brief is in the Appendix. Read it now to see the common law process at work.]

XI. Bluebooking

The real name of the Bluebook is: *The Bluebook: A Uniform System of Citation* (16th ed. 1996). It was put together by editors of the law reviews of Columbia, Harvard, Pennsylvania and Yale law schools. It is followed by most lawyers and virtually every court. One of the final steps you must do is to "Bluebook" your legal writings.

You must use proper cite forms, "proper" being defined by what the Bluebook says. You may think it tedious, but your legal writing grade will be based upon it, and your future employers will evaluate your writing in part based upon Bluebooking. They will notice careless mistakes in Bluebooking and will assume that carelessness is one of your traits. The same holds true for judges: presentation affects the perception of the substance. Incorrect citation format distracts from the message. *Do it right.*

The Bluebook appears a daunting mess, with its hundreds of pages of rules and exceptions. "The mass of particular rules... has made the Bluebook so lengthy and complex, that its own purpose—helping both writer and reader—has been defeated." Book Review, *Lowering One's Cites: A (sort of) Review of the University of Chicago Manual of Legal Citation*, 76 Va. L. Rev. 1099, 1104 (1990). However, it's not that hard. It is just made to appear that way, like most of law and law school.

Here are some common sense Bluebook guidelines that no one even tells you in law school. First, just because a case you're reading cites a case one way does *not* mean that's the correct way under the Bluebook. Remember that. For example, if at the top of the page of the case you're reading in one of the Reporters it says "Am. Intern. v. Jones Company, Inc.," that does *not* mean that's the proper Bluebook citation. It's not.[40] Likewise, just because the case your reading does block-indented quotes a certain way, or cites cases a certain

---

[40] The correct cite—so long as the case name is *not* being used in a sentence (Bluebook rule 10.2)—would be: "*American Int'l Co. v. Jones Co.*" Bluebook Rule 10.2.1(c) says you do not abbreviate the first name of a case unless it is an organization with widely recognized initials; Bluebook Rule 10.2.1(h) says you cannot drop the first "Co.,"; Bluebook Rule 10.2.2(a) says to abbreviate "Company;" and Bluebook Rule 10.2.1(h) says to drop the "Inc." because it follows "Company."

way, does not mean that's the correct way to do it. That would be too easy. (The *Stanback* case, quoted above, is full of Bluebook errors.) Instead, you have to ignore what the judges who came before you have done, and you have to do it right.

Second, whenever you *first* mention a case, you must give its complete cite. So this is wrong:

> In *Mayo v. Satan and His Staff,* the court denied leave for a plaintiff to proceed in forma pauperis in a civil rights action against Satan. 54 F.R.D. 282, 283 (W.D. Pa. 1971).

Instead, it *must* be like this:

> In *Mayo v. Satan and His Staff,* 54 F.R.D. 282, 283 (W.D. Pa. 1971), the court denied leave for a plaintiff to proceed in forma pauperis in a civil rights action against Satan.

Third, there is one way to do "short cites" that is *always* right, so you might as well just do it that way all of the time, until you have time to read the Bluebook to find out what other ways you can do it. Once you have cited a case in full one time, you shouldn't repeat its full cite the rest of the time that you cite it. The Bluebook gives you several options for short cites, but some are right only some times. You can *always* cite a case by citing its name, then the volume and reporter it is in, and then "at __" and cite to the page number you are referring the reader to. You can omit the name of the case in cites which are close enough to each other that it will not confuse the reader to omit it. So this, for example, could be your memorandum about *Kent © Norman v. Reagan,* 95 F.R.D. 476, (D. Or. 1982):

In *Kent © Norman v. Reagan,* 95 F.R.D. 476, 476 (D. Or. 1982), Kent © Norman[41] sued President Reagan for causing "'civil death' without legislation." The plaintiff sought certain relief against Reagan due to his alleged involvement with White Line Fevers From Mars, which allegedly had shipped marijuana and cocaine in fruit boxes for Mother's day. *Kent © Norman,* 95 F.R.D. at 476. The plaintiff also included parking tickets in his file. *Kent © Norman,* 95 F.R.D. at 476. Dismissing his suit for want of prosecution, the court reasoned:

---

[41] "The plaintiff's name apparently includes the copyright sign." *Kent © Norman,* 95 F.R.D. at 476, n.1.

There are also certain other claims which the court is at a loss to characterize, and can only describe. There is included in the file a process receipt which bears the "Received" stamp of the Supreme Court of the United States. On this form are the notations, apparently written by plaintiff, "Taxes due" and "D.C. Circuit was green" as well as "Rule 8 ... Why did you return my appeal form? Why isn't the '1840' W. 7th mailbox still next to the 1830 one?" and "Something suspicious about that mailbox." There are also other notations on the form. There is also the following "claim":

> The birds today
> Are singing loudly,
> The day is fresh
> With the sounds
> Upon the wind
> The crickets.
> The blackbirds
> The woodpeckers
> Beauty in every
> Spark of Life
> Are appreciated
> Their sounds are beauty
> The ants are silent
> But always searching
> The birds noise a song
> and the fade of the automobile tires
>   Chirp. A shadow from
> a passing monarch butterfly
>   Breathless in Colorado.
>   Kent © Norman
>   1981

It is possible, of course, that this is not intended as a claim at all, but as a literary artifact.

Kent © Norman, 95 F.R.D. at 477. The court dismissed the suit.

This passage used proper short cites for *Kent © Norman*. It is repetitive, but it is right.

The fourth Bluebook hint concerns block-indented quotes. You should block indent all quotes of fifty or more words. Bluebook Rule 5.1(a). Although you will read opinions which give all kinds of different treatment to quotes of 50 or more words, there is only one way to do it right: you should block, single space, and indent the quote, not use any quote marks around it, and then after the quote double space and put the cite at the left margin. *See id.*

The fifth Bluebook hint is to be sure to use the correct "signal." "Signals" are the words that precede your case citations, such as *"see; see, e.g.; see also*; and *cf." See* Bluebook Rule 1.2. Each signal has a very specific meaning. Here is the most relevant Bluebook rule in its entirety:

1.2 Introductory Signals

(a) Signals that indicate support.

[no signal]   Cited authority (i) identifies the source of a quotation, or (ii) identifies an authority referred to in text.

E.g.,   Cited authority *states* the proposition; other authorities also state the proposition, but citation to them would not be helpful or is not necessary. *"E.g.,"* may also be used in combination with other signals, preceded by a comma[.]

Accord   *"Accord"* is commonly used when two or more cases clearly *support* the proposition but the text quotes only one; the others are then introduced by *"accord."* Similarly, the law of one jurisdiction may be cited as being in accord with that of another.

See   Cited authority *directly states* or *clearly supports* the proposition.

See also Cited authority *constitutes additional source material that supports* the proposition. *"See also"* is commonly used to cite an authority supporting a proposition when authorities that state or directly support the proposition already have been cited or discussed. The use of a parenthetical explanation of the source material's relevance (**rule 1.5**) following a citation introduced by *"see also"* is encouraged.

Cf.   Cited authority *supports a proposition different from the main proposition but sufficiently analogous to lend support.* Literally, *"cf."* means "compare." The citation's relevance will usually be clear to the reader only if it is explained. Parenthetical explanations (**rule 1.5**), however brief, are therefore strongly recommended.

(b) Signal that suggests a useful comparison.

Compare . . .	*Comparison of the authorities cited will*
[and] . . .	*offer support for or illustrate the proposition.*
with . . .	The relevance of the comparison will
[and] . . .	usually be clear to the reader only if it is explained. Parenthetical explanations (**rule 1.5**) following each authority are therefore strongly recommended.

(c) Signals that indicate contradiction.

But see Cited authority *directly states* or *clearly supports a proposition contrary* to the main proposition. *"But see"* is used where *"see"* would be used for support.

But cf. Cited authority *supports a proposition analogous to the contrary* of the main proposition. The use of a parenthetical explanation of the source material's relevance (**rule 1.5**) following a citation introduced by *"but cf."* is strongly recommended.

"But" should be omitted from *"but cf."* whenever it follows *"but see"*.

(d) Signal that indicates background material.

See generally Cited authority *presents helpful background material related to the proposition*. The use of a parenthetical explanation of the source material's relevance (**rule 1.5**) following each authority introduced by *"see generally"* is encouraged.

(e)   Combining a signal with *"e.g."*

"E.g." can be combined with any signal, including "[no signal]," to indicate that other authorities also state, support, or contradict the proposition but that citation to them would not be helpful or is not necessary.

(f)   Signals as verbs. Signals may be used as the verbs of ordinary sentences, in which case they are not italicized (**rule 2.1(d)**). When signals are used as verbs, matter that would be included in a parenthetical explanation should be made part of the sentence itself...

Bluebook Rule 1.2 (examples omitted).

Not to be outdone by the obsessive compulsive Law Review types at Yale, Harvard, Penn, and Columbia, the obsessive compulsive Law Review types at the University of Chicago decided to publish their own *Manual of Legal Citation*— informally called, just so everyone knows there's competition here—the "Maroon Book." The Maroon Book purports to permit a free-wheeling, do-what-you-feel-is-best-so-long-as-it's-clear approach to citation. *See generally, Lowering One's Cites,* 76 Va. L. Rev. at 1099-1100 (reviewing the Maroon Book). One commentator observed the stupidity of it all, and suggested using the following cites, among others:

Will not see in   Use to support statements such as "no court has ever held..." and then cite to any random page or case.

See, e.g., [Future Volume] F.2d [Future page] This is when a writer believes someday the courts will come around to resolving the issue presented.

See, sort of   A weak signal only used because law review editors insisted on citing the case.

Really should see   Cite is directly on point

See, for the hell of it   Cite wasn't right on point, but makes a good read.

Lowering One's Cites, 76 U. Penn. L. Rev. at 1108-10
    Until we are able to use these "common sense" signals, we are stuck with the Bluebook. Sorry.

A.   Writ Histories and Other State Idiosyncracies.

Some states have their own "bluebooks" which must be followed in state court. In Texas and a few other states, the state supreme courts act much like the United States Supreme Court, deciding which cases to hear based on a procedure much like an application for *certiorari*. In Texas, for example, the loser in the appellate court may file what is known as a petition for "a writ of error." Whenever a losing party in the appeals court wants to appeal to the Texas Supreme Court, it files a petition for a writ of error with the Texas Supreme Court, which will either grant the writ—meaning that the appeal will be heard by the court—or it will deny the writ. If it denies the writ, it will issue an order which just says that the writ was denied for one of three or four reasons. Each reason has a term which has changed over time. *See generally*, Gunn, *"Unpublished Opinions Shall Not be Cited as Authority": The Emerging Contours of Texas Rule of Appellate Procedure 90(i)*, 24 St. Mary's L.J. 115, 126-130 (1992). In many states, you also must include this sort of procedural history, even if you are writing something which will be filed in federal court.

XII. Writing Hints

A. Write with Your Reader in Mind: Make it Easy.

1.   Use Plain English. As Justice Scalia noted, too many lawyers apparently believe that "it is essential to legal English that one write as pompously as possible, using words and phrases that have long since disappeared from normal English discourse." Garner, *Judges on Effective Writing,* Tex. B. J. 1194, 1194 (Dec. 1992). One of the worst side effects from reading cases is that you will read what judges have written and think that it is good writing. "The reason legal writing has gotten to such a low point is that we have had very bad teachers—judges who wrote years ago and wrote badly. We learned bad habits from them and their opinions in law school." *Id.* (quoting Bablitch, J.).

Accordingly, avoid using legalese when an ordinary English word will work just as well. Use English, not Latin or Greek. Use a short word to replace a long one. Keep it simple. You are trying to *explain*.

2.   Simplify.

- Avoid "double verbs" (usually this involves a nominalized ("ion") noun):

  "proceeded to write" instead of "wrote"
  "continued to argue" instead of "argued"
  "reached a conclusion" instead of "concluded"
  "made a determination" instead of "determined"
  "made a resolution" instead of "resolved"

- Read every sentence to yourself, and ask yourself what it means. If the little voice in your head answers back with something different than what you have written, then change what is written until the voice matches it exactly.

  If you write one sentence and then begin the next sentence with "In other words" or "Put another way," chances are that second sentence is clearer, and you can safely delete the first one.

  Delete introductory clauses which add nothing, such as "it is important to emphasize that" or "the court should be aware that." Avoid sentences which begin with "There are" or "There is" or "It is."

- Omit most dates from statements of fact. Unless a date is critical, leave it out. If you put a date in the facts, the reader will assume it is important and focus on it too much.

- Use very few footnotes. They distract.

3. Use Road-map Sentences. Road-map sentences direct the reader:

"The court correctly granted summary judgment for three reasons."

"Whether the search was unlawful depends on whether it was reasonable, whether the police had a good faith belief, and whether there was probable cause."

The court's decision was correct. The plaintiff failed to produce summary judgment evidence supporting any of the four elements of negligence: duty, breach of duty, causation, and damages.

These sentences let the reader know that the writer's next step will be to go through each of the three reasons, the three-part test, or the four elements. These types of sentences keep the reader on course, and guide him through the maze of legal reasoning.[42]

4. Use Topic Sentences. Topic sentences are like road-map sentences, but rather than guide the reader through the entire memo, topic sentences guide your reader through each paragraph, letting him know what the paragraph discusses.

---

[42] An aside. It relates to maps, and that is about its only reason for being included here, besides the fact that I like it and you may use it in a speech some day.

A group of mountaineers was lost. Tempers were rising, fear growing. The expedition's leader told everyone to calm down and that he would figure out where they were. He took a map from his backpack and patiently scanned the horizon, repeatedly comparing the map to what he saw before him. After ten long minutes, he announced, "I've figured it out. I know where we are."
The group gathered around. "Do you see that mountain over there?" he asked, pointing to a prominent peak in the distance.
"Yes," they all responded, hopeful that their anxiety was about to end.
"We," the leader concluded, "are on top of it."

Every paragraph should discuss one topic, and only one topic. A topic sentence should let the reader know what the paragraph is about.

5. Use Headings. Headings should function as landmarks which break your writing into logical, visually appealing bits and guide your reader through your work. Never waste any words in a heading: if the heading is in a memorandum, it should inform; if it is in a brief, it should persuade. So don't just say "Whether the client is liable for battery depends on what the cases say." Instead use the heading as a summary for what follows: "Our client will prevail on her claim for battery unless ....."[43]

6. Vary Sentence Length. Use short sentences as often as possible, but avoid sounding like Hemingway. Short sentences are not "simple." Long sentences are not "sophisticated." In fact, short sentences are often better and

---

43 For an example of completely useless headings, see *United States v. Abner,* 825 F.2d 835 (5th Cir. 1987), known as the "Talking Heads" opinion. The law clerk who wrote *Abner* worked into the opinion the names of various Talking Heads songs, including "Fear of Music," "Speaking in Tongues," and "Remain in Light," even though those headings have absolutely nothing to do with the opinion. (The names of other songs are worked into the text. How many can you spot? I am told there are 25). *Cf. Matter of Salkin,* 430 N.W.2d 13, 14 (Minn. Ct. App. 1988) (in commitment proceeding, man claimed he "had been adopted as one of the Talking Heads").

However, the Fifth Circuit later redeemed itself by issuing *Texas Pig Stands, Inc. v. Hard Rock Cafe Int'l, Inc.*, 951 F.2d 684, *reh'g denied*, 966 F.2d 956 (5th Cir. 1992), which contains several useful and informative headings, such as "This Little Piggy Went to Market" (951 F.2d at 687), "Collateral Estoppel—Does the Pork Stop Here?" (951 F.2d at 690), "Unjust Enrichment—Did Hard Rock Bring Home the Bacon?" (951 F.2d at 694), and "D-D-Dt D-D-Dt That's All, Folks!" (951 F.2d at 698). *See, e.g., Croft & Scully Co. v. M/V Skulptor Vuchetich*, 664 F.2d 1277 (5th Cir. 1982) (in suit involving damage caused to cases of soft drinks on a ship, court used headings such as "Pepsi Cola Hits the Spot—On the Pavement"); *United States v. Grissom*, 645 F.2d 461 (5th Cir. Unit A May 1981) (headings relating to Jack and the Beanstalk); *National Papaya Co. Domain Indus., Inc.*, 592 F.2d 813 (5th Cir. 1979) (using headings concerning Sam Spade); *Noble v. Bradford Marine, Inc.*, 789 F. Supp. 395 (S.D. Fla. 1992) (headings inspired by Wayne's World, including "Hurling Chunks" and "A Schwing and a Miss").

more effective at conveying a complicated idea because they break the complicated idea into its component parts. Vary the lengths of your sentences.

7.   Use Concrete, Specific Labels. For example, don't refer to company that sued your client as "appellant" in your responsive brief. Call it "plaintiff" or "Jones Company." If there's a contract involved, call it "the Contract." Pick the most specific label you can imagine.

The easiest way to let the reader know that you're going to use a label is as follows: "In accordance with the agreement to sell the house ('the Contract'), Mr. Smith paid $500 on August 31, 1993." Just put the label in parentheses and quote marks: don't use "hereinafter referred to as." If you tell the reader you're going to use a label, then *always* use it and use it consistently.

8.   Don't Overdo It with capital letters, italics, bold, and underlines. People with Macintosh computers are especially susceptible to this. It is really hard to read print that looks like this:

> **PLAINTIFF** INSURANCE COMPANY OF TEXAS, INCORPORATED wrote the AGREEMENT BETWEEN THE PARTIES, said *AGREEMENT* being *dated July 5, 1993*, and forwarded by <u>United States Mail</u> said ***contract*** to DEFENDANT BIG MANUFACTURING COMPANY, a <u>corporation</u> incorporated in accordance with and under the laws of the *STATE OF DELAWARE*....

Don't capitalize something unless it must be capitalized. Don't capitalize the names of parties in pleadings or briefs, unless it is required by the rules (and I know of no requirement). Don't use bold within the body of the text (you may want to use it for your main headings). Don't use *both* italics and underlining within the body of the text: use one or the other. Too many tricks with fonts and typeface makes the document harder to read, not easier.

If you think this doesn't bother readers, think again. In *Casas Office Machines, Inc. v. Mita Copystar Machines, Inc.*, 847 F. Supp. 981 (D.P.R. 1993), the court lashed out against an attorney who had violated the Bluebook by using many different fonts and type styles:

> Furthermore, Casas is ORDERED to refrain from unnecessary adornments to the text of its briefs. Casas utilizes so many typographic emphases that a reasonable reader is left bewildered. Some statements are in bold. Others are underlined. Some are in bold and underlined. Some are even set in enlarged type, utilizing different fonts, and then emphasized in bold print and underlined. The court understands that the advent of the computer age has changed the legal field and the way that briefs are prepared and edited,

and recognizes that the great majority of these changes have increased efficiency and clarity in the presentation of legal arguments. Here, however, Casas' excessive use of the computer mandates that the court ORDER Casas to adhere to the advised Bluebook provisions for court submissions. ("Generally, only two type faces are used in court documents and legal memoranda—ordinary type, such as courier, and italics (indicated in word-processed or type-written materials by underscoring)." a Uniform System of Citation, pp. 11 et seq. (15th Ed. 1991)). Any further submissions utilizing more than two type faces will not be accepted, and in addition Casas will be sanctioned for such submissions.

847 F. Supp. at 990. Keep it simple for your reader, both in terms of the message and the means of delivering the message.

9.   Keep Subjects With Verbs. As part of the writing process, you will often think of the sentence you want to say, but as you are typing it, you'll think of a qualifying phrase that needs to be in there, too. You'll just go ahead and put it in the middle because that's where you thought of it. Thus, you'll end up with sentences like this: "The argument, which plaintiffs make at the beginning, middle, and end of their incomprehensible brief, is wrong." This puts too much strain on your reader. Get long clauses out of the middle of sentences when it becomes hard to follow. Similarly, as a general rule, put dates in the beginning of sentences, not at the end or in the middle: "On October 19, 1993, Jones sued ...."

Likewise, if there are qualifying or conditional words, make sure they are close to their antecedents. Otherwise, the meaning can become unclear. For example, notice the different possible meanings in these sentences where one word is moved:

> *Only* the lawyer signed the contract on Thursday.
> The *only* lawyer signed the contract on Thursday.
> The lawyer *only* signed the contract on Thursday.
> The lawyer signed *only* the contract on Thursday.
> The lawyer signed the *only* contract on Thursday.
> The lawyer signed the contract *only* on Thursday.
> The lawyer signed the contract on *only* Thursday.
> The lawyer signed the contract on Thursday *only*.

As you see, each time the word "only" is moved, the meaning changes. It important to keep in mind that slight changes in word order can greatly affect meaning:

To a scientist, the fundamental fact of human language is its sheer improbability .... I can arrange a combination of words that explains how octopuses make love or how to build an atom bomb; rearrange the words in even the most minor way, and the result is a sentence with a different meaning or, more likely, word salad.

Steven Pinker, *Grammar Puss*, The New Republic 19 (Jan. 31, 1994).

Be careful. Be clear. Keep the subjects and verbs together, and keep qualifying words close to their antecedents. You don't want to describe how octopuses make love when your purpose is to explain why your client did not breach the contract.

10. Be Concrete. Below is what is called "an abstraction ladder." On either end, it is abstract because it is either too general or too specific:

Wealth

   Assets

      Farm Assets

         Livestock

            Cattle

               Holsteins

                  Cows

                     Elsie

                        Beef

                           Molecules

                              Atoms

You need to figure out what level of abstraction works best for the purpose o your analysis. Most often, it will be on the level of Elsie, the specific cow a issue. Thus, you usually should not write about the "plaintiff" (probably at the level of "cow") or, worse, "appellant" (probably at the level of "livestock"

Write about Elsie whenever you can. Be as concrete as you can be. Avoid abstractions.

11. Watch the Length of Your Paragraphs. Too often too many ideas are put into one paragraph. A paragraph should seldom exceed two-thirds of a page. Shorter paragraphs are better, and should predominate.

A single sentence paragraph can be appropriate and effective, but be careful about using them, as they can look awkward.

12. Avoid using Statutes or Cases as the Subjects of Sentences. For example, do not write "The Texas Deceptive Trade Practices Act, 17 Tex. Bus. Comm. Code Ann. § 33.44(a)(13) defines 'consumer' as 'someone who buys something.'" That imposes on your reader the burden of wading through the cite to find where in the sentence the meat really begins. Instead, say "A consumer is defined as 'someone who buys something.' Tex. Deceptive Trade Pract. Act, 17 Tex. Bus. Comm. Code Ann. § 33.44(a)(13)." If the reader is not familiar with the definition, or questions its source, she can simply glance at the cite to see your source.

Similarly, do not make cases the subjects of sentences. Compare these two approaches: (1) "Where a plaintiff seeks to buy a product, but is prevented from actually acquiring it due to the wrong-doing of the defendant, the plaintiff still qualifies as a 'consumer' under the DTPA. *Smith v. Jones,* 828 S.W.2d 835, 838 (Tex. 1992)." (2) "In *Smith v. Jones,* 828 S.W.2d 835, 838 (Tex. 1992), the court held that where a plaintiff seeks to buy a product, but is prevented from actually acquiring it due to the wrong-doing of the defendant, the plaintiff still qualifies as a 'consumer' under the DTPA."

The first sentence states the rule as a rule—and not as just what some court said—and it does not make the reader have to wade through the cite in the middle of the sentence. Thus, it emphasizes the message, not the messenger—*i.e.*, it emphasizes the substance, not the name of the case. Unless you intend to talk about the facts of a case at length—and you will do that only when the case is *very* similar factually—do not make cases the subjects of sentences.

13. Make Your Point and Stop. Say it once, and say it right. Often, when reviewing my first draft, I find that I made the same argument twice in a row. As part of the revision process, determine which is the *best* way to say it, and say it only that way. As the court observed in *Oklahoma Natural Gas Co. v. Federal Energy Regulatory Comm'n.,* 940 F.2d 699, 700 (D.C. Cir. 1991), increased wording does not help us very much to understand the...position; it is as if on learning that a listener does not under-stand English, the speaker tries shouting."

Although you may think that your legal issue is so complex that only dozens of pages will do, think again:

(1) The story of the creation of the world is told in the book of Genesis in 400 words; (2) the world's greatest moral code, the Ten Commandments, contains only 279 words; (3) Lincoln's immortal Gettysburg Address is but 266 words in length; (4) the Declaration of Independence required only 1,321 words to establish for the world a new concept of freedom. Together, the four contain a mere 2,266 words. On this routine motion to amend a civil complaint, [plaintiff's counsel] has filed a brief (not the primary one, just a reply brief) that contains approximately 41,596 words spread over an agonizing 124 pages. In this case, the term reply "brief" is obviously a misnomer. Rather than impressive, the "brief" is oppressive.

Marson v. Jones & Laughlin Steel Corp., 87 F.R.D. 151, 152 n.1 (E.D. Wis. 1980). Brevity is not only appreciated by the courts, it is usually practiced by them.[44]

Another aspect of brevity is dropping losing or weak arguments. Making *every* argument means making each one equally important, and thus diminishes the strength of the better argument.

By the way, since we are talking about brevity, the shortest sentences which use all of the letters of the alphabet without breaking any grammatical rules are: "How razorback-jumping frogs can level six piqued gymnasts!" and "Pack my box with five dozen liquor jugs," and "Jackdaws love my big sphinx of quartz." The latter is the shortest. *Help Folder*, MacUser 158 (March 1994).

---

[44] The following parentheticals contain the *entire* decisions of these courts. *Devine v. Byrd*, 667 F. Supp. 414 (N.D. Tex. 1987) ("A judge should not talk too much. Therefore... This *pro se* § 1983 suit seeks 'good time credit.' But the plaintiff is now dead. That means this suit is, too. The first is with prejudice. The second, without. Dismissed.") (footnotes omitted); *Denny v. Radar Industries, Inc.*, 184 N.W.2d 289, 290 (Mich. App. 1971) ("The appellant has attempted to distinguish the factual situation in this case from that in *Renfroe v. Higgins Rack Coating and Manufacturing Co., Inc.*, 17 Mich. App. 259, 169 N.W.2d 326. He didn't. We couldn't." Affirmed.); *Robinson v. Pioche, Bayerque & Co.*, 5 Cal. 460 (1855) ("The court below erred by giving the third, fourth, and fifth instructions. If the defendants were at fault in leaving an unguarded hole in the sidewalk of a public street, the intoxication of the plaintiff cannot excuse such gross negligence. A drunken man is as much entitled to a safe street as a sober one, and much more in need of it. The judgment is reversed and the cause remanded.").

B. Use Simple English.

1. Words to Avoid.

- "Herein," "wherein," "hereinafter," and the like.

- "Action" instead of "claim" or "lawsuit."

- "ion" words: Any word ending with "ion" is an *indication* that you avoided a verb. It also *indicates* you avoided a verb.

- "Such" and "said," as in "such action" or "said contract."

- "Upon" for "on."

- Any word that you do not know the exact and specific meaning of.

2. Do Not Use More Words Than Necessary.

- "As a result of" for "because."

- "At the present time" for "now."

- "By the time" for "when."

- "Due to the fact that" for "because" or "due to."

- "During the time that" for "while."

- "Filed a lawsuit against" for "sued."

- "In connection with" for "with."

- "In order to" for "to."

- "In view of the fact that" for "because."

- "In the event that" for "if."

- "One of the reasons" for "one reason."

- "Provided that" for "if."

- Contractions (Can't; don't; won't; *etc.*)

- Alright: it is not a word. All right are.

3. Problem Words.

- **Affect/Effect.** Both words are both nouns and verbs. "Affect" as a noun will almost never come up in legal writing. As a verb, "affect" means to have an effect on ("The new regulations will *affect* all oil and gas producers."), and "effect" means to cause ("Jeff Fisher will *effect* a change in the Oilers' attitude.").

- **Alternate/Alternative**. "Alternate" as a verb means to change back and forth, as in "In Mr. Hricik's extraordinarily delightful book, he alternates between serious and humorous examples." As an adjective (for example, "alternate argument") and adverb (for example, "he alternately argued for and against the death penalty"), it has the same general meaning: flipping back and forth. On the other hand, "alternatively" means a choice between two or more things (as in "The alternatives are pepperoni, sausage, mushroom, and onion"). That means you can pick from among those ingredients, even having more than one. "Alternatives" means smorgasbord. However, if you had said "The alternates are pepperoni, sausage, mushroom, and onion," that would mean that we could only have one item from among the group. "Alternates" means Little Caesar's.

- **Ambiguous**. "Ambiguous" is a legal term of art that means a contract may be interpreted in two different ways. Do not use it to describe a contract unless that is what you intend to say.

- **And/or.** Never use this "word" in your writing. Use "and" or "or," whichever it is that you really mean. For example, "he wanted pepperoni, sausage, or both."

- **Any and all/Each and every**. Each and every time you use both words, or any, each, every, or all of them, it is redundant.

- **As per**. Do not use this phrase in your writing. It usually makes sentences longer or nominalizes a verb. For example, "As per your instruct*ions*, I..." should be, "As you instructed, I ...." "As per the parties' contract, ..." should be, "As agreed, the parties ...."

- **Claim/Action**. Do not use these words to mean "lawsuit." A claim is a part of a lawsuit. "Action" is vague. Use whatever word you need to use to be precise.

- **Clear/Obvious/Apparent/Inarguably**. It adds nothing to say "Clearly, plaintiff's argument is wrong." Saying it is clear or inarguable does not make it so, may strain your credibility, and wastes the reader's time.

- **Corporations and companies** are "its" not "they's." So do not say "IBM knew that they were liable." Instead, say "IBM knew that it was liable."

- **Double negatives**. Watch out for using more than one negative word in a sentence. For example, "The corporation did not know that it would not win the suit" can become, "The corporation did not know it would lose the suit." Often you can simplify by turning negative sentences into positive statements.

- *Etc.* Never use the abbreviation "*etc.*" in your writing. Don't use "*et cetera*" either. It indicates sloppy and incomplete thoughts.

- **Facetiously**. This is the only word (I know of) that has all the vowels in the right order (aeiou and sometimes y). Get it: factitious, facetiously. Just thought you should know.

- **Firstly/Secondly/Thirdly**. "First," "second," and "third" do the same thing in fewer letters, so use them instead.

- **Got**. Do not use "got" to mean "must," as in "he has got to go to the movie." It's wordy and colloquial.

- **His/Her or She/He**. Don't do this. Either write so that you don't have to use the pronoun, or use either "he" or "she." If you are writing about a man, however, make sure you call him a he, and likewise for a woman. It is not sexist to be accurate about someone's actual gender.

- **I/We**. Do not say "we have a claim for negligence against Mr. Smith" if you are talking about *your client's* claim. It is his/her/its claim, not yours.[45]

---

45   In one deposition, the witness kept referring to his actions as "our" actions. After stating that "No, sir, we did not. We just advised the dealer of his need to meet policies and procedures," the interrogating lawyer said: "Who is this 'we'? Do you have a frog in your pocket?"

- ***I.e./e.g.*** Do not use these abbreviations for Latin words in your writing, except as a Bluebook signal. Either delete them, or say what you mean to say with English words. By the way, *i.e.,* means "that is" and *e.g.,* means "for example."

- **In conclusion**. Just delete it.

- **In connection with/In this connection**. You can probably change "in connection with" to "about" or "concerning" and you can probably just drop "in this connection."

- ***Inter alia***. Do not use this Latin phrase. Use "among other things" or "including."

- **"ize" words**. Use words ending with "ize" only if they are in a good dictionary. A few have become accepted (sterilize, for example). Most have not. Do not let them materialize in your writing until they are in an acceptable dictionary.

- **Judgment/Judgement**. Unfortunately, sometimes jurisdictions have rules with the "e," and sometimes without it. Make sure you use whatever is correct under the rules where you are operating.

- **Moreover**. Do not use this more than once in a paper. Try "likewise," "further," "in addition," "second," or any other similar filler words, or just delete it.

- **Memo**. Memo is colloquial, but may be in use in your office, depending on how stuffy it is. The best bet: use "memorandum" (which means one memo) or "memoranda" (which means two or more memos) until you are told otherwise.

- **Me/I/the author**. *Do not use the first person in a legal memorandum.* Primarily, its use is redundant: obviously, it's *you* who is speaking, so there is no reason to say "I did not find a case which addressed these issues." Just say, "No located case addressed these issues."

- **Real/Really**. Use these words really sparingly, and only when you are really sure they add something really important to the real meaning of the sentence.

- **Shall/May**. Shall means "must" and means there's a requirement. May indicates an option. Be careful to use these words as you mean them, particularly when writing about a contract. There is a big difference between

"Upon receipt of the car, Bob shall pay $500" and "Upon receipt of the car, Bob may pay $500."

- **Splitting infinitives**. An "infinitive" is any verb preceded by "to." These are infinitives: to argue, to attack, to contend, to list. No absolute rule prohibits splitting infinitives. Here's my rule: put the adverb either before "to" or after the verb, but not between them, *unless* it sounds horrible not to do it. Imagine *Star Trek* if Kirk had said "to go boldly where no man has gone before." Sometimes you have to split those infinitives.

- **Than/Then**. "Than" is used to compare; "then" is a time word. So these are correct: "Rather than write five briefs every day, he then quit the firm." "She would rather have beer than wine."

- **That/Which/Who**. Be careful about which of these you use in a sentence. If you're in doubt, change the sentence to avoid having to figure out which one is right. A simple rule of thumb on "that" versus "which" in descriptive clauses: if the clause is not introduced by a comma, the right word is "that"; if it is introduced by a comma, the right word is "which." ("The foul call that led to Maxwell's ejection was bad even by NBA standards." "The foul call, which was bad even by NBA standards, led to Maxwell's ejection.") Also, never use "who" as a pronoun referring to companies. Companies deserve "which" or "that," depending on the sentence.

- **Their/There/They're/There's**. "Their" is a possessive used to replace the possessive name of the person or thing: "Their argument is wrong" instead of "The plaintiffs' argument is wrong." "There" refers to a place: "I was there when Aspen's Planet Hollywood first opened." "They're" is a contraction of "they are:" "They're coming around the mountain." "There's" is a contraction of "there is:" "There's little chance that anyone will ever read this sentence."

- **There are**. Chances are, you could drop these two words from every sentence where they appear and change one other word to a verb and you'll have a better statement of what that sentence means. You should rarely use "there are" or other "to be" verbs.

- **Therefore**. There is nothing wrong with this word, but it is over used. See if "accordingly," "thus," or "consequently" will work in its stead.

- **Try and**. This is wrong. You mean "try to."

- **Unique**. If something is unique, then so it is. It is not "very unique."

- **We/I**. Seldom use this word. If you do use it, remember that "we" the law firm is not "we" the client. So, for example, do not say "We have been sued" unless your firm is the defendant.

- **Whether or not**. Most of the time, you should just say "whether." You need to include "or not" only if it is necessary.

- **Whom/Who**. Good luck. Just remember Hricik's Rule of Avoidance: When in doubt, change the sentence so you don't have to use the word you're unsure about.

- **Would of**. This is wrong. You mean "would have."

C. Proofread.

Let your writing set for a day or two and then proof it.
Carefully.
Slowly.
Read the block and indented quotes word-by-word.
You would be amazed at some of the howlers that get by even the best lawyers:

- An order from the United States Court of Appeals for the District of Columbia Circuit is styled: *Border County Chapter of the Izaak Walton League of America, Inc. v. The Unclear Regulatory Commission.*

- An advertisement for a legal secretary by a large Houston law firm seeks a legal secretary trainee with accurate "transcrition" skills.

- The Department of Energy reported that it was amending regulations "correcting the self-correcting refund language" of certain regulations.

- A plaintiff in a case sought all "copulations of data."

- A deposition notice stated that the notary would "administer oats" to the witness.
- A deed which conveyed the seller's "soul and separate" property.
- A plaintiff in its pleading sought "primitive damages" because he would not "be able to hold grossful employment."

Proofread your writing. Don't write something that someday I'll add to this list.

XIII. Conclusion

You have been reading about law school and legal reasoning. I hope that you realize that for most of the book, you have been reading <u>legal</u> <u>writing</u>. You have read real memoranda, real briefs, and two opinions; and you have seen actual law school outlines. Exposure to these legal documents, along with the discussion of legal reasoning and the judicial system, is precisely the kind of information I wish I had seen before starting law school.

A few other humorous cases deserve mention, but I lacked the creativity to work them into the text. So that they are not lost among the tens of thousands of volumes of reporters filled with perhaps more important but certainly less entertaining cases, here they are. They provide a fitting ending.

In the beginning, there was Judge Goldberg, who wrote *Zim v. Western Publishing Co.,* 573 F.2d 1318 (5th Cir. 1978), which reads like the book of Genesis. For example:

> *Then there rose up in Western a new Vice-President who knew not Zim.* And there was strife and discord, anger and frustration, between them for the Golden Guides were not being published or revised in their appointed seasons. And it came to pass that Zim and Western covenanted a new covenant, calling it a Settlement Agreement. But there was no peace in the land. Verily, they came with their counselors of law into the district court for judgment and sued there upon their covenants.
>
> And they put on the district judge hard tasks.

573 F.2d at 1321 (emphasis in original).

Taking a page from a different epoch and adopting the voice of a literary god, Mark Twain, in *State v. Knowles,* 739 S.W.2d 753 (Mo. App. 1987), Judge Nugent wrote a statement of facts which gave life to an otherwise dull issue. He wrote:

> As Mark Twain might have put it, this is a tale about what gets into folks when they don't have enough to do.
>
> Old Dave Baird, the prosecuting attorney up in Nodaway County, thought he had a case against Les Knowles for receiving stolen property, to wit, a chain saw, so he ups and files on Les.

Now Les was a bit impecunious, so the judge appointed him a lawyer, old Dan Radke, the public defender from down around St. Joe. Now, Dan, he looks at that old information and decides to pick a nit or two, so he tells the judge that the information old Dave filed against Les is no good, that under the law it doesn't even charge Les with a crime. Dan says Dave charged that Les "kept" the stolen chain saw and that's not against the law. You don't commit that crime by "keeping" the chain saw, says Dan; the law says you commit the crime of "receiving" if you "retain" the saw, and that's not what Dave charged Les with, and the judge should throw Dave out of court. And that's exactly what the judge did.

But old Dave was not having any of that. No Sir! That information is right out of the book. Word for word! Yes, sir!

Bystanders could plainly see the fire in old Dave's eyes. He was not backing down. Sure. Dave could simply refile and start over with a new information by changing only one word. Strike "kept"; insert "retained." But that is not the point. Dave knows he is right.

And so he is.

So we'll just send the case back to Judge Kennish and tell the boys to get on with the prosecution. And here's why . . . .

739 S.W.2d at 754 (citation omitted).

In one of the most vivid introductions to a circuit court opinion (read this aloud), Fifth Circuit Judge John Brown wrote:

It was a dark and stormy night. A patchy, low-lying fog covered the murky waters of the river and obscured the banks. Ships, passing in the night, were but phantoms, vague outlines disappearing into the mist. Ships' whistles, echoing across the dark expanse, seemed like mournful cries from another world. Then suddenly, looming out of the darkness, another ship appeared. The distance was too small; time too short; before anyone could do more than cry out, the unthinkable occurred. The ships collided. The tug, helpless, drifted downriver. Floundering like some giant behemoth wounded in battle, the tanker came to ground and impaled itself on some voracious underwater obstruction. And still the whistles, echoing, seemed like cries from another world.

Conclusion

Allied Chemical Corp. v. Hess Tankship Co., 661 F.2d 1044, 1046-57 (5th Cir. 1981).

Taking a page from the poet Oates, Judge Gillis' opinion in *Fisher v. Lowe,* 333 N.W.2d 67 (Mich. App. 1983) (footnote omitted), reads in its entirety as follows:

> We thought that we would never see
> A suit to compensate a tree
> A suit show claim in tort is prest
> Upon a mangled tree's behest;
> A tree whose battered trunk was prest
> Against a Chevy's crumpled crest;
> A tree that faces each new day
> With bark and limb in disarray;
> A tree that may forever bear
> A lasting need for tender care.
> Flora lovers though we three,
> We must uphold the court's decree.

Affirmed.

Judges seem particularly proud of their imitations of famous poets. *See, e.g., Shafer v. Commander, Army & Air Force Exchange Service,* 667 F. Supp. 414, 417 n.1 & 433 n. 46 (N.D. Tex. 1987) (Ogden Nash and Edgar Allen Poe); *In re Love,* 61 B.R. 558 (Bankr. S.D. Fla. 1986) (bankruptcy opinion set to "The Raven" by Poe); *Helton v. State,* 311 So.2d 381, 382-83 (Fla. Ct. App. 1975) (another opinion set to "Twas the Night Before Christmas"). *See also Ford v. Rowland,* 562 So.2d 731 (Fla. Ct. App. 1990) (analyzing allegedly defamatory poem set to "Twas the Night Before Christmas," but containing lines such as "off in a corner in ill-fitting clothes, sat Diane and Tom stuffing crack up their nose."); *Howard Gault Co. v. Texas Rural Legal Aid, Inc.,* 615 F. Supp. 916, 925-26 (D.C. Tex. 1985) (bad poetry); *City of Canadian v. Guthrie,* 87 S.W.2d 316 (Tex. Ct. App. 1932) (memorializing for all eternity some very bad poetry by the court, the parties, and others).

Other judges are proud of working into their opinion words which are related to the subject matter of the case. *See, e.g., United States v. Syufy Enterprises,* 903 F.2d 659 (9th Cir. 1990) (court worked in as many movie titles as it could into suit alleging antitrust violations in movie industry); *Productos Carnic v. Central Am. Beef & Seafood Trading Co.,* 621 F.2d 683 (5th Cir. 1980) (meat metaphors); *Chemical Specialties Mfg. Ass'n, Inc. v. Clark,* 482 F.2d 325, 328-29 (5th Cir. 1973) (using the names of detergents in suit concerning ordinance requiring their labelling) (Brown, J., concurring). *See also National Lampoon, Inc. v. American Broadcasting Co.,* 376 F. Supp. 733 (S.D.N.Y. 1974) (reciting various humorous bits from the National Lampoon).

Judicial humor can literally get out of hand. For example, a joke opinion actually got published in the Southwestern Reporter. The case of *Catt v. State,* 691 S.W.2d 120 (Ark. 1985) is not real. In fact, if you try to Shepardize *Catt v. State* on Westlaw, it pretends like there is no such opinion. Apparently, the Westlaw company is so embarrassed by the fact that it published the opinion in the first place, it simply pretends it is not there.

The reason for its embarrassment must be because anyone reading the opinion—which West dutifully summarized and created headnotes for—would realize that the case is a joke. In *Catt,* the Arkansas Supreme Court supposedly decided which of two twin brothers was guilty of a drug offense. The twins were named Kilkenny and Gallico Catt. It is impossible to summarize the facts and yet do the opinion justice. In this case, all I can do is urge that you read it, and particularly read how the court reasons that both twins were guilty even though one twin must have committed both the crimes, and that it is possible that two crimes can each be lesser included offenses of each other.

Finally, and seriously, as you practice law, recall these words from the Seventh Circuit, which are far too infrequently heeded or recalled:

> About half of the practice of a decent lawyer is telling would-be clients that they are damn fools and should stop.

McCandless v. Grant Atl. & Pac. Tea Co., 697 F.2d 198, 201-02 (7th Cir. 1983). *See McDonald v. John P. Scripps Newspaper,* 257 Cal. Rptr. 473, 474 (Cal. Ct. App. 1989) (in suit by loser of county spelling bee, court observed: "Question—When should an attorney say 'no' to a client? Answer—When asked to file a lawsuit like this one.").

With that, the book ends.

Good luck!

(1) Δ argues π failed to introduce sufficient evidence to show a pattern and practice.

(2) π's legal theory at trial was that Δ violated §703(a) by refusing to recruit, hire, transfer, or promote minorities equally.

(3) The factual question, thus, is whether there was a pattern or practice of disparate treatment and, if so, whether disparity was racially premised. McDonnell.

    (a) Disparate treatment compared to disparate impact:

        i) Disparate treatment (e.g., this case): emper treats some people less favorably than others b/c of their race/etc.

            a) Proof of motive is critical, though can be inferred from differences in treatment.

        ii) Disparate impact (e.g., Griggs): The challenged practices are facially neutral in their treatment of different groups, but fall more harshly on one group and can't be justified by business necessity.

        iii) either theory may be applied to a particular set of facts.

(4) Burdens of proof:

    (a) π bore initial burden of proving PFC

        i) B/c π alleged a system-wide pattern & practice, it had to prove by a preponderance of the evidence that the discrim was Δ's standard operating procedure—the regular not the unusual practice.

            a) π had to prove more than the merely accidental or occasional discrim acts.

    (b) APPLIED: π made out PFC b/c it showed:

        i) π proved 5% (314) of all of Δ's empees were B, & 4% (257) were Hispanic (H). Yet, only .4% (8) of the line drivers were B and only .3% (5) were H, and all but one B had been hired since the suit was filed.

        ii) W/only 1 exception, Δ hadn't had a B line driver until 1969.

        iii) There were terminals in areas populated mostly by Bs where all drivers were W

        iv) 83% of Bs and 78% of Hs were in lower pay jobs, whereas only 39% of Ws held such positions.

        v) In addition to statistics, π showed 40 specific instances of discrim, where Bs and Hs had applied for line driving jobs ignored or were misled, and other instances where Bs and Hs had requested <u>transfers</u> and were given trouble.

(c) Δ argues statistics, alone, can never prove pattern and practice, nor even establish PFC case which shifts burden onto Δ.

   i) Court:

      a) The evidence wasn't solely statistics.

      b) "statistical analyses have served & will continues to serve an important role....'"'

      c) It's proper to use statistics when the disparity they reveal reaches proportions comparable to here.

(d) Δ argues that the statistics here are misleading b/c they fail to take into account Δ's business situation as of the effective date of T7: Δ admits that it had all W drivers when T7 became effective, but alleges that b/c it hasn't hired many people that the disparity is due to this, and not discrim.

   i) Court: <u>This would be forceful</u> if Δ had done virtually no hiring since T7 enacted, but the record shows Δ hired many new, almost all W, drivers.

      a) But, evidence shows Δ continued its pattern & practice after T7.

      b) The fact that it has very recently hired Bs & Hs doesn't help earlier, post-Act discrimees.

(e) Court rejects Δ's argument that the mere affirmations of its officials that it hired only the best qualified as insufficient to dispel π's PFC.

(f) Court also upheld trial judge's judgment not to be persuaded by Δ's testimony that the Bs and Hs who testified of direct discrim were not, in fact, discrimed against.

e. Class Summary:

(1) To make out PFC, π must show statistical disparity: there may or may not be a formal policy that π can point to.

(a) It is inferred from the disparity that Δ was unlawfully motivated and hence the discrim was 'because of' the sex/race/whatever.

(b) In theory, if no discrim, then %-age of minorities hired would <> = % in labor pool.

    i) E.g., labor pool is 40% B, but Δ's work force is only 10% B.

      a) Use binomial distribution to figure out how improbable this disparity is:

      b) The more improbable, the greater the inference of unlawful motivation.

   (c) Suppose π showed that Chicago is 40% B, but Sidley & Austin is only 5% B.

    i) Is this a PFC (must Δ therefore respond?), or has π not made it out?

   (d) How it works:

    i) First, π must prove what %age of minorities is in relevant labor pool. <u>Hazelwood</u>.

      a) Δ will try to make the pool contain fewer minorities, so that the disparity will seem to be less.

      b) e.g.:

    ii) π shows 5% attys are B, but Chicago is 40% B.

      a) Has π made out PFC? If so, then Δ must disprove the disparity; or

      b) Has π failed to make out PFC?

    iii) RULE: π must make a <u>threshold plausibility</u> sufficient to infer discrim:

      a) If π's proof isn't plausible enough, then no burden on Δ.

      b) If π's proof is plausible, then Δ must explain why it's not the right comparison <u>or</u> that it is right, but the disparity isn't due to Δ's discrim

    iv) Benefit of alleging systemic over individual discrim relates to remedies & class actions

   (e) Class-wide remedies can require Δ's policies be restructured.

∴. Defenses to Disparate Treatment Cases

1. <u>Bona Fide Occupational Qualifications</u>

  a. <u>Phillips v Martin Marieta</u> (S.Ct.)

   (1) Facts: π, F empee, sued Δ, emper, b/c Δ told π it wasn't accepting applications from Fs w/pre-school kids, but Δ had M empees w/pre-school kids. Δ's workforce is nearly entirely Fs.

  b. Issue: Did π make out a PFC?

  c. Held: Yes.

  d. Rationale:

179

(1) §703(a) requires persons of like qualifications be given empment opportunities irrespective of sex.

   (a) Therefore, the CtApps erred reading it to permit an emper to have one hiring policy for Fs and another for Ms, each having preschool kids.

   (b) If having kids is demonstrably more relevant to job performance for a F than for a M, then the policy may be permissible under §703(e) as a BFOQ.

      i) But, that's a matter of evidence for Δ to prove it's reasonably necessary for the operation of his business.

(2) Concur: Majority fell into the trap of thinking T7 permits discrim based on the ancient canards of the proper role of Fs: there can be no BFOQ based on stereotypes.

(3) Class Summary:

   (a) It's no defense that the workforce is nearly entirely Fs.

   (b) PFC established by on-record disparate treatment

      i) Δ bears burden of persuasion on the BFOQ.

   (c) Remanded for BFOQ, but concur says can be no BFOQ. Is the concur really a dissent?

   (d) Is every generalization a stereotype?

      i) E.g., young Fs drive better than young Ms. Why not hire individuals and use an on the job test?

         a) Or, use as a requirement for empment that person have no prior wrecks.

         b) But, what if no-prior-wrecks isn't predictive of accidents, but sex is?

      ii) 16.04.2(a)(1)ii): no generalization is permitted even if 100% accurate.

         a) 9th Cir used this standard for a long time: it can be a BFOQ only if it's true 100% of the time (e.g., wet nurse, surrogate mother).

      iii) See <u>Criswell</u>, <u>infra</u>, where court in age discrimination act case uses <u>Weaks</u> - <u>Diaz</u>:

         iv) "all or substantially all" Fs are unable to perform the job (<u>Weaks</u>)

         a) where it's impossible or impractical to do individualized testing, emper can use a general rule.

         b) essence of the business must be involved. (<u>Diaz</u>).

         c) E.g., pizza driver position

        d)   Ms more likely to have wrecks, but not substantially all

        e)   emper can argue impracticable to test individually (it's always possible to)

        f)   impracticability = too costly

        g)   E.g., child care: impracticable to test b/c how do you discern whether the M or F will be more affected?

   h) It's impracticable to test whether the existence of a child will more appreciably affect a M or a F (but, is it unlawful discrim to presume F will be more?)

     v) By permitting the emper rely on the generalization, you let the generalization continue to have validity.

        a)   <u>Cf</u>. <u>Manhart</u>: can't treat F dif from M even though actuarials show F live longer & would thus get more money after retiring.

 (e) Actor/Actress: race can never be a BFOQ, but sex can.

     i) EEOC says not stereotypes, yet it's a BFOQ for authenticity/genuineness

        a)   Professor: where does that come from? Is it societal, need for belief?

     ii) On the Race-sex analogy:

        a)   Some cases, e.g., <u>Manhart</u>, use reasoning that states 'the challenged activity would be inappropriate as a race line, therefore it's inappropriate for sex.'

        b)   Professor: this is wrong: e.g., we segregate bathrooms by gender.

        c)   cultural norms override in the sex area, but not in gender.

        d)   but, cultural preference is not a BFOQ defense.

APPENDIX B
[LEGAL ETHICS OUTLINE]

I. **WHO SHOULD BELONG?**

A. **APPLICATION TO THE BAR** - character and fitness to shield clients from potential abuses, public image.
   1. **No material falsity (omit or commit).** DR1-101(A), MR8.1(a).
   2. **Correction of misapprehensions.** DR1-102(A)(4), MR1.8(b)
   3. **Requested information**
      a. DR1-103(B): must reveal any unprivileged knowledge regarding another lawyer upon proper request.
      b. MR8.1(b): must comply with any lawful demand for information.
   4. **Recommendations**
      a. DR1-101(B): subject to discipline for giving reference for person known to be unqualified in character, education, or other relevant criteria.
      b. EC 1-3: should satisfy himself that the applicant is of "good moral character."
      c. MR8.1: must respond to lawful demand for information.
   5. **Whistle Blowing**, on:
      a. <u>Applicants</u>. EC 1-3: Although atty shouldn't become self-appointed investigator, should report all unfavorable information lawyer possesses.
      b. <u>Other Lawyers</u>
   6. Code: affirmative duty to report any violation. DR1-103(A), EC 1-4.
      a. Code DR 1-103:
         (1) Atty possessing <u>unprivileged</u> knowledge of a violation of DR 1-102 must report it.
            (a) DR 1-102: atty shall not engage in conduct involving dishonesty, etc, nor conduct prejudicial to administration or justice, nor adversely effecting his fitness to practice law.
         (2) Atty possessing <u>unprivileged</u> knowledge or evidence shall reveal it upon request of investigating tribunal.
   7. Rules: MR8.3(a), 8.4: duty only covers conduct which involves a substantial question of lawyer's honesty, trustworthiness or fitness as a lawyer.
      a. <u>Own Conduct</u> - DR1-103(A): yes.
      b. <u>Client Confidences</u>
         (1) DR1-103: not clear if "privilege" means only attorney-client evidentiary privilege or broader stuff protected by Canon 4 (probably the latter, if the former, the duty would vary among jurisdictions depending on local rules of evidence).

        (2) MR8.1(b), 8.3(c): do not apply to information protected by MR1.6.

    c.   EC 1-6: if applicant or atty is under temporary mental or emotional disability, atty should take diligent steps to ensure he is not licensed or, if licensed, doesn't practice.

B. **Competence** - DR6-101(a), MR1.1.
1. Lawyer is forbidden to exonerate himself or limit liability to client for malpractice. DR6-102(a); EC 6-6.
    a. Lawyer can prospectively limit malpractice if client is independently represented. MR1.8(h).
    Ratio: w/independent advice, no danger of overreaching.
2. **Neglect**
3. What is neglect?
    a. Keep client informed. EC 9-2, 7-8, MR1.4(a), (b). Subject to rule of reason.
    b. Act with diligence.
4. Code is stronger than rules: DR6-101(a)(3) merely says atty must not neglect a client, but MR1.3 imposes an affirmative duty of diligence and promptness.
5. Atty should see matter through to completion, and if doubtful whether termination of client relationship has occurred, atty should consult in writing w/client. MR1.3; cf EC 2-31 (criminal appeal).
6. MR: personal problems, workload, procrastination aren't excuses. MR 1.3.
    a. Neglect involves indifference and a consistent failure to carry out obligations which lawyer has assumed for client; or conscious disregard for responsibility owed client. ABA Formal Op. 1273 (p. 37). Not if inadvertent or result of an error of judgment made in good faith.
    b. Not waivable and even refusal to pay fee does not justify neglect. DR2-110(a), (c)(1)(f), MR1.16(b)(d), (c), (d).
    c. Accepting matters not trained in: MR1.1
7. Code: atty can take matter not trained in if study will make him competent w/out undue client expense. EC 6-3.
8. Atty can associate w/other atty who is competent, if client consents. DR 6-101(A)(1); MR1.1.
9. In emergency, can advise to extent emergency. MR1.1.
    a. Neglecting matter entrusted to atty. DR 6-101(A); Comment to MR 1.1; MR 1.3.
    b. Habitually failing to pursue legal actions. <u>Schullman</u>.
    c. Not diligently guarding financial position of client. Greene

      d.   Not limited to conduct in professional capacity as a lawyer. DR1-102(a)(3), (4).

  10. How should atty be disciplined?

      a.   Proposed standards for imposing sanctions on neglect— p. 38. Focus on:

         (1) duty violated;

         (2) lawyer's mental state;

         (3) actual or potential injury caused by the misconduct;

         (4) aggravating or mitigating circumstances.

      b.   Cases: Some courts refuse to consider mental or emotional strain. <u>Snyder</u>. While in <u>Walker</u> alcoholism was mitigator, and in <u>Loew</u> "burn out" was a mitigator.

II. LAWYER'S OBLIGATIONS TO CLIENT - DUTY OF LOYALTY

A. DUTY OF CONFIDENTIALITY

  1. Absent client consent, atty can't revel information relating to representation of a client. DR 4-101(B); MR1.6.

      a.   Attorney/client privilege: Duty of confidentiality is broader.

  2. DR4-101(A), (B): confidences and secrets.

  3. MR1.6(a): any information relating to the representation of a client.

      a.   Privilege is exclusion as to disclosure of information; confidences may not be used or disclosed.

  4. Rationale

      a.   encourage client to talk freely with lawyer. EC 4-1; MR1.6, comments 2, 3, 4, 5.

      b.   Truth seeking function in system of values - restraints on way we get information (5th and 6th amendments). Give lawyer (agent) information to make him effective.

      c.   Uneducated would be hurt - can't stand up for themselves and afraid to go to lawyer.

  5. Applies to prospective and former clients

  6. May disclose to other lawyers in firm unless client otherwise directs. Lawyer must exercise reasonable care to prevent his employees or associates from violating the obligation re: client confidences. DR4-101(D); EC 4-5; MR5.3. The disciplinable violation is the failure to supervise

B. PROHIBITIONS: Confidences can't be used or disclosed:

  1. Disclosure is prohibited by DR 4-101(B)(1); MR 1.6(a).

  2. Can't use client secrets or confidences to disadvantage of client. DR4-101(B)(2), MR1.8(b).

     a.   Includes former client if information has not become generally known. MR1.9(b); EC 4-6.

3.   Can't use client confidence for lawyer's own advantage - even if client doesn't suffer detriment. DR4-101(B)(3), MR1.8, comment 1 - can't exploit information relating to representation to client's disadvantage.

C. **EXCEPTIONS: When confidences can be used or disclosed:**

1. **Client consents - if full consultation..** DR4-101(C)(1); EC 4-2; MR1.6(a).

     a.   Implied consent:

2. DR 4-101(A), if not protected as privileged, client doesn't specifically request confidentiality, information is not embarrassing and information is not likely to be detrimental.

3. MR1.6(a), disclosures impliedly authorized in order to carry out the representation, i.e. in negotiation or undisputed fact (comment 7).

4. **Other provisions permit**

     a.   Rules:

5. Lawyer acting as intermediary. See Comment 6 to 2.2.

6. Lawyer evaluating matter affecting client for use by another. 2.3.

7. To remedy false evidence given to tribunal. 3.3(b).

8. If lawyer assists in crime or fraud, but not information protected by 1.6. 4.1(b).

     a.   Code

9. Client consents after full disclosure. DR4-101(C)(1).

10. Lawyer can't conceal that which law requires him to reveal. DR7-102

11. **Court Orders**: DR4-101(C)(2); MR1.6(b)(5), comments 19, 20.

12. **To Collect Fee**: DR4-101(C)(4); MR1.6(b)(1) (to extent necessary, no blackmail).

     a.   Purpose: to prevent client who is beneficiary of a fiduciary relationship from exploiting that relationship to detriment of lawyer (MR1.6, comment 1.8)

13. **To Respond to a Charge of Wrongful Conduct**: DR 4-101(C)(4), MR1.6(b)(2). SHd reveal only to extent necessary. Not necessary accuser bring formal proceedings or actually file suit against lawyer.

14. **When Client Intends to Commit Future Crime**

     a.   Code: DR4-101(C)(3) - lawyer may reveal client's intention to commit a crime as well as information necessary to prevent it. **No distinction between types of crimes**. May require disclosure if lawyer knows, beyond a reasonable doubt, that the client will commit the crime.

     b.   Rules: MR1.6(b)(1), (2) . allowed disclosure in order to prevent the client from committing a criminal act that the lawyer believes is likely to result in **imminent death** or **substantial Bodily harm**, or another law mandates disclosure (comment 20).

15. Lawyer given discretion - not supposed to subject to reexamination, but Cf Tarasoff. p. 218

16. **Withdrawal** - fact of withdrawal may amount to disclosure of client confidences.

    a. If client will use lawyer's services to further client's criminal or fraudulent conduct, the lawyer must withdraw. MR1.6, comment 19; MR1.16(a); DR2-110(B)(1); DR7-102(A)(7). Comment 15 - may give notice of withdrawal.

17. If people were defrauded by client during representation, atty may give notice of his withdrawal to them, may disaffirm any opinion or document previously given. Comment to MR 1.6.

    a. MR1.16(d): after withdrawal, must take reasonable steps to protect client's interest. MR1.8(b): lawyer may not use confidential information to disadvantage of client unless client consents.

APPENDIX C
[ADMINISTRATIVE LAW OUTLINE]

1. <u>Delegation of Authority</u>: Has Congress delegated to the agency the particular authority it seeks to exercise?
   a. Is the delegation overly broad (does the agency have standards to apply)? <u>Crowell</u> ; <u>Schechter</u> ; <u>Panama Refining</u>.
      (1) But, see more lenient case of <u>Amalgamated Meatcutters</u>.
      (2) See Rehnquist in <u>Benzene</u> and <u>Cotton Dust</u>. Are the 3 purposes violated?
   b. Did the agency act within the scope of the authority delegated?
      (1) <u>Benzene, Cotton Dust</u>.
      (2) Is there a constitutional issue implicated? (property, liberty, search & seizure).
         (a) If so, ct will construe the delegation as not authorizing the agency's act. <u>Kent</u> (liberty to travel); <u>Hampton v Mow Sun Wong</u>.
         (b) But if the statute clearly infringes, it will be read as doing so. <u>Zemel</u> (liberty to travel); <u>Schor</u> (right to trial).
         (c) If the agency is adjudicating.
            i) Does its authority infringe on article III courts?
               a) <u>Northern Pipeline</u>; <u>Schor</u>.
            ii) Is the authority not unconstitutionally vague? <u>Boyce</u>.
      (3) If definitions are made, are they w/in the authority delegated? <u>Addisson</u> <u>Skidmore</u>; <u>Nierotko</u>.
   c. Congressional Issues:
      (1) Congress can't have a legislative veto. <u>Chadha</u>.
   d. Presidential Issues:
      (1) Only the President can remove executive officials.
         (a) <u>Myers v U.S.</u>; <u>Humphrey's Executor v U.S.</u>; <u>Wiener v U.S.</u>

2. **Has the Agency provided the necessary hearing**?
   a. Does agency's enabling statute require a certain type of hearing and was it provided?
   b. Does APA require a certain type of hearing and was it provided?
   c. <u>Due Process Constitutional Protections</u>: Liberty & Property are protected by Due Process, and depriving of either will require some kind of process.
      (1) First, is due process due? (property or liberty?)
         (a) PROPERTY interest deprived?
            i) Gov't Empment:
               a) Property is deprived only when person has an property interest in it.
            ii) Statute gave job except for removal for cause. <u>Loudermill</u>.

189

      iii) "Common law" of tenure give property interest. <u>Sinderman</u> (733.54).

      iv) No property interests: <u>Bailey</u>; <u>Roth</u>.

      v) Welfare: <u>Goldberg</u>; <u>Mathews</u>.

          a) But, <u>Lyng</u> applicants don't have protected property interest.

          b) No property right to stay in unqualified nursing home. <u>O'Bannon</u>.

      vi) Note: Even though <u>Loudermill</u> rejected <u>Arnett's</u> bitter w/the sweet, under Rehnquist's literalist approach to statutory construction he can still restrict when due process is triggered by narrowly reading the conferring of the property right.

    (b) LIBERTY interest deprived?

      i) For deprivation of liberty, π must show stigma by publicity. <u>Bishop</u>.

          a) No badge of disloyalty: <u>Cafeteria Workers</u>;

          b) Good name not hurt: <u>Roth</u>.

          c) Paddling students is deprivation. <u>Ingraham</u>.

          d) Academic dismissal assumed to deprive. <u>Horowitz</u>.

          e) High School Suspensions (reputations): <u>Goss</u>.

          f) Excluding/deporting Aliens: <u>Wong Yang Sung</u>.

d. Even if liberty or property is involved, only adjudicative facts require a hearing.

  (1) Adjudicative facts relate to particular parties. <u>Londoner</u>.

  (2) Legislative facts are determinations of policy or general application.

    (a) Where a rule applies to "more than a few people, it is impracticable that everyone should have a direct voice." <u>Bi-Metallic</u>; <u>Minn Bd</u>; <u>Florida E. Coast</u>; <u>O'Bannon</u>.

  (3) **APA**

    (a) <u>Adjudication</u>: §554(a) requires a trial type hearing in "every case of adjudication by statute to be determined on the record after an opportunity for agency hearing."

    (b) <u>Rulemaking</u>: §553 requires at most a legislative type hearing.

      i) But, Constitution may require a hearing where the APA doesn't: e.g., the rulemaking procedure affects property or liberty and it's not 'impracticable' to have a hearing under <u>Bi-Metallic</u>.

        a)   In other cases (e.g., a non-tenured job, so there's no property interest), constitution won't require a hearing but a statute might.

e. **How Much Process is Due?**

   (1) <u>Constitutional Due Process</u>: If due process is triggered and it's not impracticable to grant individual hearings, then what kind of hearing is due?

      (a) This is determined by a <u>balancing</u> of the: <u>Mathews</u>.

         i)   Nature of the affected private interest;

         ii) Risk of error to that interest from the existing procedure;

         iii) Likelihood the proposed process would be better, and

         iv) Burden the extra process puts on gov't.

      (b) In all cases, though, the following is usually required. <u>Goldberg</u>:

         i)   Timely and adequate notice. §554b.

         ii) Hearing must be at a meaningful time and manner. §554b.

            a)   Pre-termination? <u>Goldberg</u>; <u>Loudermill</u>;

            b)   How formal of a hearing varies by need. <u>Goldberg</u>; <u>Goss</u>; <u>Loudermill</u>

            c)   Where facts disputed, oral confrontation. <u>Goldberg</u>.

         iii) Decisionmaker must state reasons & indicate what evidence used.

         iv) Decision maker shouldn't have participated in the decision under review.

   (2) <u>APA requirements</u>:

      (a) <u>Adjudication</u>: Does a statute require decision or record 'after opportunity for hearing'?

         i)   If not, <u>no</u> APA procedures are required. <u>WNCN</u>.

         ii) If yes, then APA 554/556-7 apply.

      (b) <u>Rulemaking</u>:

         i)   There is no constitutional trial-type hearing required if it involves only legislative, not adjudicative, facts.

            a)   But, if there are constitutional implications, then trial-type hearing may be required if it's 'practicable' under <u>Bi-Metallic</u>, <u>Florida E. Coast</u>, and <u>Minn Bd</u>.

         ii) APA requirements:

            a)   553(c) requires that interest parties be given opportunity to submit written info.

         iii) It is the agency's discretion whether to grant oral hearing.

a) If agency chooses not to, lots of deference. <u>Vt Yankee</u>.

iv) Only if it's 'quasi-judicial' decision affecting a few people on individualized grounds or if the decision not to grant a hearing is a 'wholly unjustified departure' from a longstanding policy to give such hearings will agency's decision not to grant hearing be overturned. <u>Vt Yankee</u> (614).

v) Only if a statute explicitly requires the rules be made 'on the record' after opportunity for agency hearing will the higher formal rulemaking requirements of §556-7 apply. <u>Florida E. Coast</u>.

a) If a statute requires 'hearing' it does not require §556-7. In such cases, the hearing required will vary depending on whether it's adjudicatory or legislative and upon the strength of the language in statute. <u>Florida E.Coast.</u>

3. Has the agency violated any constitutional or statutory rules in its actions?

   a. Will its choice b/w rulemaking & adjudication be upheld?

   (1) Adjudication: Generally, agency can choose to make policy by adjudication in its 'informed discretion.' <u>Chenery II</u>.

   (a) But, if the retroactive new policy has serious adverse consequences, then ct may find that agency abused its discretion. <u>Chenery II</u>, <u>Bell Aerospace</u>; <u>Arizona Grocery</u>.

   (b) In <u>Wyman-Gordon</u>, held that a prospective rule (that didn't apply to the parties in <u>Excelsior</u>) cannot be adopted by adjudication.

   (c) In <u>Chenery II</u>, ct identified types of subject that policy can be made for on a case-by-case (adjudication) basis:

   i) can't be foreseen; those that it only has a tentative judgment b/c of lack of experience, and those problems so specialized and varied that a general rule won't work.

   (2) Rulemaking: Purpose of rulemaking is to create general prospective rules. APA ensures public participation (informal notice & comment or formal. See above).

   (a) Has the agency consistently used one or the other and this is a big departure? <u>Vt Yankee</u>; <u>Wyman-Gordon</u>.

   (b) There are constitutional implications of what type of proceeding may be required. See <u>Bi-Metallic</u> and all, above.

b. Has it observed any statutory/constitutional limitations on investigations?
    (1) Did it demand unreasonable amount of unrelated info from party?
        (a) Old standard: <u>American Tobacco</u>: fishing expeditions prohibited.
        (b) New standard: <u>Morton Salt</u>: does the underlying statute authorize the agency to make investigations other than in cases/controversies?
            i) If so, and if demand is w/in that authority and reasonably relevant, then it's okay.
    (2) Search Warrant: <u>Marshall v Barlows</u>; <u>Dow</u>
    (3) Freedom of Information Act: APA§552; <u>Chrysler v Brown</u>.
c. Was the decision-maker biased or interested?
    (1) <u>Withrow</u> (880.64): no bias because plaintiff must show the risk of bias was intolerably high or risk that the decision maker would be psychologically wedded to his decision.
    (2) <u>Gibson</u> (897.63): pecuniary interest in decision maker shows bias.
d. Was there an adequate separation of functions of investigatory & adjudicatory?
    (1) Were the agency's enabling statute separation principles violated?
    (2) Were APA separation principles violated? (554d).
        (a) <u>Wong Yang Sung</u>: Error b/c decisionmaker was also prosecutor.
    (3) Were constitutional principles of separation violated?
        (a) <u>Withrow</u>: Fact that Bd certified complaint didn't preclude it from investigating.

APPENDIX D

WNS, INC., Plaintiff-Appellant,
v.
James Larry FARROW and Mary Dee Farrow, Defendants-Appellees.

No. 88-6065.

United States Court of Appeals,

Fifth Circuit.

Sept. 22, 1989.

Franchisor brought state court action in Texas alleging fraud and breach of contract on part of Georgia franchisees in misrepresenting their intentions to apply for and operate franchise, and franchisees removed case to federal court and then moved to dismiss for lack of personal jurisdiction. The United States District Court for the Southern District of Texas, at Houston, Lynn N. Hughes, J., granted the motion to dismiss, and franchisor appealed. The Court of Appeals, Johnson, Circuit 5. Judge, held that franchiser had established prima facie case of personal jurisdiction in Texas over Georgia franchisees and exercise of personal jurisdiction over franchisees would be constitutionally permissible.

Reversed and remanded.

1. Constitutional Law 305(5)

In Texas, sole inquiry for Court of Appeals to determine whether federal court sitting in diversity could exercise jurisdiction over nonresident defendant was whether exercise of personal jurisdiction over nonresident defendant comported with federal constitutional requirements, as Texas long-arm statute had been interpreted to extend as far as was permitted by due process. U.S.C.A. Const.Amends. 5, 14.

2. Federal Courts 76.10

Court of Appeals was concerned only with whether specific jurisdiction, rather than general jurisdiction, could be exerted over nonresident defendants in diversity action, where claim asserted against nonresident defendants arose out of or was related to alleged contacts by defendants with Texas, the forum state.

3. Federal Courts 96

Once motion to dismiss for lack of personal jurisdiction has been presented to district court by nonresident defendant, party who seeks to invoke jurisdiction of district court bears burden of establishing contacts by nonresident defendant sufficient to invoke jurisdiction of court.

4. Federal Courts 96

In satisfying burden of establishing contacts by nonresident defendant sufficient to invoke jurisdiction of court once motion to dismiss for lack of personal jurisdiction has been presented to district court by nonresident defendant, when jurisdictional issue is to be decided by court on basis of facts contained in affidavits, party seeking to invoke jurisdiction need only present facts sufficient to constitute prima facie case of personal jurisdiction.

5. Federal Courts 96

Franchisor established prima facie case of personal jurisdiction in Texas over Georgia franchisees by alleging, with affidavit support, that franchisees committed intentional tort of fraud at least in part through their activities in Texas, and exercise of jurisdiction was constitutionally permissible; Texas contacts of franchisees included their contacting franchisor in Texas about becoming franchisees, their traveling to Texas to participate in franchise negotiations resulting in preparation of three agreements, one franchisee's attending week long training seminar in Texas on mechanics of operating franchise, and franchisees partially performing agreement by making payments to franchisor in Texas.

6. Federal Courts 96

In interpreting whether plaintiff has established prima facie case of personal jurisdiction, uncontroverted allegations in complaint of plaintiff must be taken as true, and conflicts between facts contained in affidavits of parties must be resolved in favor of plaintiff.

Lee L. Kaplan, David Hricik, Baker & Botts, Houston, Tex., for plaintiff appellant.

Daniel J. Kasprazak, Glenda Hobbs Kirsch, John T. Johnston, Calvin, Dylewski, Gibbs, Maddox, Russell & Verner, Houston, Tex., for defendants appellees.

Appeal from the United States District Court for the Southern District of Texas.

Before CLARK, Chief Judge, JOHNSON and SMITH, Circuit Judges.

JOHNSON, Circuit Judge:

Plaintiff WNS, Inc. (WNS) appeals an order of the district court dismissing its lawsuit against defendants James Larry Farrow and Mary Dee Farrow for lack of personal jurisdiction. Persuaded that sufficient contacts exist between the Farrows and Texas to support the exercise of personal jurisdiction over the Farrows in federal district court in Texas, we reverse and remand.

WNS, Inc. v. Farrow

I. FACTS AND PROCEDURAL HISTORY

The jurisdictional issue presented by the instant appeal evolves out of the attempt by plaintiff WNS to bring suit against the defendant Farrows in federal district court in Texas. WNS filed its action against the Farrows on December 18, 1987, asserting both tort and contract claims arising from transactions and negotiations occurring in Texas and Georgia between WNS and the Farrows regarding the purchase and operation of a "Deck the Walls" franchise. The following is a brief summary of the facts relevant to the instant appeal.

WNS is a Texas corporation located in Houston, Texas, which licenses the Deck the Walls trade name, and franchises a comprehensive system for opening and operating a Deck the Walls store. In maintaining this system, WNS provides franchisees desiring to operate a Deck the Walls store with a complete program for operating such a business. In the instant appeal, the Farrows, who are residents of Georgia, contacted WNS at its Houston office in March 1986 for the purpose of one or both of them applying to become Deck the Walls store franchisees. As part of the process of becoming a Deck the Walls franchisee, an individual applicant is required by WNS to travel to Houston for an extensive formal interview. Accordingly, on or about March 7, 1986, the Farrows travelled to Houston for the purpose of meeting with WNS employees for the above formal interview and allegedly to negotiate and structure a franchise agreement.

At this point, it should be noted that the Farrows dispute the above proposition that they travelled to Houston for the purpose of becoming Deck the Walls franchisees; instead, the Farrows maintain that they travelled to Houston merely for a "social visit" to learn more about the virtues of the company from the WNS staff. WNS asserts, however, that in addition to negotiating and structuring a franchise agreement with WNS during the Houston visit, the Farrows also completed an application for a Georgia franchise of Deck the Walls which both Mr. and Mrs. Farrow signed. Moreover, WNS maintains that, during the Houston visit, the parties negotiated specific terms for the following three contracts: (1) a franchise agreement to buy a franchise for $171,857 to operate a Deck the Walls store in Georgia, (2) a loan/lease agreement to enable the Farrows to operate the Deck the Walls store in Georgia before permanent financing was in place, and (3) a sublease agreement for a space in a shopping center in Georgia for the Deck the Walls store.

Thereafter, the Farrows returned to Georgia and subsequently mailed a cashier's check to WNS in partial payment of their financial obligations under the franchise agreement. On the same day that the Farrows mailed the above cashier's check WNS transmitted to the Farrows a copy of the franchise agreement for their signatures. In April 1986, the Farrows sent to WNS in

Houston a second cashier's check. Mrs. Farrow subsequently attended a one-week training course in Houston to learn the mechanics of operating a Deck the Walls store. Apparently, both Mr. and Mrs. Farrow originally signed up for the training course, but only Mrs. Farrow attended.

Following the one-week training session in Houston, Mrs. Farrow returned to Georgia and, on May 13, 1986, signed an authorization to occupy certain leased premises for the Deck the Walls franchise in Georgia which designated both the Farrows as franchisees. Mrs. Farrow also signed the franchise agreement. Mr. Farrow, however, did not sign the above two documents. Upon receipt of the franchise agreement in Houston with only the signature of Mrs. Farrow, WNS, through its attorney, informed the Farrows that it had understood both Farrows were applying to be franchisees. Thereafter, Mrs. Farrow operated a Deck the Walls franchise in Georgia until April 1987, at which time WNS took possession of the Georgia store and terminated the sublease. It was at this time that WNS discovered that Mr. Farrow had been operating a competing framing store in Georgia in purported violation of the franchise agreement.

Ultimately, WNS filed suit against the Farrows in state district court in Texas alleging fraud and breach of contract on the part of the Farrows in misrepresenting their intentions to apply for and operate a Deck the Walls franchise. After the Farrows removed the instant case to federal district court in Texas, the Farrows filed a motion to dismiss the suit for lack of personal jurisdiction on the basis that they were not residents of Texas, and had not engaged in business in Texas. The federal district court subsequently granted the motion to dismiss of the Farrows. WNS now appeals.

II. DISCUSSION

[1] "A federal court sitting in diversity may exercise juris-diction over a nonresident defendant, provided state law confers such jurisdiction and its exercise comports with due process under the Constitution." *Interfirst Bank Clifton v. Fernandez,* 844 F.2d 279, 282 (5th Cir.1988), *opinion withdrawn in part on other grounds,* 853 F.2d 292 (1988). In Texas, since the Texas Long-Arm Statute has been interpreted to extend as far as is permitted by due process, the sole inquiry for this Court becomes whether the exercise of personal jurisdiction over a nonresident defendant comports with federal constitutional requirements. *Id. See Hall v. Helicopteros Nacionales de Columbia, S.A.,* 638 S.W.2d 870 (Tex.1982), *rev'd on other grounds,* 466 U.S. 408, 104 S.Ct. 1868, 80 L.Ed.2d 404 (1984).

[2] Due process requires that a district court seeking to exercise personal jurisdiction over a nonresident defendant must first conclude that the

nonresident defendant has purposefully established "minimum contacts" with the forum state "such that the maintenance of the suit does not offend 'traditional notions of fair play and substantial justice.'" *International Shoe Co. u Washington,* 326 U.S. 310, 316, 66 S.Ct. 154, 158, 90 L.Ed. 95 (1945) (quoting *Milliken v. Meyer,* 311 U.S. 457, 463, 61 S.Ct. 339, 342-43, 85 L.Ed. 278 (1940)). In this regard, the minimum contacts of a nonresident defendant with the forum state may support either "specific" or "general" jurisdiction. *Interfirst Bank Clifton,* 844 F.2d at 283. We are concerned only with specific jurisdiction in the instant appeal as the claim asserted by WNS against the Farrows arises out of or is related to the alleged contacts by the Farrows with Texas.[1]

[3, 4] Once a motion to dismiss for lack of personal jurisdiction has been presented to a district court by a nonresident defendant, the party who seeks to invoke the jurisdiction of the district court bears the burden of establishing contacts by the nonresident defendant sufficient to invoke the jurisdiction of the court. *D.J. Investments v. Metzeler Motorcycle Tire Agent Gregg,* 754 F.2d 542, 545 (5th Cir.1985). In satisfying the above burden, when the jurisdictional issue is to be decided by the court on the basis of facts contained in affidavits, a party need only present facts sufficient to constitute a prima facie case of personal jurisdiction. Addressing this issue in *D.J. Investments,* this Court stated that,

> [T]he party who bears the burden need only present a *prima facie* case for personal jurisdiction; proof by a preponderance of the evidence is not required. Moreover, on a motion to dismiss for lack of jurisdiction, uncontroverted allegations in the plaintiff's complaint must be taken as true, and conflicts between the facts contained in the parties' affidavits must be resolved in the plaintiff's favor for purposes of determining whether a *prima facie* case for personal jurisdiction exists.

D.J. Investments, 754 F.2d at 545-46 (emphasis in original, citations omitted).

[5] In the instant appeal, WNS maintains that it presented to the district court a prima facie case for specific jurisdiction over the Farrows by alleging that the Farrows purposefully committed the tort of fraudulent misrepresentation, at least in part, in Texas, and by establishing that the Farrows had substantial contractual connections with Texas by virtue of their negotiations with WNS to become Deck the Walls franchisees. Without

---

1 In contrast to specific jurisdiction, "[g]eneral jurisdiction refers to a suit which does not arise from the nonresident's contacts with the forum, and is asserted only over defendants who maintain 'continuous and systematic' contacts in a particular forum." *Interfirst Bank Clifton,* 844 F.2d at 283.

addressing whether the alleged contractual connections by the Farrows with WNS in Texas satisfy the due process requirement of "minimum contacts," we conclude that WNS has established a prima facie case of personal jurisdiction over the Farrows in Texas by alleging, with affidavit support, that the Farrows committed the intentional tort of fraud, at least in part, through their activities in Texas. In this regard, the Farrows engaged in activity that had reasonably foreseeable consequences in the State of Texas, and through which the Farrows "purposefully availed themselves of the benefits and protections of the forum state's laws." *D.J. Investments,* 754 F.2d at 547. *See Burger King Corp. u Rudzewicz,* 471 U.S. 462, 105 S.Ct. 2174, 85 L.Ed.2d 528 (1985); *Keeton v. Hustler Magazine, Inc.,* 465 U.S. 770, 104 S.Ct. 1473, 79 L.Ed.2d 790 (1984).

Specifically, WNS alleges that the Farrows purposefully travelled to Texas to obtain proprietary information regarding a Deck the Walls franchise for the purpose of opening a competing store in Georgia by misrepresenting to WNS staff that they were interested in becoming Deck the Walls franchisees. In support of the above allegation, WNS submitted to the district court an affidavit by Joseph James Dugan, the director of store planning at WNS, wherein Mr. Dugan stated that,

> At all times during the negotiation and interview process, the training process, and the transfer of possession and operations ... until Mrs. Farrow contacted us in the latter part of May, 1986 stating otherwise, WNS acted upon the belief, based on the *Farrows' fraudulent representations at the interview in Houston and subsequent thereto,* that both the Farrows were applying in good faith for a Deck the Walls franchise which they intended to operate in compliance with the terms of the Franchise Agreement.

(Emphasis added). Further, in their original petition, WNS specifically alleged fraud on the part of the Farrows in representing to WNS in Houston that they desired to become Deck the Walls franchisees. Finally, to further support their contention that the concerns of due process would be satisfied in exercising personal jurisdiction over the Farrows in Texas, WNS points to the following contacts by the Farrows with WNS in Texas: (1) the Farrows contacted WNS in Houston about possibly becoming Deck the Walls franchisees, (2) the Farrows travelled to Houston to participate in franchise negotiations with WNS resulting in the preparation of three distinct agreements between the parties, (3) Mrs. Farrow attended a week long training seminar in Houston on the mechanics of operating a Deck the Walls franchise, and (4) the Farrows partially performed the above three agreements by making payments to WNS in Texas. In rejecting the position of WNS regarding the exercise of personal jurisdiction over the Farrows, the district court reasoned that,

If the promise was in Texas, the breach was in Georgia, the plaintiff is going to have to prove attach any part of the tort to Texas, that at the time of making the promises, that they intended not to obey them because its a future performance case and none of the evidence suggests that at the time of making the promises that they didn't intend to follow them.

[6] What belies the above position of the district court, however, is the fact that, in interpreting whether the plaintiff has established a prima facie case of personal jurisdiction, uncontroverted allegations in the complaint of a plaintiff must be taken as true, and conflicts between the facts contained in the affidavits of the parties must be resolved in favor of the plaintiff. In the instant appeal, while the Farrows dispute the fact that they did not intend to keep their promise to WNS at the time they applied to become Deck the Walls franchisees, WNS maintains otherwise, and for purposes of determining whether the district court has personal jurisdiction, the version of the facts advanced by WNS at this time must be favored. *D.J. Investments,* 754 F.2d at 54546. Accordingly, we conclude that WNS has established a prima facie case of personal jurisdiction in accordance with the due process requirement of "minimum contacts."

Having determined that "minimum contacts" exist to support the exercise of personal jurisdiction in Texas over the Farrows, the inquiry for this Court next becomes "whether it would be 'fair' to require [the Farrows] to defend this suit in [Texas]." *Bean Dredging Corp. v. Dredge Tech Corp.,* 744 F.2d 1081, 1085 (6th Cir. 1984). In resolving the above inquiry,

A court must consider the burden on the defendant, the interest of the forum state, and the plaintiff's interest in obtaining relief. It must also weigh in its determination 'the interstate judicial system's interest in obtaining the most efficient resolution of controversies; and the shared interest of the several States in furthering fundamental substantive social policies.'

Asahi Metal Ind. Co. v. Superior Court of California, 480 U.S. 102, 107 S.Ct. 1026, 1034, 94 L.Ed.2d 92 (1987) (quoting *World-Wide Volkswagen Corp. v. Woodson,* 444 U.S. 286, 292, 100 S.Ct. 559, 564-65, 62 L.Ed.2d 490 (1980). Applying the above factors to the instant appeal, we conclude that the exercise of personal jurisdiction over the Farrows would be constitutionally permissible. Most importantly, we note that Texas has a significant interest in redressing injuries that occur within its borders at the hands of nonresidents.

For the above reasons, the order of the district court dismissing the action of WNS against the Farrows for lack of personal jurisdiction is reversed and remanded for proceedings not inconsistent with this opinion.

REVERSED AND REMANDED.